Elementary School Guidance

Elementary School
Guidance

ERVIN WINFRED DETJEN

Principal of the Gavin H. Cochran School
Louisville, Kentucky

MARY FORD DETJEN

Guidance Counselor of the Alex G. Barret
Junior High School, Louisville, Kentucky

New York   Toronto   London   1952
McGRAW-HILL BOOK COMPANY, INC.

VI

TO ALL CHILDREN
who have problems
and
TO ALL TEACHERS
who help to solve them

Preface

This book is written for all teachers—experienced, inexperienced, and prospective—who are interested in improving the mental health of children.

Most emotional maladjustments originate early in life and become more deep-rooted and more difficult to treat as time goes on. Problems that have their source in childhood should not be allowed to continue into adolescence and young adulthood. The sooner remedial measures can be taken, the more effective they will be and the less time they will require. For this reason, the material in this book has been planned primarily for elementary school teachers and for college students who plan to teach in the elementary grades. However, because the problems of children of all ages are similar in nature, most of the techniques suggested here can be adapted for use in the junior high school.

The aim of this book is threefold. Its first purpose is to suggest ways in which teachers and prospective teachers may learn about the background, the environment, the physical condition, and the social status of children in order that they may supply some of their unmet needs, interpret their emotional disturbances to parents, and be more sympathetic with those whose situations cannot be altered. Teachers who know something about the factors that have influenced the lives of children are better prepared to accept without emotion their undesirable behavior. They are more inclined to contribute to the security of insecure children, to give warmth and affection to the unloved ones, and to find ways of helping the confused and thwarted ones.

The second purpose of this book is to suggest ways in which adults can give children more opportunities to bring their grievances to the surface, to get rid of negative feelings, and to work out their own solutions to problems. Sometimes it is extremely difficult even for skilled psychiatrists and psychologists to ferret out the root causes of emotional problems and undesirable behavior patterns. Teachers cannot be expected always to bring to light the obscure factors that are responsible or to detect all the contributing forces that aggravate behavior problems. However, they can do much toward alleviating emotional ills by using permissive classroom procedures. Cases of maladjustment often respond readily to the relationship treatment. The teacher who can inspire confidence in her pupils and can counsel with them successfully can do a great deal for their mental health even though she knows little about their backgrounds.

The third purpose of this book is to help boys and girls to get along better with one another. Children have more insight than is sometimes realized by their elders. Through informal group discussions and explanations, it is possible to help them understand why people act as they do, to make them conscious of their own feelings and behavior traits, and to enlist their cooperation in creating an atmosphere of friendliness throughout the school.

Most teachers try to provide for the emotional and social needs of their pupils as the occasion arises. This can be done most effectively when the characteristics and the problems of all the children are considered individually. By making a definite plan and setting aside a specific time each day or each week for group guidance, it is possible to obtain a great deal of helpful information about the children in a class. By means of questionnaires, dramatizations, informal play, and other activities of the guidance period, teachers' opinions of children's needs may be confirmed or disproved and many individual problems may be discovered for the first time. Personal child-to-child reactions, which are so important to mental health, may also be detected through the medium of group-guidance projects. Data thus gathered by the observant teacher can be recorded and filed for future use in counseling with parents and teachers and as an aid to the principal and the guidance personnel of the school.

The first part of each chapter of this book contains a discussion of some phase of child behavior, child psychology, or child guidance. At the close of each chapter are suggested pupil activities designed to help the teacher get a better understanding of the child, his pattern of living, the thinking of his parents, the influence of his playmates, and many other factors in his environment. Although remedial measures are suggested for different types of maladjustment, specific treatment of each case necessarily requires much thought and ingenuity on the part of the teacher.

There is enough material in this book for the use of one class for an entire year. The interests and the needs of the pupils should determine the number of lessons covered and the amount of time devoted to each. For example, a primary class might spend several weeks on the problem of temper tantrums and other forms of aggression but might not need the lesson on daydreaming and might omit it altogether. A class of older children might need to spend much more time on the problem of developing responsibility than on ways of overcoming fears. It is advisable that some of the lessons be carried on by all classes throughout the school at the same time. School morale may be built up by having the chapter on friendliness, for instance, presented simultaneously in all classes.

The success of the lessons will depend to a large extent upon the cleverness and the enthusiasm of the teacher who presents them. The suggested activities are intended merely as a guide. Some of them are geared to the kindergarten and primary grades, some to the intermediate, and some to the upper grades. The resourceful teacher will adapt them to her particular group or devise other more suitable plans. No one teacher is expected to use all the activities but rather to select a few of the most appropriate ones for her own class.

It is not necessary that all group-guidance lessons be labeled as such. Real guidance is not accomplished as a cold, methodical chore, but it comes as the result of a warm, understanding relationship between student and teacher. Some of the most effective guidance may be brought about incidentally by means of casual conversation with the children or through correlation with language, health, art, writing, arithmetic, and other lessons.

Because some teachers find it difficult to take an objective view of children's behavior, they are prone to consider as their greatest problems the actions that antagonize and frustrate them. They tend to magnify the importance of rudeness, impertinence, and talkativeness, and to overlook withdrawing tendencies, fears, resentments, and other types of behavior which are real threats to happiness and good mental health. In writing this book the authors have endeavored to treat the behavior problems which appear most serious from the standpoint of both the teacher and the mental hygienist.

It is not the aim of this book to provide a group of impressive ready-made guidance lessons to be presented to the children or a set of tricks for helping teachers to handle all classroom situations. But if these lessons cause children and teachers to understand and like each other better and to be happier, more considerate, and more friendly in their associations, they will have served their purpose.

The teachers of the Gavin H. Cochran School, Louisville, Ky., were the first to use this material. For their willingness to try out the theories and activities presented here and for their original ideas and helpful suggestions the authors are deeply grateful.

Throughout the writing of the manuscript Dr. Hilda Threlkeld, Dean of Women and Professor of Education, University of Louisville, has been a constant source of encouragement and inspiration. The authors are truly indebted to her for guidance and counsel in all their literary ventures.

Appreciation is also due Dr. Noble H. Kelley, Head of the Department of Psychology, Southern Illinois University, Carbondale, Ill., for a critical reading of the manuscript; Miss Lillian McNulty, Assistant in Curriculum for Audio-Visual Education, Louisville Public Schools, for professional advice in the field of visual aids; and Mrs. Virginia P. Turner, Librarian, Louisville Public Schools, for valuable assistance in research.

ERVIN W. DETJEN
MARY FORD DETJEN

LOUISVILLE, KY.
March, 1952

Contents

CHAPTER 1

Studying the Home Environment of Pupils

Aims of This Lesson:

To acquire helpful information concerning the home life and background of each child in the class.

To interpret this information in terms of the emotional and social needs of the child.

To help each child solve his problems or learn to rise above difficult situations in his life which cannot be changed.

Some teachers contend that they can teach subject matter without being familiar with the background of the children in their classes. This may be true so far as the mere presentation of a lesson is concerned. But the most effective teaching is done by one who understands the problems of the individual child and knows the difficulties he must overcome before learning takes place. If the teacher knows that a child's annoying attention-getting behavior springs from his need for affection, that his tardiness is due to the fact that no one was up to prepare his breakfast, that his daydreaming is really an escape from unpleasant or intolerable situations, or that his stealing is the result of jealousy, the desire for prestige, or the fact that he has nothing of his own, she may find some way of relieving the underlying cause of the trouble. At least, she is likely to be more patient, sympathetic, and understanding.

Only a small part of a child's time is spent in school. In order to interpret his behavior in the classroom, it is helpful to know him as he is at home, on the playground, and in the neighborhood. Not only should the teacher

1

make an effort to learn something about the present environment of all her pupils, but she should also try to become familiar with the history of their important preschool years.

A problem child usually comes from a problem home. The insecurities and frustrations that originate from an undesirable home life carry over into school and sometimes assume such proportions that they block all academic progress. A child who is unhappy, maladjusted, and mentally ill simply has no zest for learning. When his need to feel loved, respected, worth while, and successful has not been met at home, he will try in one way or another to satisfy it elsewhere. If he does not gain attention, affection, and recognition at school, he may then resort to truancy, cheating, stealing, fighting, daydreaming, or some similar type of behavior.

Many teachers fail to study conditions which affect the child's out-of-school life because they do not realize the importance of doing so, because they do not know how to go about making such a study, or because they do not feel that they have the time for it. Classroom situations cannot always be remedied merely by dealing with the present behavior. In spite of scolding, preaching, nagging, threatening, and punishing, the problem may persist or take some other form. Time spent in studying a child's background and the elements that influence his immediate behavior may actually be time saved. When the causes of emotional disturbances can be discovered, they can be treated at their source before more serious problems develop.

One factor which affects the life of the child is the social and economic status of his home. The teacher frequently judges the family's standard of living on the basis of the father's occupation. This is the most easily obtained index to the financial security of the family, their social position in the community, and the comforts and cultural advantages which they enjoy. The amount of income, of course, must be considered in terms of the number of persons in the family and of any unusual sources of expenditure. It must be remembered, too, that the morale of the home and not the economic condition is the key to the mental health of the child. Many families are happy and well adjusted in spite of undesirable living conditions, and many are discontented and frustrated in the midst of luxury. Special attention may have to be given to children at the two extremes of the economic scale. For instance, those from very poor homes may need help from the school in getting glasses, dental work, medical care, lunches, or clothing. Children from very wealthy homes, on the other hand, may be just as much in need of a different kind of help because they have been overindulged, overprotected, or neglected.

The adequacy of a child's home life depends upon a great many things. It makes a difference, for example, whether the family lives in a residential or a business district, whether they are crowded into a small apartment or have a large house with plenty of outdoor play space, and whether their home is convenient and attractive or entirely lacking in comfort and beauty. A child is concerned about the way his home compares with the homes of his friends. He may be emotionally disturbed by feeling that he lives in the least desirable dwelling in the neighborhood. Or he may get the impression that he is socially superior to the other children if his home is conspicuously better than theirs.

When studying the environment of a child, it is important to learn something of the composition of his family. This involves finding out about the number of brothers and sisters and the number of adults including grandparents, boarders, or others who live in the home. It is helpful, too, to know whether parents are living together, whether the child has stepparents, and whether the children are left in care of another person while the mother is employed. Teachers find that a great many emotional problems carry over into school when homes are broken by death, separation, or divorce, when relatives live in the home, and when both parents are absent much of the time. To be sure, the damage caused by such conditions is sometimes exaggerated. In many cases divorce is preferable to constant friction in the home. Contrary to popular belief, the only child may not be overprotected and unsocial, the oldest may not be the favored one, and the youngest may not be spoiled. The nature of the child, the wisdom of the parents, and many other factors determine the effects of abnormal home situations and of the child's place in the family. But the fact remains that the school will need to make different contributions to a recently adopted child who has been reared in an orphanage, to an oldest daughter who must hurry home to take care of the children while her mother works, and to a motherless boy who lives with his father in a boarding house.

The relations of parents to each other, of parents to children, and of children to each other are important factors in the emotional make-up of the child. When investigating a home situation, the teacher should find out about the parents' physical health, emotional stability, intelligence, and judgment in dealing with children. It is important to know whether they are warm, affectionate, overindulgent, domineering, indifferent, neglectful, or hostile toward the child. Some parents show a thorough understanding of the child's problems, while others never seem to see his viewpoint or to appreciate his abilities and limitations. Naturally, homes that are characterized by harmony, love, and understanding tend to produce happy, well-adjusted children. But when parents quarrel, disagree on the rearing of their offspring, show partiality, and compare one child unfavorably with another, they pave the way for feelings of inferiority, jealousy, resentment, and rebellion.

The most frequent cause of ill feelings between brothers and sisters is jealousy. A child may feel that he is being deprived of parental love and attention by the arrival of a new baby, by the illness of another child in the family, or by the enviable status of a more favored one. The teacher may recognize negativistic attitudes, daydreaming, nail biting, shyness, destructiveness, and fighting as symptoms of jealousy. If she realizes that a youngster feels himself supplanted by another child at home, she may give him some extra love and attention. If she knows that he resents a brother or sister who is put up as an example to him, she may be able to find ways to build up his ego.

Children tend to imitate the behavior and to adopt the customs which they see from day to day. If orderliness, cooperation, consideration, and courtesy are practiced at home, the same traits are usually evident at school. A child is likely to be alert or listless, calm or tense, punctual or slow, according to the pattern of his home. His attitudes toward school and education, toward religion, and toward life in general are largely reflections of his parents' viewpoints. His prejudices, his superstitions, and even his vocabulary come directly from home. If a child throws things when he is angry, sulks when his feelings are hurt, or gives up immediately when things are not going his way, it is usually because he has seen adults react in the same manner under similar circumstances.

By listening to children talk with each other and by observing them at play, it is easy to tell whether they hear stimulating conversation or gossip and small talk, whether their leisure-time activities are of a high type or are limited to cheap movies and other forms of ready-made entertainment, and whether they see examples of kindness and generosity or of backbiting and intolerance in their homes and neighborhoods.

It is possible to learn about some of the things that are bothering children from snatches of conversation heard in passing. The teacher cannot help but understand their needs and emotional disturbances a little better when she overhears such remarks as, "Daddy was so drunk that he kept the whole family awake all night," "I wish we could have flowers at our house, but there is so much junk in our back yard that there just isn't room for plants," or "I hope the alimony check comes today so I can have some new shoes."

Teachers cannot be expected to know how to relieve all human difficulties or to solve all emotional problems, but they can be sympathetic, willing to listen, and available for private talks when pupils need them. Because tensions are often decreased by "talking things out," children should be encouraged to chat about themselves at odd times—before and after school and at recess. They may not always relate accurate facts, but they will express feelings. If they have complete confidence in the teacher, they will reveal many significant things about their out-of-school life during quiet personal interviews with her.

Since a good counseling technique is one of the most important tools of guidance, it behooves all teachers to become familiar with the latest approved methods. Some excellent books on counseling are listed in the bibliography at the end of the chapter.

The teacher should do very little talking during the interview. She should never appear shocked at anything the child says, should not prod him to tell more than he wants to tell about himself or his environment, should not stop him from talking about parents or teachers, and should not try to correct his feelings. She should let him pour out his resentment, anger, animosity, or any other pent-up emotion. Her only reply should be to let him know that she understands how he feels. By reflecting his feelings she helps him to clarify his thinking about his problem. For example, a child may say, "My father would not let me explain about the windowpane. He whipped me because he thought I broke it. I hate him!" The teacher might say in reply, "I understand. You don't like your father because you think he treated you unfairly." Sermonizing, moralizing, or shaming the child for his feelings would probably put an end to the story and the teacher would get no further insight into the situation. The child would not only get no help but, feeling rebuffed and misunderstood by his teacher as well as his father, he would be hurt even more.

Every person has certain fundamental needs which must be satisfied somehow. By finding out which basic needs of a child have not been met at home, the teacher will know how the school can best make up for these needs. It is difficult, if not altogether impossible, to alter an unsatisfactory home environment. But when a teacher discovers in a child's life a distressing situation which cannot be changed, she may be able to help him face his problem calmly and courageously or to create in him a desire to rise above his environment. Although the school can never substitute for the home, it can provide some of the deficiencies which a child feels. At least, the teacher who is aware of undesirable home conditions may be more understanding and tolerant, may offer more sympathy, affection, reassurance, and encouragement where it is especially needed, and may try to provide more opportunities for joy and happiness in school.

It is desirable for teachers to visit in the homes of their pupils, to talk with the parents, and to see the children in their normal surroundings. In a small community the teacher may already be familiar with the living conditions and the family relations of her pupils. In a city school system it is not always possible or practical to visit in all the homes. Contacts must then be made through the visiting teacher or the social worker. In any event, calls should not be limited to the homes of problem children. Parents are likely to be on the defensive when they feel that a home visit indicates trouble at school. It is important to know the home background of all the children in the class.

If it is impracticable for the teacher to visit in the homes, the next best thing is to arrange for conferences with the parents at school. This may be done by inviting certain ones to come at definitely scheduled times during the first days of the term when children are not present. Or mothers may be invited to come after school in groups of five or ten to talk informally about any questions that are initiated by the group. It sometimes helps to invite a few parents at a time to spend an entire morning or afternoon visiting their children's room when nothing special has been planned. In this way they can better understand the teacher's motives and can know what to expect and to require of their children.

Naturally, parents are more interested in a project in which they are active participants. It gives them a feeling of belonging and of being needed if they are called upon occasionally to help with such things as decorations, refreshments, costumes, and transportation for field trips. It also gives the teacher additional opportunities to meet and talk with the parents informally.

Either during a home visit or at a small group meeting at school each mother may be asked to answer a mimeographed list of questions concerning her child (see page 14). The purpose of the questions is to help find out which needs of the child are being met at home and what the parents would like to have the school do toward the child's further development. It is more satisfactory to give the explanation and to ask for the information in this way than it is to send a questionnaire home to be filled out. Immediately after a home visit, a group meeting, a private interview, or a casual contact with a parent, significant facts and remarks that indicate feelings should be recorded. The alert teacher will jot down notes of impressions gained when parents accompany children to school on registration day or at any other time.

When getting information from a parent about a child, it is important that the teacher phrase her questions thoughtfully. She must not give the impression that she is prying into the private life of the family, but must make it evident that she is attempting to gain a better understanding of the child's behavior so that she will know how to help him. Parents welcome an opportunity to talk with a teacher who is friendly and warm, who is sincerely interested in their child, and who considers that their problem is one of mutual concern. The teacher can put parents at ease by finding something kind to say about their child and by assuring them that his behavior is normal and not unusual.

The child's mother is the one who knows him best. By listening to the mother talk the teacher can learn much about the things the child likes, the things that make him happy or unhappy, the things he does which worry his mother, the things he does which especially please her, his fears, his hobbies, and his talents. During an informal conversation it is possible to learn a great deal about the parents' opinions and attitudes toward the child, about the amount of time they spend with him, and about any trying situations to which the child must adjust. Parents' feelings toward their children are sometimes expressed in the most unexpected ways. A few casual remarks may be enough to indicate that a child is constantly nagged, cowed, distrusted, or belittled. Such feelings are of great importance to the teacher because a child's relation with his parents colors his relations with all other adults. If he is rejected and unloved at home, the teacher will have to make a special effort to win his friendship and confidence before she can teach him. If he is considered a bad child at home, she will have to help him live down his feeling of worthlessness and build up his self-esteem.

Sometimes teachers feel that they are wasting time when they must listen as parents ramble on and on about themselves and their personal problems. But in this way parents often unconsciously give a very good picture of their home life. Teachers should try to analyze everything that is said, remembering that anything which concerns the parents may be felt by the child. There are reasons for the parents' actions just as there are reasons for the children's behavior. They, too, sometimes feel frustrated, defeated, and in need of sympathy and understanding. It is not necessary for the teacher to offer advice or to suggest a solution to the problem when conferring with a parent. She should, however, listen attentively and sympathetically and show by her remarks that she understands the feelings expressed. Simply by talking, a parent is usually able to clarify his thinking, to get a better insight into his problem, and often to find the solution for himself. As he becomes less anxious and worried, he will release pressure on the child who, in turn, will become less tense and nervous.

One of the most important things a teacher can do in her contacts with the home is to inform parents of the purposes and goals of present-day education as they relate to the needs of children. Adults are prone to judge the school by the standards of the schools which they themselves attended and, consequently, to misinterpret some of the modern procedures.

Parents need to know how the child's mental health is affected by his home life. They often fail to see the connection between their child's behavior or his failure in school and some emotional disturbance at home. Instead of treating the underlying cause of the trouble, they may make matters worse by severe punishment and scolding. Sometimes the teacher's viewpoint can be effectively presented by recommending or providing for parents suitable books and magazine articles on the subject of mental hygiene, discipline, and modern trends in education (see reading lists for parents at the close of Chapters 1 and 19).

In addition to visiting in the homes and interviewing the parents, it is suggested that teachers learn as much as possible about the background of the pupils in their classes by talking with the visiting teacher, the school nurse, and the former teachers of the children, by examining their previous school records, and by carefully observing their classroom and playground behavior.

An individual folder for each child should be filed in the classroom. This folder should contain significant information obtained from the parents, the visiting teacher, the school nurse, and the child himself. Autobiographies, diaries, questionnaires, representative samples of work, stories, poems, drawings which express feelings and desires, and anything else which throws light on home backgrounds, personalities, interests, ambitions, abilities, and problems should also be included. If intelligence tests, achievement tests, personality tests, behavior rating scales, and home environment scales are used, the results should be recorded in this file (see pp. 12-16).

While it is somewhat time-consuming to keep complete accounts of the development of all the children in a class, it is suggested that anecdotal records be made from time to time at least on those who are maladjusted or socially unaccepted. These should be short, clear, accurate accounts of significant comments of the child, descriptions of typical or unusual behavior, examples of leadership or other characteristic abilities, and quotations from interviews with parents. Making these chronological entries should not be a hardship on the teacher because not more than one or two incidents worthy of note will usually occur in one day. But if these are recorded without bias or personal feeling and with enough background to make the comments understood later, they may be invaluable in interpreting the behavior and the development of certain children. By forming the habit of writing anecdotal records, the teacher will become more conscious of the children as individuals and will have some means of studying trends in their behavior patterns. Such records give meaning to test scores and rating sheets and are helpful to teachers who receive them later.

One teacher made the following entry in a child's folder:

December 1. Today we were seated informally in the front of the room discussing reasons for feeling happy or unhappy. I had asked the question, "Why do you think some children seem unhappy?" Carolyn, who is extremely quiet and reserved, waited until the others had finished their discussion. Then she commented, "A child might be unhappy because she has a new baby at home and whenever she says, 'Mama, I want to show you something,' her Mama answers, 'Don't bother me now. I'm busy feeding the baby.'" (Carolyn has a new baby sister.)

December 5. Carolyn's mother was invited to come to school. Both parents came. They were quite surprised to know that Carolyn felt any jealousy toward the new baby but realized that of necessity some of the attention to which she had been accustomed had recently been withdrawn. The mother agreed to be more conscious of Carolyn's requests for attention and suggested that before feeding the baby she would ask Carolyn if she were hungry and would also like some lunch.

By keeping fairly complete records on all children, the teacher is sure to have a better understanding of their behavior problems. She will have at hand valuable information to use for conferences with parents, to provide the principal with data for guidance purposes, to explain emotional problems to the school psychologist, and to pass on to the children's next teacher.

General information obtained by observation and from parents, children, and other sources may be recorded on a form similar to the following:

Child's name——————— Address——————— Telephone———————
Grade——————— Year——————— Age——————— Date of birth———————

Home life:
  Child lives with———————————————————————————————
  Type of neighborhood——————— Type of home———————
  Occupation of father——————— Occupation of mother———————
  Religion of father——————— Religion of mother———————
  Education of father——————— Education of mother———————
  Attitude of parents toward each other———————————————
  Attitude of parents toward child———————————————
  Attitude of parents toward school———————————————
  Relatives or other adults who influence child———————————
  Other children in the family———————————————
  Child's relations with brothers and sisters———————————
  Child's home duties———————————————
  Wishes child has expressed about his home———————————
  Answers on home rating scale indicate a need for———————
  Other information———————————————

Schoolwork:
  Intelligence quotient——————— Test——————— Date———————
  Achievement-test scores——————— Test——————— Date———————
                 Reading——————— Arithmetic———————
                 Total grade placement———————
  Personality rating——————— Test——————— Date———————
    Traits which need attention———————————————
  Behavior rating——————— Test——————— Date———————
    Behavior which needs attention———————————————
  Subject in which best work is done———————————————
  Subject in which child needs help———————————————
  Work habits———————————————
  Special abilities, interests, or talents———————————————

Social adjustment:
  Child's status in his community———————————————
  Attitude toward classmates———————————————
  Accepted, rejected, or ignored by classmates———————————
    Possible reasons———————————————

Emotional adjustment:
Parent's description of child at home——————————————
Child's disposition——————————————
Emotional problems——————————————
    Apparent cause——————————————
    Treatment applied——————————————
    Results——————————————

ACTIVITIES SUGGESTED

The activities and questions suggested here will not be suitable for every class. It is not expected that any teacher will use all of them. Choose the ones that you consider best for your particular group. Substitute any others which are likely to be more effective. If necessary, change the wording of the questions to suit your grade level. The explanations and instructions should be presented in such a way that the pupils will not suspect that the purpose of the activities is to give the teacher an insight into the type of home from which the child comes, his feelings and attitudes toward his home and family, and the extent to which his basic needs are being met. Some of the activities can be used in connection with regular class work. Significant information may be obtained simply by talking with pupils in a casual, friendly manner.

1. Ask the children to write or tell "The Story of My Life," stating where they were born, the different places they have lived, the schools they have attended, the kinds of work their fathers and mothers do, the other persons who live in their homes, how they feel about their brothers and sisters, what they like or dislike about their homes, the things they like to do, the things they do not like to do, any good and any bad qualities they feel that they have, what they would like to be when they grow up, and what they would like to do for their families when they are older.

Children of the lower grades who are too young to write may be asked to tell the teacher or the class about their homes, the persons with whom they live, the names and ages of their brothers and sisters, their neighborhood playmates, their pets, and the things they most enjoy doing at home. The one who is speaking may be guided by occasional questions from the teacher or the other children. No child who appears hesitant should be urged to participate. This activity may be used as a language lesson.

2. Ask each child to draw a floor plan of his home, putting in all doors, windows, and furniture just as they are placed in his house. In this way the teacher may get some idea of the physical setting in which a child lives without asking questions directly. This activity may be used in connection with an art lesson, or the drawings may be made to scale in an arithmetic class in the intermediate grades.

Younger children may be asked to build their own homes with blocks and then to explain their buildings to the teacher.

3. During a language lesson each child may be asked to write or talk on one of the following subjects:

"What I Would Do if I Had $10,000."
"What I Do to Help at Home."
"Some Good Times I Have Had with My Family."
"Some Things I Would Like to Change about My Home."
"What I Like Most about My Home (or Family)."

Instead of writing or speaking, some of the children may prefer to draw pictures about one or more of these topics and then explain the drawings to the teacher. Those who do not draw well may like to cut pictures from newspapers or magazines to illustrate what they do to help at home or good times they have with the family.

4. Using finger paint, water colors, or crayons, the children may draw as they feel about their homes and anybody who lives there. The observing teacher will be able to learn a great deal about problems at home from the nature of a drawing, the characters portrayed, and the feeling which the child puts into his drawing. The coloring is also significant. Bright colors are frequently chosen by the happy child, dull ones by the unhappy one.

5. A great deal may be learned about their environment by watching children as they play house or dramatize different home situations. Certain groups may be asked to dramatize mealtime, bedtime, an evening when the whole family is at home, getting ready for school, helping mother, entertaining company, or some other bit of home life. The players should be arranged in groups of the same number of members as their own families at home. Each child should be allowed to portray the character of his choice.

6. Tell the children to write on slips of paper the three wishes they would make for themselves or for members of their families if a good fairy or some

very powerful person offered to make these wishes come true. Remind them that they should not waste their wishes on foolish things, like the old people in the fairy tale who wished the pudding on and off the nose.

This activity may be introduced to younger children by telling the story of Cinderella and following it up by having the teacher act the part of the good fairy. Each child may take a turn at coming to the teacher and whispering his wish to her. These wishes are often very enlightening.

Study each wish and try to interpret it in the light of the child's age and his obvious needs. Talk with the children about how to make some of the wishes materialize. Impress upon them the fact that we cannot have things simply by wishing for them, but that if we really plan and work, we can often make our dreams come true. In some cases the wishes may be of such a nature that the teacher will want to confer with the parents and plan some solution. After the lesson is finished the wishes should be recorded in the children's folders.

One first-grade teacher originated a Magic Corner in her room. In front of a star-spangled blue curtain stood a little "throne" on a platform. Each day during rest period, while all heads were down on their desks, the teacher touched a different child with her magic wand. The chosen child then tiptoed to the magic chair, sat down, and quietly told his secret wish to the teacher. On the closing day of school a sixth-grade girl, dressed as a fairy, led each child to the chair, called his name, and invoked the Magic Corner to give him a gift. Individualized gifts, compatible with the wishes which had been expressed during the year, were handed through the folds of the curtain by a mother who was concealed there.

7. As another means of finding out the kinds of life the children lead ask each one to keep a diary over a period of two or three school days or a week end. It will be found that some children have all of their time supervised and planned for them while others waste many hours not knowing what to do with themselves. You may be able to suggest some interesting and profitable activities to these children.

8. One of the following inventories may be used for rating the social, economic, and cultural aspects of the children's homes:

> *The Minnesota Home Status Index,* by Alice M. Leahy, University of Minnesota Press, Minneapolis, 1936. (This scale requires an interview with a parent. It is useful in the lower grades, where pupils cannot read and cannot write answers to a questionnaire.)

The Sims Score Card for Socio-economic Status, by Verner M. Sims, Public School Publishing Company, Bloomington, Ill., 1927. (This questionnaire can be answered by elementary school children in the fourth grade and higher.)

9. In order to have on file a rating of each child's behavior and attitudes for use throughout the year, one of the following scales may be used:

Telling What I Do Test, by Harry J. Baker, Public School Publishing Company, Bloomington, Ill., 1930. (Primary Form, grades 4 to 6, and Advanced Form, grades 7 to 9.)

The Haggerty-Olson-Wickman Behavior Rating Schedule, World Book Company, Yonkers, N.Y., 1930. (For kindergarten through high school.)

The Winnetka Scale for Rating School Behavior and Attitudes, by Dorothy Van Alstyne and others, Winnetka Educational Press, Horace Mann School, Winnetka, Ill., 1937. (For nursery school through sixth grade.)

10. As a means of determining the needs and problems of elementary school children, you may use the *SRA Junior Inventory,* by H. H. Remmers and R. H. Bauernfeind, Science Research Associates, Inc., Chicago, 1951. (This is a check list of children's health, social, school, personal, and home problems.)

11. When parents are invited to school for private or small group conferences they may be given mimeographed sheets containing questions about their children and asked to fill them out while there. They should, of course, be fully aware that the information is wanted solely for a better understanding of the child. If you do not have group meetings but talk casually to single parents as the occasion arises, you should have in mind some questions which you would like to ask. The following are suggested:

a. How does your child feel about school?
b. What, if anything, does he dislike about school?
c. Does he like the teacher? The principal? The children?
d. How do you think other youngsters feel about your child?
e. How does your child get along with other children in the home? In the neighborhood?
f. Does he have enough contacts with other children?
g. Does he prefer to stay indoors and read or to play outdoors with the crowd?

h. How does this child compare with his brothers and sisters?

i. Do your children realize that there is a difference in their abilities?

j. Do you work outside the home? During what hours are you away from home? Who has charge of the children?

k. How much time do you spend with your children?

l. How much time does your husband spend with the children?

m. What kind of activities do you and your husband share with the children?

n. Does your child take any private lessons? What kind?

o. Does he have any physical condition that might interfere with his school work?

p. What does he do during his leisure time?

q. Does he have any regular duties at home?

r. Does he receive an allowance?

s. Is your child jealous? Of whom?

t. Is he afraid of many things? What?

u. Does he cry easily?

v. What are some of his good characteristics?

w. What do you consider his worst faults?

x. Does he have any definite interests?

y. What are your ambitions for him?

z. In what particular way would you like the school to help your child?

12. Some information may be obtained by having mimeographed questionnaires filled out by the pupils themselves. Emphasize the fact that honest and accurate answers should be given in all cases. Tell the children that nothing they write is to be read or discussed in class and that the purpose is merely to help you to know and understand your pupils better so that you can be of more help to them. The questions may have to be interpreted to some groups. The following are suggested, provided the information has not already been obtained from some other source:

a. With whom do you live?

b. Are your mother and father both living?

c. How many brothers and sisters do you have?

d. Besides your father, mother, brothers, and sisters, who else lives in your home?

e. Do you have any hired help in your home?

f. What kind of work does your father do?

g. Does your mother work away from home? What does she do?

h. Is any member of your family crippled or sick a great deal of the time? What is the trouble?

i. Do you frequently stay at home with a sitter while your parents go out?

j. Do your father and mother like to hear about the things you do at school?

k. Does your father or your mother help you with your homework?

l. Do you often go places or do things with your father?

m. Do you often go places with your mother?

n. How often do you go to motion-picture shows?

o. How much schooling did your father have?

p. How much schooling did your mother have?

q. Do you go to church? What church?

r. What regular duties do you have at home?

s. What things do you do that seem to annoy your parents?

t. Do your parents frequently scold or punish you? How do they punish you?

u. Do your parents often praise you?

v. What do you do that seems to please them especially?

w. Can you think of anything that would make your home happier? What?

13. When groups of parents, teachers, or prospective teachers study problems of mental health and family relations, a good approach can be made by the use of appropriate films. See Activity 13, pages 244 to 245.

FOLLOW-UP

Continue to talk with parents and children about their problems. One or two interviews are not enough. Make a record of any important bit of information you may happen to obtain. It will probably prove useful in connection with later lessons.

BOOKS FOR PARENTS

BACMEISTER, RHODA W.: *Growing Together,* Appleton-Century-Crofts, Inc., New York, 1947.

———: *Your Child and Other People,* Little, Brown & Company, Boston, 1950.

BARUCH, DOROTHY WALTER: *New Ways in Discipline,* McGraw-Hill Book Company, Inc., New York, 1949.

BAUER, W. W.: *Stop Annoying Your Children*, Bobbs-Merrill Company, Indianapolis, 1947.

BENEDICT, AGNES E., and ADELE FRANKLIN: *The Happy Home*, Appleton-Century-Crofts, Inc., New York, 1949.

BUXBAUM, EDITH: *Your Child Makes Sense*, International Universities Press, Inc., New York, 1949.

DAVIS, ALLISON, and ROBERT J. HAVIGHURST: *Father of the Man*, Houghton Mifflin Company, Boston, 1947.

DUNBAR, FLANDERS: *Your Child's Mind and Body*, Random House, New York, 1949.

FRANK, MARY, and LAWRENCE K. FRANK: *How to Help Your Child in School*, The Viking Press, Inc., New York, 1950.

GESELL, ARNOLD, and FRANCES L. ILG: *The Child from Five to Ten*, Harper & Brothers, New York, 1946.

GRUENBERG, SIDONIE M.: *We, the Parents*, Harper & Brothers, New York, 1948.

JENKINS, GLADYS GARDNER, HELEN SHACTER, and WILLIAM W. BAUER: *These Are Your Children*, Scott, Foresman & Company, Chicago, 1949.

LANE, BESS B.: *Your Part in Your Child's Education*, E. P. Dutton & Co., Inc., 1948.

PATRI, ANGELO: *How to Help Your Child Grow Up*, Rand McNally & Company, Chicago, 1948.

SMART, MOLLIE, and RUSSELL SMART: *Living and Learning with Children*, Houghton Mifflin Company, Boston, 1949.

BIBLIOGRAPHY

ARBUCKLE, DUGALD S.: *Teacher Counseling*, Addison-Wesley Press, Inc., Cambridge, Mass., 1950.

AXLINE, VIRGINIA MAE: *Play Therapy*, Houghton Mifflin Company, Boston, 1947.

BLAIR, ARTHUR WITT, and WILLIAM H. BURTON: *Growth and Development of the Preadolescent*, Appleton-Century-Crofts, Inc., New York, 1951.

BUHLER, CHARLOTTE, FAITH SMITTER, and SYBIL RICHARDSON: *Childhood Problems and the Teacher*, Henry Holt and Company, Inc., New York, 1952, Chaps. 5, 12.

FOSTER, JOSEPHINE C., and NEITH E. HEADLEY: *Education in the Kindergarten*, American Book Company, New York, 1948, Chap. XXI.

GLUECK, SHELDON, and ELEANOR GLUECK: *Unraveling Juvenile Delinquency*, Commonwealth Fund, Division of Publication, New York, 1950, Chaps. V, VIII, IX, X, XI.

HILDRETH, GERTRUDE: *Child Growth through Education*, The Ronald Press Company, New York, 1948, Chap. 21.

18 ELEMENTARY SCHOOL GUIDANCE

KILPATRICK, WILLIAM HEARD, and WILLIAM VAN TIL: *Intercultural Attitudes in the Making*, Harper & Brothers, New York, 1947, Chap. II.

PORTER, E. H., JR.: *An Introduction to Therapeutic Counseling*, Houghton Mifflin Company, Boston, 1950.

ROGERS, CARL R.: *Client-centered Therapy*, Houghton Mifflin Company, Boston, 1951.

STRANG, RUTH: *An Introduction to Child Study*, The Macmillan Company, New York, 1951.

TORGERSON, THEODORE L.: *Studying Children*, The Dryden Press, Inc., New York, 1947, Chaps. 2, 4 to 6.

WITMER, HELEN LELAND: *Psychiatric Interviews with Children*, Commonwealth Fund, Division of Publication, New York, 1946.

CHAPTER 2

Understanding the Physical Needs
of Children

Aims of This Lesson:

To become alert to any physical conditions of pupils which may impair their learning efficiency and their mental health.

To cooperate with parents, doctors, and nurses in correcting physical defects.

To help pupils who have become emotionally maladjusted as the result of physical inadequacies.

In our zeal to improve the mental health of children, we are likely to overlook the importance of their physical fitness. There is such an interrelationship between mental hygiene and physical hygiene, however, that it is necessary for teachers to be equally concerned about them. The normal educational, social, and emotional development of a child is greatly affected by his physical condition. Many a youngster who is casually labeled by his teacher as lazy, inattentive, disinterested, or dull would make a very different showing if some physical deficiency were only observed and corrected. Low scholarship, reading disability, nervousness, or a lackadaisical attitude may be the result of defective hearing, poor eyesight, faulty eating habits, or too little sleep. Anything which improves the general health of a child is likely to increase his energy, his happiness, his interest in schoolwork, and his learning efficiency. On the other hand, anything which disturbs his mental health is likely also to affect him physically. Much of the so-called "illness" which causes absence from school is due to psychological factors.

The amount of time which the teacher devotes to the physical needs of her pupils is somewhat determined by the health program of the school. Most

19

city school systems have periodic physical examinations made by physicians, follow-ups made by school nurses, the services of public clinics, and free dental care for those who are unable to pay. Some systems provide special classes for the blind and partially sighted, for the deaf and hard-of-hearing, for speech defectives, and for the badly crippled. Some have health programs which provide for immunization against various diseases, for detection of tuberculosis, and for home instruction of the seriously handicapped. In smaller communities where there are no such services the classroom teacher has a greater responsibility for evaluating and helping to meet the physical needs of her pupils. But even in schools where there is an adequate health service, examinations are not made every day and teachers need to be constantly on the alert for physical conditions that should be corrected.

A classroom teacher cannot be expected to play the role of an amateur physician and to suggest diagnoses. Certainly she should never presume to prescribe or give medicine of any kind to a pupil. But she should know enough about the symptoms of ill-health to recognize them in children whom she sees every day. It is the teacher's responsibility to report any indications of illness, to recommend pupils for physical examinations, and to urge parents to see that treatment is carried out. Because of her strategic position as an observer, she can furnish valuable information to the physician, the nurse, and the home.

After a teacher has known her class long enough to be familiar with the normal appearance of each pupil, it is easy for her to detect any signs of abnormality. She should give special attention to a usually healthy child who shows symptoms of drowsiness, headache, flushed face, paleness, sneezing, coughing, bad breath, discharging ears, rash, watery eyes, or sore throat. These signals of ill-health should be called to the attention of the parents. Since many communicable diseases start in this way, a child who has symptoms similar to those of a common cold should be sent home or referred to a physician.

While the more obvious physical problems are being observed and corrected, the child of lowered vitality often remains unnoticed. His round shoulders, slow and draggy gait, and constant feeling of tiredness indicate a general weakness due to faulty nutrition or some other condition of poor hygiene. Very pale mucous membranes along the gums and inner surfaces of the eyelids are other signs of poor nutrition. The child who often feels cold in a room that is comfortable for others and whose hands, arms, and lips appear purplish may be in need of additional food, clothing, or rest. He may be helped by a midmorning lunch, an extra rest period, or some other special consideration at school. Although physical weakness in children is sometimes caused by malnutrition, the physician may discover that it is due to an anemic, tubercular, cardiac, or glandular condition. Any child who is unhealthy in appearance, irritable in disposition, and disinclined to play deserves study.

Although it is important to know whether a child is overweight or underweight, this is not usually a matter of much concern if he has energy, vigor, clear eyes, glowing skin, and a good color. Growth is not always regular and seldom conforms exactly with standard height-weight-age tables. The so-called "average" children for whom these tables are planned are comparatively few. But if a pupil loses weight or fails to gain over a period of several months, the teacher should find out if anything is wrong.

Imperfect vision is often the cause of academic failure, social maladjustment, and emotional disturbance. Any teacher should be able to detect nearsightedness, farsightedness, squint-eyes and cross-eyes. She may suspect poor vision or susceptibility to eyestrain when a child shows a lack of interest in work requiring good eyesight, is inattentive during blackboard lessons, is irritable over his lessons, cries frequently, blinks continually when reading, holds his book too close or too far from his face, reads only a short time without stopping, often loses his place on the page, rubs his eyes frequently, and confuses figures and letters in reading and spelling. Complaints of blurred vision, headache, dizziness, fatigue of the eyes, and styes indicate faulty vision. A child who wears glasses may show the same symptoms because his glasses need changing, because they were not made correctly, or because they have become bent.

Whether or not a teacher has observed signs of poor eyesight among her pupils she should test all of them in order to spot any who may need professional attention. Two tests which are fairly simple to administer and interpret are (1) the Eames Eye Test obtained from the World Book Company, Yonkers-on-Hudson, N.Y., and (2) the Snellen Charts available from the American Medical Association, Chicago, or from the National Society for Prevention of Blindness, New York. For children who do not know their letters the examiner may use the Snellen test card with the letter E printed in different sizes and turned in different directions so that the pupils may indicate in which direction the arms of the E are pointed.

When the teacher discovers that a child is having sight difficulty, she should, of course, get in touch with the parents and advise that they consult an oculist. Many children have seriously defective vision before their parents are aware of it. The teacher can also help the child by seating him so that he gets a good light without glare, by allowing him to rest frequently, and by talking and reading to him more, giving him more charts and large-type texts to read, and requiring him to read less of the usual book assignments.

Subnormal hearing may be the real cause of apparent dullness, listlessness, and inattention. Some of the things which cause a teacher to suspect impaired hearing are defects in speech, poor grades in subjects that are taught orally, failure to answer when questioned, errors in carrying out instructions, and irrelevant interruptions. Defective hearing may be accompanied by earache, mouth breathing, and discharges from the ear. Because loss of hearing is sometimes not noticed until there is considerable impairment and because deaf children are sensitive and will not mention it, all children should be given periodic auditory tests.

Hearing can be tested most accurately by the audiometer, an instrument which consists of a phonograph with special records and earphones for the pupils. Before attempting to use this device, a teacher should receive instruction from someone who is familiar with such testing. For information concerning the audiometer, write to Volta Bureau, Washington, D.C., or to the American Society for the Hard of Hearing, Washington, D.C.

A less scientific but fairly accurate method of measuring hearing acuity is the watch test. While a card is held at the side of a child's eye as a blinder, a loud-ticking watch is placed level with his head at about arm's length from him and is then brought closer until he indicates that he can hear the ticking. The distance at which several children who apparently have normal hearing can hear the watch in a quiet room is used as the standard. Any child who can hear the ticking of the watch at only half or less than half the standard distance should be referred to a physician for examination.

The teacher can help the child with hearing difficulties by seating him near the front of the room, standing near him when presenting lessons and giving directions, and urging him to watch the lips of persons who are speaking to him. She can help to make him independent by interesting him in many things that do not require hearing and she can tactfully and privately appeal to the other children to help.

Many children have dirty, unsightly, decayed, or protruding teeth. If not given the proper care, such teeth may mar the facial appearance and speech and cause embarrassment, suffering, and loss of time from school. Teachers can exert a great influence toward getting children to keep their teeth clean, improve their diet, and have needed dental care.

Teachers are often concerned about children who display nervous symptoms such as fidgeting, biting their fingernails, pulling their knuckles, gritting and grinding their teeth, twitching their eyelids, and making jerky movements of the eyes, mouth, or nose. Some of the most common tics, or constantly repeated spasmodic motions, are sniffing, throat clearing, coughing, shoulder shrugging, neck twisting, and restless movements of arms or legs.

Although severe cases of nervous disorder should be referred to a psychiatrist, the minor ones can be helped a great deal by a thoughtful teacher. In the first place, the nervous child usually needs to have his general health built up. Eyestrain, defective teeth, bad adenoids, vitamin deficiency, or insufficient sleep may be contributory.

Children often imitate the mannerisms of their associates. There is no need for great concern over nervous habits which healthy, well-balanced children have temporarily copied from others. But when a tic, whether imitated or original, becomes chronic, the subject invariably shows other evidences of emotional disturbance.

Some nervous tensions stem from deep-seated problems in the child's past or from difficult circumstances in his present environment. A youngster may be tense, restless, irresponsible, disinterested in schoolwork, and unable to get along with his teachers or classmates because he feels insecure, unloved, or afraid. The underlying cause of the trouble may be pressure from strict parents, schoolwork that is too difficult, too many outside activities such as dancing and music lessons, or too much domination from adults. If the irritation which these things cause in the child is not released in some other form of behavior, it may be bottled up within him until it finally comes to the surface in the form of a tic.

Since the child has very little control over nervous habits, it is useless to scold or punish him for them. Telling him to stop making aimless movements merely serves to call attention to the habit and to make it stronger. The nervous child needs affection and a minimum of nagging and disapproval. His schoolwork should be interesting, adapted to his abilities, and not too strenuous. He should also have ample opportunity for a satisfying social life with other children.

A conference with the parents may help them to understand that they can do more than anyone else for the nervous child. High-strung, excitable parents generate tensions that are responsible for many nervous disorders in their children. Teachers may be able to point out to such persons the importance of trying to slow down the general tempo in the home, of speaking and moving more slowly, and of allowing children to develop at their own speed. They may also help parents to realize the necessity of providing an atmosphere that is happy and agreeable and free from bickering and quarreling.

Speech defects may be due to either physical or psychological conditions. Some of the physical causes are malformations of the throat and vocal organs, nasal obstructions, abnormalities in the structure of the tongue, harelip, and cleft palate. Grave physical disorders should be referred to a physician. Some complicated disturbances respond to careful training in speech clinics.

Unless they are allowed to persist until they become deep-rooted habits, such minor speech defects as indistinct articulation and baby talk tend to disappear as a child grows older. Lisping, which is the most common speech defect of young children, is often due to the influence of poor speech habits in the home or to imitation of playmates. Classroom teachers who have had some training in speech education can do a great deal to correct lisping and other defects before they develop into permanent habits. Any reforms, of course, should be undertaken during the early years while speech habits are still pliable.

Stuttering, which is the most common speech disability, is generally considered to be due to a psychological condition. It frequently has its origin in some nervous shock, frightening event, disagreeable experience, or sudden change in family life. It may start as the result of a serious accident or the arrival of a new baby in the home. Or stuttering may develop more slowly due to the effect of constant nagging, too close supervision by parents or teachers, compulsion to meet hopelessly high standards, unfavorable comparisons with brothers or sisters, or a feeling of failure. Arguing, bickering, and unhappiness at home may cause the sensitive, highly excitable child to stutter. His inability to speak normally then, in turn, increases his emotional tension and aggravates the trouble. Whether or not the original cause can be determined and corrected, the fact remains that the stutterer is likely to be an anxious, fearful, or emotionally immature child who needs help in his present situation.

Remedial procedure depends entirely on the individual case. It is well, however, to take care of the physical aspects first. Since malnutrition, anemia, lack of proper rest, and general debility make a child more susceptible to stuttering, the teacher should check with the parents to see that the stutterer has a healthful diet and plenty of sleep.

Because his speech defect is a symptom of some trouble at home, at school, or in the neighborhood, the stuttering child needs help in making a better personal adjustment. The parents should be asked to ignore the stuttering. Any pressure from them, any indication that they are unduly worried about the handicap, or any attempt to have the child overcome the difficulty by repetition of certain words will only make matters worse. The stutterer needs to feel that his family is proud of some special ability he has, not embarrassed because of his speech. By consulting with the parents, it is possible to see that tension is reduced at home and that some definite plan is made for building up the child's confidence.

Many children stutter only under certain conditions. They can sing, do choral reading, or talk with people they know well without any indication of the defect. But when they are speaking alone to persons who they think may be critical or unsympathetic, they feel self-conscious and the stuttering becomes worse. It is often accompanied by grimaces, tossing of the head, blinking of the eyes, or some other sign of tension. Naturally, a child who has this difficulty is embarrassed in the presence of his classmates and begins to develop a feeling of inferiority. It then becomes the problem of the teacher to build up his confidence by giving him jobs of responsibility which do not require speech, by emphasizing the things which he can do well, and by making him feel that he is a part of things, both academic and social.

The child who stutters should not be excused from any of the regular class requirements because of his speech. One of the things which he most needs is practice in talking to people who treat the stuttering as if it were of no importance. The class should be told that everyone stutters sometimes and that many children stutter when they are young but overcome it as they grow older. The child should not be rushed, shamed, interrupted, or corrected when he stutters, nor praised when he does not. No suggestions for improvement should be offered in front of the class. The best procedure is to treat the stuttering casually and to try to remedy the underlying cause. The teacher who speaks slowly, distinctly, and calmly and who avoids speech mannerisms of her own will unconsciously help children who are victims of minor speech disorders.

Crippled children also require thoughtful consideration from the teacher. If they have received no special medical or surgical care, the parents should be informed of any clinics or welfare agencies where the handicap can be studied and treated. It may be necessary to take special measures for the comfort and convenience of handicapped children at school. For example, if a child has difficulty in getting up steps, it may be possible to have an older boy carry or accompany him, to suggest that he use a different entrance than the other children, or to arrange for him to arrive earlier or later than the others. Without making it too obvious, games and other activities should be planned so that the crippled child can participate in some way. But extra provisions other than those that are absolutely necessary should not be provided.

Handicapped children have the same interests and emotions as others and they should be made to feel and act as nearly normal as possible. Although the teacher should be kind, sympathetic, and understanding, she should not do anything for the crippled child which he can do for himself, should not allow him privileges beyond reason, and should not lower any standards that are possible for him to attain. She should do everything possible to help him retain his independence, self-respect, and self-confidence.

Because a handicapped child gets an unusual amount of attention from his parents and is necessarily cut off from many social contacts, he naturally becomes absorbed in himself. If he learns to use his handicap as an excuse for shirking responsibility and as a means of getting favors and attentions from others, he is likely to become selfish, lazy, useless, and bitter. A person with such an unhealthful attitude soon comes to feel inferior, discouraged, and beaten. He may retreat from life because he believes that he is too helpless to compete with others.

The happiness of the handicapped child depends upon the way he reacts to his disability. Parents who assume an unemotional attitude toward the child's handicap and teachers who recognize his need for satisfactory compensation can do a great deal toward giving him courage. They can see to it that he keeps busy and interested in the things that children of his age like to do and that he learns the joy of contributing to the happiness of others.

The entire class may be inspired by hearing stories about people who have been successful in compensating for physical handicaps. Sometimes by working hard at it, a person may overcome a weakness or disability. For example, a pale, sickly boy who could not participate in the strenuous games at school decided to concentrate on building a strong body. He read volumes on the subject, ate the proper food, got the required amount of sleep, exercised systematically, and let nothing interfere with his goal. Before he graduated from high school he had become an unusually strong and vigorous fellow and had taken part very successfully in track meets, boxing matches, and other athletic contests.

Persons who have a physical handicap that cannot be overcome may make up for this lack by becoming especially proficient at something else. All about us there are examples of blind persons who have gotten college educations, badly crippled persons who have succeeded in business, and paralytics who have been able to carry on some useful form of work from a wheel chair. The teacher should make it her mission to see that each child who has a physical deficiency is started on the road toward making some sort of desirable and satisfying compensation.

It has been estimated that two-thirds of all school children have some physical defect which is more or less damaging to personality. A child with a clubfoot, congenital lack of fingers on one hand, a birthmark on the face, or some other physical irregularity which has nothing to do with his ability to learn may become a personality problem. It is easier for children to accept much more serious disabilities that are not so obvious. Looking different than others is the thing that hurts most. Even crooked teeth, freckles, excessive height, weight, tallness, shortness, or any other deviation from the normal may be the cause of poor mental health. Children with physical defects, no matter how minor, are usually extremely sensitive to the attitudes of others. They are the victims of many curious stares and whispered remarks. They have to become accustomed to the nicknames given them by unthinking classmates and to the tactless, inconsiderate remarks which are sometimes addressed to them by adults. The effect of all this on the child depends upon his concept of his own worth, his social and emotional maturity, and his ability to think and act independently.

Children can be made to feel successful in spite of physical defects. They can be taught to realize that, whether or not it is evident to the casual observer, everyone has some incapacity with which he must contend. Each person has to learn how to master his deficiency and live with it without allowing it to get the better of him.

Along with the many other duties of the busy teacher, it is her responsibility to learn the signs and symptoms of the most common diseases which develop during school life and to be prepared to instruct pupils and parents regarding a communicable disease at the time it is prevalent in the community. Educational material for this purpose is available from the state health departments and other government sources.[1]

[1] James Frederick Rogers, *What Every Teacher Should Know about the Physical Condition of Her Pupils,* Pamphlet No. 68, U.S. Office of Education, Washington, D.C., 1945.

In each child's cumulative record folder there should be recorded any significant information concerning his health from the preschool period to the present. This history, obtained from parents and from records of physical examinations at school, should include diseases which a child has had, those against which he has been immunized, any chronic ailments from which he suffers, and any physical handicaps, abnormalities, or weaknesses of which the teacher should be aware. The school should also have on record the name of each child's family doctor so that in an emergency the child may be cared for by his own physician.

It is sometimes helpful to keep a record of one's impressions of children who need medical or dental attention. This may serve as a reminder to speak to parents about having the child examined, to find out whether recommended treatment has been carried out, and to bring neglected cases to the attention of the school nurse or physician. A chart similar to the one below may be used.

HEALTH CHART

Date	Pupil	Signs & Symptoms	Physician's Diagnosis	Nurse Notified	Treatment and results

ACTIVITIES SUGGESTED

The activities used in connection with this chapter must depend to a large extent upon the particular needs of the group. The most frequent causes of absence and the most prevalent defects of the children will determine the points of emphasis. For example, balanced diet, good posture, or nervous stability may be the goal on which the group most needs to concentrate.

You will need to be constantly on the alert for any deviations from the habits and the behavior which you normally expect. For instance, you will know that something is wrong with those certain children who fail to join in wholesome laughter and joyous play and who cannot be kindled with enthusiasm for any classroom project. Watch the children as they play. Estimate their ability to throw, catch, run, and jump. Notice the ones who stand on the side lines or sit on the steps while the others play. Take a good look at these children, talk to them, and try to find out what the trouble is. If certain children seem habitually sluggish in the classroom, study them. Perhaps they are handicapped by infected tonsils, glandular difficulties, or impaired vision or hearing. At least, you may interest their parents in having physical examinations for them.

All the activities suggested below will not be suitable for any one group. Use only those which fit your needs.

1. Talk with the children about posture, gait, disposition, facial expression, and energy as indicators of good or poor health. Ask certain ones to demonstrate how they stand, walk, and look when they are feeling well and when they are feeling ill. This approach will lead naturally into a discussion of health and will be likely to reveal some of the physical problems of the pupils.

2. Have on hand a supply of pamphlets, charts, and other educational materials concerning communicable diseases to be used whenever there is an epidemic in the community. Instruct the children regarding the symptoms, treatment, and control of the disease. Impress them with their responsibility for preventing the spread of the disease. Lessons of this type can be used frequently in connection with the common cold.

Health posters, pamphlets, and mimeographed materials may be obtained from the American Medical Association, Chicago 10.

3. Talk with the children about the difference between illness that is real and that which is feigned. Ask about the reasons for their most recent absences from school and what they did while at home. Lead the discussion into a consideration of the kind of illness which is brought on by dread of having to face a difficult situation at school. (Use a story about a child who is quite ill at ten o'clock on a school morning but able to play baseball in the afternoon.) Also discuss the person who enjoys illness because he gets so much sympathy from his mother or the one who frequently wants to go to the nurse's office because he likes to get attention. Explain how children who use illness as a means of escape or as an attention-getting device grow into adults who use illness as a way out of situations that they do not like to meet.

If you suspect that certain children are using illness as a means of escape, make opportunities to have quiet, personal interviews with them. By giving a child enough opportunities to discuss his symptoms and his feelings about home, school, and classmates, you may be able to uncover the root of the trouble and to help him come to grips with his real problem.

4. Observe the children in the lunchroom to see which ones buy balanced meals and which ones make poor selections. As another means of finding out about their diet, ask the pupils to discuss the foods they like best and eat most often. Also ask them to write a list of the foods which they usually have for breakfast, for lunch, and for dinner at home. As a language lesson each child may write a paragraph describing "My Breakfast" or "My Dinner."

It is sometimes possible to obtain food models from a dairy company or other organization. The younger children may use these for dramatizations in which they select the food, set the table, and serve the meal. This will give you an idea of their preferences and habits and will furnish an approach for talking about proper diet.

Charts depicting the basic foods may be secured from state health departments upon request.

5. Introduce the subject of physical handicaps for class discussion. Call attention to the ways in which certain handicaps limit one's activities and social contacts. Show how it is possible for a handicapped person to become shy, withdrawing, bitter, and cruel, and to want to hurt others as he has been hurt, how desperately some handicapped children need companionship, and how it must feel to be teased, laughed at, or left out of things because of a physical defect. Suggest that the pupils look not only in their own classroom but throughout the entire school and the community for such children and befriend them, being careful never to appear condescending.

Numerous pamphlets and reprints which will be helpful to parents and teachers of crippled and handicapped children may be obtained from The National Society for Crippled Children and Adults, Inc., Chicago 3. The various state societies for crippled children will be glad to make their services and facilities available to those who need them.

6. Tell some stories of persons who have succeeded in spite of, or perhaps because of, physical handicaps.

7. As one means of spotting the children with hearing difficulties, use a game in which you tell the children to do what you say and not what you do. Or watch the children while you give directions without allowing them

to see your lips. A child who must watch the others in order to know what to do may be hard-of-hearing.

Help with hearing problems may be found in some of the publications of the American Speech and Hearing Association. Requests should be addressed to the office of the secretary-treasurer of the association, Speech Clinic, Wayne University, Detroit.

8. Plan a campaign for motivating children to take proper care of their teeth. A great many helpful suggestions and materials for this activity may be obtained from the American Dental Association. These aids include teaching outlines for conducting dental health programs on different grade levels, attractive story books, filmstrips, motion pictures, colored posters, charts, leaflets for seatwork and coloring, recordings, records of radio transcriptions in which terse dental health messages are inserted in well-known children's stories, and certificates to be given to children who have kept their teeth clean a specified length of time. Descriptions and prices of these materials may be secured from the American Dental Association, Chicago 11. Samples of most of the material are supplied free on request.

9. By asking the children to answer a questionnaire similar to the following, you may discover the physical needs of some of your pupils.

   a. Do you have headaches after reading or seeing a movie? [1]
   b. Are you unable to see the blackboard clearly?
   c. Does light hurt your eyes?
   d. Do your eyes often twitch?
   e. Do you usually have to watch the lips of a person in order to hear him well?
   f. Do you often have sore throat?
   g. Do you often have toothache?
   h. Do you often feel tired in the morning?
   i. Do you sometimes get so sleepy that you almost fall asleep in school?
   j. Is it hard for you to breathe with your mouth closed?
   k. Do you often feel cold when others in the room seem warm enough?
   l. Do you bite your fingernails?
   m. Are you often not hungry at mealtime?
   n. Do you lie awake a long time after going to bed?

[1] Pamphlets, reprints, posters, and other materials concerning the protection of the eyes may be obtained from the National Society for the Prevention of Blindness, Inc., New York.

10. Small children who cannot read or write well may have dictated to them such questions as the ones below. They may answer on a sheet of paper by drawing a face with an upturned mouth or by making a mark with a red crayon to indicate a satisfactory response. Unpleasant answers may be expressed by a face with a drooping mouth or by making a mark with a black crayon.

    a. Do you have toothaches?
    b. Do you have headaches?
    c. Does light hurt your eyes?
    d. Do you get very sleepy at school?
    e. Do you often feel sick at your stomach?
    f. Do you often feel tired in the morning?
    g. Do you often feel that you don't want any dinner?
    h. Are there many times when you cannot understand what the teacher or the children say?

11. In order to have a more complete record and a better understanding of the health problems of each child, you may ask the parents some of these questions:

    a. Does your child have any observable or known physical defects?

        Vision ——————
        Hearing ——————
        Teeth ——————
        Speech ——————
        Muscles ——————
        Glands ——————
        Other ——————

    b. What serious diseases or accidents, if any, did he have in his preschool years?
    c. Does he now suffer from a chronic disease of any sort?
    d. If he has a physical disability, does it affect his mental attitude?
    e. Has he been absent from school a great deal because of illness in other years?
    f. What do you consider his physical strong points?
    g. What do you consider his physical weaknesses?
    h. How much sleep does your child get?
    i. Does he have a good appetite? Are there many foods that he refuses to eat?

j. Does he cry frequently, bite his fingernails, or show any other signs of being nervous?

k. Does he often seem listless and tired?

l. Are there any physical problems with which you feel that the school might help your child?

m. If your child stutters,[1]

    i. When did he begin to stutter?

    ii. Is he imitating a stutterer at home or at school?

    iii. Does he show any unreasonable fears?

    iv. Have there been any changes in the family which would cause him to feel jealous or insecure?

    v. Do you punish him for his speech?

    vi. When talking with what particular person or groups does he stutter most?

12. Interesting books on health and safety should be made available for the use of the pupils. Examples:

    LEAF, MUNRO: *Health Can Be Fun,* J. B. Lippincott Company, Philadelphia, 1943.

    LEAF, MUNRO: *Safety Can Be Fun,* Frederick A. Stokes Company, Philadelphia, 1942.

13. Recordings can be used effectively with this lesson. For example, Robert Dwan's recording *Why Do I Have to Go to Sleep?* produced by Decca Records, Inc., New York, explains why everything that lives must have rest. By means of a story it shows the necessity of sleep and rest for the various organs of the human body. This science story for intermediate grades is accompanied by a teacher's guide.

    Songs of Safety, written by Irving Caesar, with music by Gerald Marks, and sung by Frank Luther, is another Decca recording which emphasizes important lessons for children of the kindergarten-primary grades. Teacher's guide.

    Health Can Be Fun, by Frank Luther, Decca Records, Inc., New York, is an interesting presentation of basic health ideas for primary- and intermediate-grade children. Teacher's guide.

14. Suitable films may be used in connection with this lesson. The following are suggested:

[1] *If Your Child Stutters* and other educational leaflets may be obtained from the National Hospital for Speech Disorders, New York 3.

Cleanliness and Health (for primary, intermediate, and junior high school), 16 mm., sound, 10 min., Coronet Films, Chicago, 1949. This is a story of David's visit to a doctor and of what he learned about the existence of dangerous tiny organisms and the importance of cleanliness to good health.

Dental Health: How and Why (for intermediate, junior, and senior high school), 16 mm., sound, 10 min., Coronet Films, Chicago, 1949. This film gives an up-to-date account of diet and its relation to the growth and decay of teeth, new sodium fluoride applications, and the latest techniques of oral hygiene. It has been awarded the Seal of Approval of the American Dental Association.

Immunization (for elementary grades), 16 mm., 11 min., Encyclopaedia Britannica Films, Inc., Wilmette, Ill., 1947. This picture, which opens in the sickroom of a child, first shows the external symptoms of disease, then the period of convalescence after the child has developed active immunity to the disease, and concludes with the warning that contagious diseases cannot be stamped out unless people avail themselves of the protection afforded by vaccination. Animated drawings illustrate different disease germs, white cells, antibodies, and vaccines.

Let's Have Fewer Colds (for primary and intermediate grades), 16 mm., sound, 10 min., Coronet Films, Chicago, 1950. This film shows how children can reduce the number of colds they get each year by such simple practices as avoiding contact with people who have colds, avoiding chilling or overheating, and establishing good health that will prevent colds.

Modern Guide to Health (for elementary grades), 16 mm., 11 min., Young America Films, Inc., New York, 1948. This animated cartoon presents such health factors as posture, selection and care of clothing, and importance of sleep and rest.

Playground Safety (for primary, intermediate, and junior high school), 16 mm., sound, 10 min., Coronet Films, Chicago, 1946. This story tells how Jack, who had broken his arm in a playground accident, taught the other students some important safety rules.

Posture Habits (for intermediate and junior high school), 16 mm., sound, 10 min., Coronet Films, Chicago, 1947. This film develops posture consciousness in the growing child. It treats standing, walking, and sitting positions, using a puppet to explain bodily structure and showing scrapbook examples of good posture among adults and why posture is important to everyone.

Safe Living at School (for primary, intermediate, and junior high school), 16 mm., sound, 10 min., Coronet Films, Chicago, 1948. This film shows how Ted and Ruth, who are on the Junior Safety Council, go on a "safety tour" to see the safety features of their school and to learn what students can do at school to live safely.

Teeth Are to Keep (for primary and middle grades), 16 mm., sound, 11 min., Encyclopaedia Britannica Films, Inc., Wilmette, Ill., 1950. Animated drawings show the Smith family on a picnic and also the children learning the four essentials of good dental care: eat proper foods, avoid sweets, brush the teeth after each meal, and visit the dentist twice a year.

Your Ears (for elementary grades), 16 mm., sound, 11 min., Young America Films, Inc., New York, 1947. This film illustrates the structure of the human ear, explains the function of each of its parts, discusses the manner in which certain diseases cause deafness, and stresses the necessity for proper care of the ears.

Your Eyes (for elementary grades), 16 mm., sound, 11 min., Young America Films, Inc., New York, 1947. This film illustrates the structure and function of the eye, explains such maladjustments as farsightedness and nearsightedness, shows how the eyeball is protected by the eyebrow, eyelash, eyelid, and tears, and stresses the importance of proper care of the eyes.

In connection with this lesson, you may also use the Jimmy Rabbit Series of colored filmstrips, Johnson-Hunt Productions, Hollywood 38, Calif., 1947. This series consists of the following:

Safety at Play reminds small children to pick up things, look in both directions at crossings, and wait their turn.

Wholesome Living emphasizes the importance of neatness, cleanliness, good posture, fresh air, and proper food.

Democratic Living reminds children of the primary grades to help at home, to share with others, to care for their playthings and books, and to clean up after their work.

The Health Adventure Series (for later elementary and junior high school grades), colored slide films, may be obtained from the Jam Handy Organization, Detroit 11. Each film is divided into units of instruction, one of which may be presented in an average class period. The first units of each film deal with the purpose and function of a specific part of the body; the last unit stresses the care of these specific parts. The following subjects are included in the series:

Part 1—The Head:
  Health—Your Teeth and Their Care
  Health—Your Eyes at Work
  Health—How Your Ears Work
  Health—Your Nose and Throat
Part 2—The Body:
  Health—Your Skin and Its Care
  Health—Your Food and Digestion
  Health—Your Bones and Muscles
  Health—Your Heart and Lungs
  Health—Sleep and Rest

BIBLIOGRAPHY

BARUCH, DOROTHY, W. W. BAUER, WILLIAM S. GRAY, GLADYS G. JENKINS, ELIZABETH R. MONTGOMERY, and HELEN SHACTER: Health and Personal Development Series, Scott, Foresman & Company, Chicago:

Happy Days (grade 1), 1948
Good Times with Our Friends (grade 1), 1948
Three Friends (grade 2), 1948
Five in the Family (grade 3), 1947
The Girl Next Door (grade 4), 1948
You (grade 5), 1948
You and Others (grade 6), 1949
You're Growing Up (grade 7), 1950
Into Your Teens (grade 8), 1951

BAUER, WILLIAM WALDO: *Contagious Diseases, A Guide for Parents,* Alfred A. Knopf, Inc., New York, 1944.
DUNBAR, FLANDERS: *Mind and Body: Psychosomatic Medicine,* Random House, New York, 1947.
HARMS, ERNEST: *Handbook of Child Guidance,* Child Care Publications, New York, 1947, pp. 135–142, 147–171.
HILDRETH, GERTRUDE: *Child Growth through Education,* The Ronald Press Company, New York, 1948, Chap. 18.

JOHNSON, WENDELL: *Speech Problems of Children,* A Guide to Care and Correction, Grune and Stratton, New York, 1950.

NEUGARTEN, BERNICE L.: *How You Grow,* Science Research Associates, Inc., Chicago, 1951. Pamphlet.

SLAVSON, S. R.: *The Practice of Group Therapy,* International Universities Press, New York, 1947, Chap. 9.

STERN, EDITH M., and ELSA CASTENDYCK: *The Handicapped Child,* A Guide for Parents, A. A. Wyn, Inc., New York, 1950.

TAYLOR, EUGENE J.: *Help at Last for Cerebral Palsy,* The National Society for Crippled Children and Adults, Inc., Chicago, 1950. Pamphlet.

VAN RIPER, CHARLES: *Helping Children Talk Better,* Science Research Associates, Inc., Chicago, 1951. Pamphlet.

———: *Stuttering,* The National Society for Crippled Children and Adults, Inc., Chicago, 1948. Pamphlet.

WARE, E. LOUISE: *Mental Hygiene for the Orthopedically Handicapped Child,* Association for the Aid of Crippled Children, New York, 1947. Pamphlet.

CHAPTER 3

Discovering the Social Needs
of Children

Aims of This Lesson:
  To understand the feelings which underlie the behavior of the group.
  To find out each child's reactions toward other members of the class.
  To discover lonely or isolated children and to help them to make satisfying
  social adjustments.

After studying the home background and the physical needs of pupils, the
next step in understanding them is to learn something about their feelings
toward one another. The teacher's job is easier, her work is more effective,
and she has fewer behavior problems when she undertakes to study the
social status of her pupils and to help them make the necessary adjustments.
Time spent in observing the way members of a class get along with each
other, in discovering social outcasts, and in helping them make a place for
themselves in the group is as justifiable as time spent in teaching subject
matter. Sometimes it is even more helpful and far-reaching.

Children need to have a satisfying relationship with their teachers. But
they need the approval of other children more than they need the good will
of adults. A child who feels perfectly secure in the love of his parents and
the respect of his teachers may be very lonely and unhappy because he is
not a part of things in his group at school. He may prefer to forfeit the
teacher's approval in order to gain social prestige among his friends. Sometimes he can accomplish this by purposely doing inferior schoolwork or attracting unfavorable attention. In this way, at least, he can be considered a
regular fellow by some of his classmates.

38

Too often teachers rely on their own adult standards in judging a child's social acceptability. They are prone to consider him well adjusted if his teacher-pupil relationship is good. But the impression which a child makes upon the teacher is not necessarily the impression which he makes upon his playmates. The most irritating pupil from the teacher's standpoint may be regarded by the children as the most friendly and likable child in the class. On the other hand, the teacher's ideal of a quiet, obedient child may be quarrelsome, contrary, and domineering with the other children. Because he is disliked and rejected by his fellows he may withdraw from social contacts with them and devote himself wholeheartedly to his lessons in order to enjoy the praise of his teacher. Even though he is not a discipline problem, he is as truly maladjusted as the class show-off and may be even more in need of help. If something is not done for this social outcast, he may develop resentments and feelings of inadequacy which will warp his personality and influence his behavior throughout life.

Instead of arbitrarily deciding that certain children are socially unadjusted, the teacher should find out how the other children in the class really feel about them. In every group there are those who are accepted and liked by their classmates, those who are actively rejected and disliked by many, and those who are simply ignored by everybody. Nothing is harder to bear than being left out. But the child who is rejected does not usually know why and, consequently, can do nothing about it. Many emotional problems can be forestalled by the teacher who finds out how individuals in her class are rated by their peers and then acts accordingly.

When it is learned that a child secretly longs for the companionship of a specific one in the group, it is possible for the teacher to plan ways of placing these children together for games or for classwork. Sometimes a child who has hitherto been unnoticed by the others can be taught some skill or given an opportunity to demonstrate some accomplishment which will give him a place of more importance in the group. Many a child has shown increased interest in his schoolwork merely because he realized that he was being recognized and appreciated. A happy, well-adjusted, well-liked child is not a problem child. In fact, the more satisfying social relationships he has, the better able he is to concentrate on his schoolwork.

It is not unusual to find several social cliques in one class. Some children are leaders in these cliques; some play only minor roles and are not generally admitted by all the members of any group; and still others are rejected by all groups. Many school problems arise from the loyalty of members of social circles to each other and from the fact that, because of their longing to be like others, they follow their leaders blindly. It is a definite advantage to the teacher to discover the existence of cliques within her class and to attempt to win the leaders. Any classroom movement that has the support and cooperation of the social group leaders is much more likely to succeed.

In one class a girl whom the teacher considered the most reliable and helpful child in the class was asked to collect money from the pupils for a class project. At the end of the week, in spite of her diligent efforts, she had managed to wheedle only 30 cents from the children. In the meantime, by the use of a mutual-rating questionnaire, it was discovered that, according to the children's standards, this girl was the most unpopular child in the room. This explained the fact that when she had volunteered to direct a little drama, none of the children would learn their parts. The next week a boy who was quite troublesome to the teacher but who had been voted by his classmates to be the best liked child in the room was given the job of collecting. The children contributed $2.80 the first morning. Later, when he was asked to take the lead in producing a skit, the group cooperated unanimously.

A teacher can learn a great deal about how children rate with each other merely by observing them. She can notice which children are chosen for committees, squads, teams, and class offices, and by whom they are selected. She can see which children come to school together, which ones eat together in the lunchroom, and which ones usually play together. Casual remarks made by the children, the tone of voice they use in speaking to each other, and the looks that pass between them often have a meaning for the wide-awake teacher. Those who tend to be unacceptable members of their own class will often play with younger children, establish friendships with pupils from other grades, or play with groups of the opposite sex. A child who hangs around the teacher a great deal may do so because he has no friends of his own age.

By observation the teacher can single out the children who take part in everything and those who are always definitely left out, but she cannot tell much about the ones who are not so obviously chosen or rejected. It is about this great middle section of children who long to be a part of things that she must be concerned. By the use of little friendship tests or quizzes in which each member of the class names those whom he would most like and those whom he would least like to have for friends or guests, the busy teacher may locate some of the lonely, neglected children.

Sociometric tests are frequently used for the purpose of finding which children secretly wish to be associated with certain others in their group. These tests are given by asking each pupil in the class to make a first, second, and third choice of a child to sit next to him, to serve on a committee with him, to be on a team with him, to go on a picnic with him, or to work together in a small group on some class project. To get the desired result, the questions must not be referred to as a "test," but must be asked casually and informally. It is extremely important to the success of the project that the choices be based on some activity in which the children will really participate. It is also essential that the pupils be assured of absolute secrecy in the use of this information.

The teacher may say, "We are going to divide the class into committees to be responsible for keeping up-to-date material on the bulletin board. Each group will serve for three weeks. In order that you may work with persons of your own choice, will you please write your name at the top of a slip of paper, then write, in order, your first, second, and third choices of persons in this class whom you would like to work with. Use the names of friends who are absent, if you wish. Those who are not here today will make their choices when they return. If you definitely prefer not to work with any particular person or persons, write their names at the very bottom of the paper. I shall try to arrange for you to be with one or more of the persons you have chosen."

For young children who cannot write, the same idea may be carried out in the form of a "whisper test." Each child comes to the teacher and whispers the name of the person whom he would most like to have for a best friend and, perhaps, the name of a person whom he would not like to have for a best friend. The teacher will, of course, record the choices so that the information can be used later.

In order to see at a glance the reactions of the pupils toward each other, it is helpful to have the choices recorded on a form similar to the one on page 42. The names of all the members of the class are listed in the same order vertically and horizontally. The names across the top are the pupils chosen, and those along the side are the ones who made the choices. First, second, and third choices are indicated by 1, 2, and 3 in the proper squares. Rejections are shown by the letter x.

From this chart of social relationships it is easy to recognize the most popular children in the group and the ones who are consistently overlooked by their classmates. The reasons for some of the preferences and the rejections will be readily understood by the teacher. It may be that some children are isolated because of religious or racial differences, because of economic factors, or because they are new to the group. Children who come from broken or unhappy homes often have difficulty in making satisfactory social

SOCIOMETRIC CHART*

Chooser ↓ \ Chosen →	Alex	Andrew	Arnold	Ben	Charles	Floyd	Frank	Fritz	Harold	Herman	Jack	Marshall	Richard	Sam	Simon	Wallace	William	Betty	Camilla	Carolyn	Cecilia	Dorothy	Hannah	Helen	Irene	Jane	Jennie	Kathryn	Linda	Nelle	Norma	Patricia	Thelma	Tilly	Verna
Alex	X										1		2					3																	
Andrew	1				X								2	3																					
Arnold									3	1	2																								
Ben			3		2										1																				
Charles						2									1			3				X													
Floyd		3	1												2																				
Frank	2			3											1																				
Fritz	2			3										1											X										
Harold		1										3	2																						
Herman												2	1		3																				
Jack	1											3	2																						
Marshall	2					X					3				1																				
Richard			1						3									2															X		
Sam		2	1								3																								
Simon	3												2											1											
Wallace		1											2			3																			
William	2													3	1																				
Betty		X	2																												1				3
Camilla																				1	X											3	2		
Carolyn																				2				1											3
Cecilia																				2													3	1	
Dorothy													3							X									2						1
Hannah																								1	2		3								
Helen																				1	X	2											3		
Irene																						1				3	2								
Jane																						2						1	3						
Jennie															2							3			1										
Kathryn																						3		1								2			
Linda																						1									2			3	
Nelle			X										2																			1			3
Norma			X																					2							1		3		
Patricia																												1				2	X		3
Thelma																								3						2	1				
Tilly															2							1									3				
Verna			X																												3		2	1	
Chosen as:																																			
1st choice	2		2	2	1				1		1		1	2	4			2	1	1		1	2	1			2			4		1		3	
2nd choice	4		1		1	1				1	4	3	3	3				3		1			2	1			1	1	1	3		1	2		
3rd choice	1		2		2			1	1	1	2		1		1		1				2		2			2	1		1	3		3		3	3
TOTAL	7	0	5	2	4	1	0	2	2	2	7	3	5	5	5	0	1	5	1	2	2	1	6	2	0	2	4	1	2	10	0	5	2	6	3
Rejections	1		3	1	1	1												1		1	2			1									2		

*Adapted from Sociometry in Group Relations, by Helen Hall Jennings, American Council on Education, Washington, D.C., 1948, p. 18.

adjustments at school. Those who enjoy a feeling of being loved and wanted at home are usually friendly, cheerful, and well liked at school. Children who are identified with the band, orchestra, glee club, basketball team, schoolboy patrol, or some other group tend to have better relations not only with pupils of that group but with the entire class. A child's ability to do anything well, whether it be academic or physical, causes the others to recognize, appreciate, and accept him.

The reasons for a child's acceptance or rejection as shown by a sociometric test are not always obvious, however. It may be necessary to get the information directly from the children who have given the ratings. This may be done by private conferences in which the teacher asks each child to tell her point-blank what qualities he likes in the children of his choice and what qualities he dislikes in those whom he rejects. A less time-consuming method is to ask the pupils to write in confidence a detailed description of the traits which have attracted them to the persons of their choice and also of the traits which have turned them against any person whom they may have professed not to like. The teacher should be careful to follow up any clue which gives an insight into a child's rejection.

By means of mutual ratings it is possible for the teacher to discover why, from the children's own standpoint, some pupils are acceptable to the group and others are not. A questionnaire such as the one on pages 48–49 may be used to find out how the youngsters rate each other as to friendliness, helpfulness, honesty, fairness, and other traits. Their comments are of special value because children are usually honest in their judgment of others; they are not afraid to express their opinions; they know and understand each other; and they evaluate each other according to youthful standards. It is natural that children should be concerned about what others think of them. Mutual ratings give an answer from the ones who mean most to them —the children of their own age. They also furnish the teacher a basis for personal guidance by indicating that a large number of children label a certain classmate as bossy, grouchy, and selfish, or another as submissive, afraid, and unfriendly. It is true that when children are allowed to give confidential answers about how they feel toward each other, they may sometimes be influenced by their most recent contacts with the children they are rating. If there has just been a squabble, the individuals concerned will not be very generous in their estimation of each other. But the trend of the ratings given by all the children is the important thing. It is the over-all picture, and not a single rating, that counts.

After a sociometric test has been used, it is essential that the teacher carry out the agreement made with the class at the time. Committees must be formed, a picnic must be planned, or reseating must take place as promised. Grouping should start with the children who have received no choices at all. In so far as possible, these children should be given their first choices. To be sure, a rejected child should not be placed with the child who rejected him. The teacher can usually manage to get the unchosen children in the company they want without allowing them to realize that they have not been chosen by anyone. Frequently as these boys and girls become better known and more at ease with their fellows, they come to be appreciated and liked enough to be among those chosen on the next sociometric test.

An effort should be made to place together those who have chosen each other. If possible, a child who has received no reciprocal choice should be given his first choice of a friend. In order to form committees so that the popular, the unpopular, and those of middle rank are equally distributed, it may be necessary to place a much-chosen child with others than the ones he most prefers. Such a child can be told in private that a number of boys and girls want to work with him and that it is impossible to please all of them. He will probably be gracious about being placed with these children who have expressed a desire to associate with him and may soon come to accept and like them.

There are few things that mean more in a child's life than to be admired by others of his own age. When a pupil is rejected by several of his classmates, it is the teacher's responsibility to study the case until the cause of his unpopularity is discovered. This can be done by developing an interest in what goes on between children and by keeping anecdotal records that illustrate typical behavior traits. If it is found that a child is unhappy and withdrawing because of an unpleasant home situation, perhaps a home visit or an interview with the parents may lead to a solution. If a pupil is rejected because of some unfortunate personality traits, it may be possible to help him recognize and correct these traits. Sometimes a rejected child has some special ability or talent that has not been noticed by the others. If so, this ability may be brought to the attention of the group by using it in a class project or activity. The lonely child who has no special skill can often be taught to do something which the other children would like to learn. At least, this will serve to build up his ego and self-esteem. An outstanding student is sometimes praised by the teacher to the point that his classmates reject him through jealousy. When this is the case, the teacher should make a conscious effort to distribute her attention more equitably.

Tension is often relieved and a better teacher-pupil relationship is fostered merely by allowing a child to sit next to his best friend. Many teachers purposely separate special friends by seating them far apart or by assigning them to different rooms whenever possible. Such an arrangement usually results in increased whispering, giggling, note writing, and other distracting behavior. Fewer discipline problems are likely to arise in a classroom in which the pupils' paramount need for social contacts is recognized. When this need is satisfied and the children realize that they are free to work with their friends, they no longer have to find ways to outwit the teacher but can settle down to the more challenging business of serious classwork. There are fewer causes for frustration, cheating, and undercover activities when children are sometimes allowed to study together. A busy teacher can well use the help of intelligent students who can clearly and patiently explain things to other boys and girls who are having difficulty.

The teacher who has been accustomed to permitting only individual work and no informal communication between pupils may find that confusion reigns when she first uses the sociometric method and introduces democratic procedures into her classroom. It may take the children a while to adjust to the new order. But after they have become accustomed to working together, there is usually a marked increase in interest, enthusiasm, and willingness to cooperate. In an autocratically controlled class situation, where the atmosphere is cold and formal, the children are harder to work with because they have the feeling that the teacher is their natural enemy and that they must gang up against her whenever possible. But they feel differently when they realize that the teacher is allowing them some freedom and is not trying to isolate them from all normal contacts with friends.

Boys and girls need the satisfying experience of teamwork. Teachers need to accept the fact that there is a direct relationship between social adjustment and classroom behavior.

ACTIVITIES SUGGESTED

The following activities will need to be altered to suit different age levels. For the younger children it is advisable to present some of them in the form of games. It may be necessary to change the wording of questions to conform to the reading ability of the children.

In activities such as these, it is extremely important to get the confidence and the cooperation of the pupils. They should be told that the information which they give about themselves and others will help the teacher to understand their feelings about each other so that she can plan ways for them to work together congenially and happily.

1. Ask each child to write on a small card the names of three persons in the class whom he would most like to have for his best friends. The names

should be listed in order of the first, second, and third choices. Then have each one draw a line across the center of the card and below the line write the name of any child whom he would not like to have for a friend. If he especially dislikes more than one, he may add other names to the list. If there are no children whom he dislikes, he should leave this part of the card blank. The pupil should sign his own name in the upper left corner of the card.

This information may be classified for the purpose of finding out which children are well liked by the others, which ones are liked somewhat by only a few, and which ones are rejected or entirely ignored (see page 42). Find the persons whom the unpopular members would like to have for friends and try to plan some means of promoting such friendships.

2. Ask the school psychologist to administer and interpret personality tests for your class and to suggest plans for the use of the results. Attitudes and feelings which might otherwise remain obscure are often discovered in this way. Test scores sometimes furnish clues to the personal problems of children and to the reasons for their being socially unacceptable. If antisocial tendencies are discovered, you may need to plan group guidance lessons accordingly. If a child is found to have many nervous symptoms, a physical checkup may be suggested. If an unhappy home life is indicated, a visit in the home or an interview with the parents may be advisable.

There are many good personality tests which may be used in connection with this lesson. The following are suggested:

> *California Test of Personality* (Primary Form, grades 1 to 3; Elementary Form, grades 4 to 6; Intermediate Form, grades 7 to 8), California Test Bureau, Los Angeles, 1942.
>
> *Hildreth Personality and Interest Inventory* (grades 4 to 8), Teachers College, Columbia University, New York, 1939.
>
> *Pintner Aspects of Personality* (grades 4 to 9), World Book Company, Yonkers, N.Y., 1937.
>
> *Rogers Test of Personality Adjustment* (grades 4 to 8), Association Press, New York, 1931.

3. Teachers of very young children can usually devise some game or activity which will help them to discover the chosen and the rejected members of the group. For example, the children may come to the teacher one by one and whisper names of their best friends while she makes a record of the choices. Since it will be necessary to take more than one time for this activity,

there may be a boys' day and a girls' day to name friends. The boys may whisper into the teacher's left ear and the girls into her right ear.

Another way in which small children may indicate their choice of friends is by playing Friendly Callers. One child says, "Here comes a caller," as he skips around (to music or clapping), calling on a given number of friends. The friends who are chosen then skip with him while the class continues to clap to the music. After the teacher has observed this combination of friends, another child is asked to be a "friendly caller" and choose his friends. The children who are not chosen at all in such games are the ones who need thoughtful study and special help.

4. By way of getting more clues to the feelings which various members of the class have for each other, ask each pupil to write a detailed description of one of the following:

The person in this class whom I admire most.
The one I like most to play with.
The one I like most to study with.
The friend I would like to invite home for dinner.
Why I consider ———— my best friend.

The name of the person described should be given in each description. Assure the pupils that the information will be treated confidentially if they so desire. The children who are not mentioned in any of the write-ups are the ones who are in need of help in the art of making friends.

5. Hold a class discussion concerning the characteristics which tend to make young persons liked by others and those which tend to make them disliked.

6. A series of sociometric studies may be made, using a variety of criteria. For example, each child may be asked to make three choices of persons in the class with whom he would like to study arithmetic or spelling, three whom he would choose to be on his team in a game, three with whom he would like to eat in the lunchroom, and three whom he would like to have sit nearest him in class. If there are any children who would definitely not be wanted in any of these situations, they, too, should be mentioned.

Whenever sociometric tests are used, endeavor to satisfy the expressed wishes of the children by making at least some of them come true. The results will justify the amount of time required to make the necessary arrangements.

If you are sure that you have the complete confidence of the children, ask them to write you a letter explaining why each choice and each rejection was made.

7. Ask the children to answer the questionnaire on this and the next page; explain that their answers are to be kept strictly confidential and that the purpose is to assist you in discovering persons who may need help. Tell the pupils that they are to answer with names of persons in their own class, using as many names as they think belong after each question. The same person may be mentioned as an answer to several questions. "Myself" may be used as an answer to any question which fits the child himself. If he cannot think of anyone who is described by a particular question, he may leave it blank. Replies may be recorded on a chart similar to the one on page 49. A mark should be placed opposite a child's name to indicate each time a trait has been attributed to him by a classmate. It is helpful to use a red pencil for positive traits and a blue one for negative traits.

If this activity is used in a lower grade in which the children are unable to write well or are uncertain of all the names of their classmates, another device may be used. A mimeographed diagram of the seating arrangement of the room may be given to each child. Instead of writing names to answer questions, the child may write the number of the question read by the teacher in the block representing the desk of the child who best fits the description. Or the names of members of the class may be placed in order on the blackboard so that the children can learn to write and associate them with the pupils before answering the questionnaire.

Some of the words or questions may need interpretation. Characters from stories with which they are familiar may be used to illustrate traits to the younger children.

My Classmates

a. What children get along best with the others in the class?
b. What children badly need the friendship of others?
c. Which children smile often and seem happy and good-natured?
d. Which ones are grouchy, sullen, and unhappy-looking?
e. Who are the most helpful to teachers and other pupils?
f. Who are the least helpful?
g. Which ones allow others to have their way most of the time?
h. Which ones always want to have their own way and boss others?
i. Which ones do not fight?

j. Which ones fight a great deal?

k. Which ones protect and help smaller children?

l. Which ones tease and pick on smaller children?

m. Which children always share and take turns when playing?

n. Which ones will not share and take turns?

o. Which ones always play fairly and observe the rules of the games?

p. Which ones often try to take unfair advantage in games?

q. Who are the most honest and trustworthy?

r. Who are the most dishonest—the ones who are likely to cheat or lie?

s. Which ones are especially good at active outdoor games?

t. Which ones would rather read, play quiet games, or watch the others play?

u. Which ones never seem to be frightened at anything?

v. Which ones are afraid of a great many things?

w. What children are especially good sports about doing their share of the work in a group project?

x. Which ones shirk and do not do their share of the job?

y. Which children are careful of the feelings of others and always try to say kind things?

z. Which ones are not thoughtful and often say things that hurt others?

d′. Which children do not try to attract attention?

b′. Which ones are always trying to get others to notice what they do?

TABULATION CHART

NAME	1. Friendly	2. Unfriendly	3. Happy	4. Unhappy	5. Helpful	6. Not helpful	7. Meek	8. Bossy	9. Nonaggressive	10. Aggressive	11. Protective	12. Bullying	13. Unselfish	14. Selfish	15. Fair	16. Unfair	17. Honest	18. Dishonest	19. Active	20. Inert	21. Fearless	22. Afraid	23. Cooperative	24. Noncooperative	25. Tactful	26. Thoughtless	27. Non-attention-getting	28. Attention-getting
Adams, Abe	/// ///	/// //	/// /						/// ///						///	/// /	/// ///	///					/		/		/// ///	
Beck, Bill		/// ///	/// //	///	///	/// ///	/// ///	///					/	/										//				/// ///
Coe, Chas.		///	/// ///		///	/// /											///	///	/// //	/// //						//		

FOLLOW-UP

Make new sociometric charts for the same group about every six weeks. In this way it will be possible for you to check on the social trends of your class, make comparisons concerning the much-chosen and the unchosen individuals, keep informed of the presence of cliques, and become aware of any significant changes of feeling among the children.

BIBLIOGRAPHY

BUHLER, CHARLOTTE, FAITH SMITTER, and SYBIL RICHARDSON: *Childhood Problems and the Teacher,* Henry Holt and Company, Inc., New York, 1952, Chap. 8.

BULLIS, H. EDMUND: *Human Relations in the Classroom,* The Delaware State Society for Mental Hygiene, Wilmington, Del., 1948, Course II, pp. 27–39.

CUNNINGHAM, RUTH, and Associates: *Understanding Group Behavior of Boys and Girls,* Teachers College, Columbia University, New York, 1951, Chaps. IV, V.

JENNINGS, HELEN HALL: *Sociometry in Group Relations,* American Council on Education, Washington, D.C., 1948.

JERSILD, ARTHUR T.: *Child Psychology,* Prentice-Hall, Inc., New York, 1947, Chaps. V, VI.

KILPATRICK, WILLIAM HEARD, and WILLIAM VAN TIL: *Intercultural Attitudes in the Making,* Harper & Brothers, New York, 1947, Chap. III.

OLSON, WILLARD C.: *Child Development,* D. C. Heath and Company, Boston, 1949, Chap. VIII.

SLAVSON, S. R.: *The Practice of Group Therapy,* International Universities Press, New York, 1947.

Staff of the Division on Child Development and Teacher Personnel, Commission on Teacher Education: *Helping Teachers Understand Children,* American Council on Education, Washington, D.C., 1945, Chaps. IX, X.

TABA, HILDA: *A Sociometric Work Guide for Teachers,* American Council on Education, Washington, D.C., 1947.

TABA, HILDA, and DEBORAH ELKINS: *With Focus on Human Relations,* A Story of an Eighth Grade, American Council on Education, Washington, D.C., 1950.

CHAPTER 4

Developing Friendliness

Aims of This Lesson:
To foster good group relationships.
To create a feeling of friendliness and good will throughout the entire school.
To encourage the social outcasts to develop traits and skills which will help them to become acceptable members of the class.

Happiness is the keynote of a successful school. If good mental health for all children is to be one of the goals of modern education, the school must be a happy institution filled with happy individuals. This implies a pleasant and understanding principal, teachers who radiate friendliness and good will, and children who know the joy of achieving on their own level and a feeling of security in their own social group. The warm atmosphere of kindness and consideration which permeates such a school can be felt when one enters the building. It cannot help but promote sound emotional development and good social adjustment in its pupils.

Most children become actual members of a group for the first time when they enter kindergarten. The social attitudes which they acquire while in elementary school often color their relations with others throughout their lives. One of the chief responsibilities of teachers is to help these boys and girls to develop the ability to get along harmoniously with each other. The earlier an attempt is made to foster good social relationships, the better and more permanent will be the results. If children are allowed to become social misfits while in the lower grades, it is extremely difficult to effect good relationships after they have reached the upper grades.

In order to be happy and carefree enough to concentrate on the business of learning, a child needs to experience a mutual feeling of warmth and

51

friendliness with a few other children in his group. At least, there must be one person who is his friend. It is to the advantage of the teacher to help her pupils, in so far as possible, to make satisfying attachments with each other. She will find that when problems of social relationships are solved, academic work usually improves and behavior difficulties tend to diminish.

By careful observation, by the use of sociometric charts, and by thoughtful study of the children's evaluations of each other, it is easy to spot those who are having difficulty in finding a place for themselves in the group. A great deal can be learned simply by taking a thoughtful look at the children in a class. The ones who are happy in the knowledge that they are admired and sought after by their classmates reveal their feelings in their sparkling eyes, light steps, and ready smiles. Those who are actively rejected or simply ignored by the rest of the group show their unhappiness in their listless expressions, lagging steps, and drooping shoulders.

Children who are unaccepted socially react in different ways. Some of them become diffident, shy, and withdrawn; others become overaggressive and domineering. The timid, friendless child often daydreams, reads a great deal, stays indoors during recess, or stands aloof while others play. He may compensate for his lack of companionship by striving for perfection in his schoolwork. If he has no close friends of his own age, the next best thing is to gain adult approval. Although the unusually good and studious children make teaching easy and pleasant, they are often the ones who are most in need of special attention. They frequently have grave emotional problems which may cause them to become neurotics in later life.

On the other hand, a child may fail to enter into class activities because he is so desperately lonely that schoolwork seems of little importance to him. After a long period of feeling that he is not liked or wanted, he sometimes becomes rebellious, resentful, and bitter. He may be bossy and rude to his classmates and defiant toward his teachers. Feeling frustrated, he starts doing many annoying things which will upset the class and attract attention to himself. If he cannot be liked, at least he can be noticed. Punishment and admonition will not solve this child's problem. If he receives no constructive help, he is likely to become a delinquent.

Each lonely child must be studied individually to find the reason for his being overlooked by others and to discover any potential interests, skills, or characteristics which, if developed, might help him to win friends. When a child is socially maladjusted, there may be several factors which need to be corrected.

Situations in the child's background or in his home environment sometimes block his social progress. For example, a child who lives in a home where there are constant bickering and quarreling may never have known genuine happiness. Because of his own unpleasant state of mind, he repels rather than attracts others. One who has been made conscious of his inferiority to a more gifted brother or sister may suffer from a general feeling of insecurity which causes him to shrink from competition with his classmates. A child who has never had the satisfaction of knowing that he is wanted and accepted at home may feel that the world is against him. As a result, he may be timid, withdrawing, and afraid of larger social contacts. Or, in an effort to bolster his own ego and to salve his feeling of being unloved, he may be defiant and insolent toward adults in authority and may affect a superior and critical attitude toward other children.

Some children are driven so hard by proud or ambitious parents that they have no fun and no friends. They are made tense and nervous by a constant pressure to lead the class at any cost. Their lives are mapped out for them and their out-of-school time is almost wholly filled with homework and music, art, dramatics, dancing lessons, or other activities. Social contacts and normal play with other boys and girls are completely crowded out.

One boy who always sat alone in the lunchroom, stood on the side lines while others played, and walked home alone after school confessed to his teacher that he would like to invite some of the boys home with him but that his mother kept the house so immaculate that she would never even let him bring any of the neighbor children in. He told how he would like to show the boys from school some of the expensive playthings which his father had bought for him and which his mother made him keep strictly out of sight. But young people were unwelcome in this home. The guests at the boy's own birthday parties had always been the grown-up friends of his parents. Family trips and excursions had never included any children of his own age. Although this boy was utterly miserable from a want of friends, he did not know what to do about it. He was completely lacking in the ability to approach other children.

Young persons tend to choose their friends from others who are near the same age, have about the same mental capacity, whose families are in the same socioeconomic station in life, and whose interests are similar. They have a tendency to reject those who differ greatly from themselves. The teacher can sometimes bring neglected children into favor with the group by helping them to look and act more like their classmates.

Personal appearance matters a great deal in a child's social relations. A girl who feels self-conscious because she is dressed differently from her classmates may suffer imagined slights and may become so irritable and touchy that she drives others away. Another girl who realizes that she is not pretty or feminine in appearance may compensate by bossing the other children, by becoming loud and boisterous, or by affecting an air of indifference. In such cases the teacher may be able to make some subtle suggestions for improvement in grooming or may tactfully point out the trouble to the parents. As a part of the group program, all the children should be made aware of the advantage of neatness, cleanliness, and a pleasing appearance in winning friends.

Any physical abnormality which causes a child to look markedly different from others may be a disadvantage to him socially unless he is a well-balanced individual who has found a satisfactory way of compensating. Some physically handicapped children are very popular with their associates. Others are avoided mainly because they drive friends away with their own feelings of inferiority and self-pity or with their unconscious desire to hurt people.

When a child says, "I do not like that boy because he is too fat," he may think that he is giving the real cause for his rejection. Actually, the excess weight may make the boy clumsy and prevent his participation in the activities which would make him accepted as a regular fellow. The weak, undernourished child may be left out because he does not have the energy to join in the games of the other children. By talking to the parents and suggesting changes in diet, more rest, or medical care, physical conditions can sometimes be improved.

Because friendships are generally based on similarity of interests and abilities, a child who is mentally slow or one who is unusually brilliant or talented may find it difficult to meet others on a common level. It is natural for children to avoid attachments with one who is so inferior that he seems dull and uninteresting or with one who is so superior that he makes others feel inadequate. It is not necessary that children of widely varying intellects become fast friends, but it is imperative that they learn to accept each other in a friendly manner and to appreciate and value the special abilities which each possesses. The child who does outstanding academic work need not affect a supercilious air toward his less gifted classmates. The dullest boy in the room may far outshine him in flying a kite, in playing marbles, or in building a birdhouse. Although these accomplishments are insignificant according to adult standards, they are vastly important to children. By recognizing them, it is possible to build up the ego of an unnoticed child.

Children should be taught the importance of being friendly with everyone. They can make new friends without losing the old ones. It is a mistake for boys and girls to limit their friends to an exclusive group and hold themselves aloof from everybody else. Although it is good to have close friends, no clique needs become so select that its members feel that anybody outside this small group simply does not exist. Life is more interesting for the person who has a wide circle of friends.

One of the first things a teacher should do at the beginning of the year is to provide opportunities for the pupils to become acquainted. Sometimes children do not even know the names of all their classmates. When asked to choose partners for work or play they make their choices from only a limited number. Using "get-acquainted" games or activities, permitting children to talk in the halls and the lunchroom, and allowing some time for friendly conversation on the playground will help.

Youngsters who have chosen each other on sociometric tests and questionnaires should be teamed up whenever possible. In grouping them for work or play or out-of-school activities, it is good practice to place a timid child with a popular one. A child who has no close friends may be asked to befriend a newcomer and help him to become adjusted to the school. Sometimes a new pupil can be made to feel at home more quickly if some child who has the same church affiliation or other common interest is asked to take him to Sunday school, to a boy scout meeting, or to some neighborhood function.

A great deal can be done toward making children conscious of their responsibility for befriending lonely classmates. Teachers can tactfully mention to certain children some specific things which they may do to help a person who is always left out. Some time when the rejected member is not present, a group of children may devise subtle ways of helping him and including him in their plans. But even when others make every effort to be friendly, a withdrawing child is often unresponsive. It is necessary to discover what is blocking his approach to children before he can be helped to overcome the difficulty.

Children who for one reason or another feel inferior and inadequate cannot be very successful at making friends until their self-confidence has been built up. The teacher can assign tasks about the school that are well within the range of ability of these pupils and then commend them for work well done. She can place them in positions of responsibility that will give them a feeling of importance and will bring them to the attention of the others. A little coaching in subjects that are difficult for a particular child may help him to overcome a feeling of inferiority and embarrassment before his class-mates. The teacher who stays after school for a short time several afternoons a week to give a little private instruction to a child who is falling behind in his work usually finds the results well worth her time.

The ability to compete with others in everyday games is of great impor-tance to children. If a teacher discovers that a friendless child has some motor skill or some ability that the others do not possess, she may be able to help him gain prestige among his fellows by planning a project that will give him a chance to display his skill. Athletic proficiency is always an asset. Children who can skate, swim, throw a ball, or do whatever is done by others of their own age are more respected by their fellows and have more opportunities to develop friendships. A child who is too shy to take part in games may first be given some easy task, such as keeping score or calling time, until he gradually gains enough courage to participate more actively.

Social relations can be improved by teaching good sportsmanship. A child is certain to be more popular if he has learned to play according to the rules, to win without boasting, to lose without grumbling, to be tolerant of a classmate's poor playing, to cooperate with the leaders, and to play as a member of the team rather than as an individual.

The teacher should diagnose the social skills of the children in her class and then set about to develop and improve those personal traits which make for good adjustment. Boys and girls need positive and concrete help in the art of making friends. They must become conscious of the fact that friends are attracted and won by a friendly, happy disposition and by courtesy, loyalty, and unselfishness. They can find in school many opportunities to observe that the more popular children are the ones who are thoughtful of other people's feelings, who show a genuine interest in others, and who are willing to share and take turns.

Special attention should be given to those children who try to attract attention by scuffling, hitting, pushing, and slapping at others. By fighting, annoying, and teasing their fellows, they are actually expressing their long-ing for companionship. These youngsters must be taught that although they may be noticed, they will not be liked for thoughtless name calling and abuse of others. Neither will they make friends by displaying an egotistical, cocky, know-it-all attitude or by strutting, showing off, and insisting upon doing things their own way. Nervous children who whine and complain that others pick on them usually feel inferior and consequently think that everybody dislikes them. Sometimes these children with emotional disturb-ances are so irritating that it is hard even for the teacher to be patient with them. However, the other children are more tolerant of them if they see that the teacher accepts and likes them. The teacher sets an excellent example by being especially warm and friendly with unpopular children.

The key to a happy school atmosphere is very often the simple fact that the teacher likes the children and lets them know it. An understanding look, a smile, and a friendly caress from the teacher always have a tonic effect. The sympathetic teacher knows which children are in need of the largest doses of affection.

Problems of social maladjustment are often created by the coldness and unkindness of some of the members of a class. By their cruel, unthinking remarks and their arrogant and haughty manners, it is possible for young persons to cause their associates much unhappiness. On the other hand, it is equally possible for a group to be so friendly that they make everyone in their midst feel comfortable, needed, and wanted. A teacher can cause a class to be so imbued with the importance of happiness that they consider it their special mission to spread good cheer until it is felt throughout the entire school. In such a situation, friendliness, thoughfulness, and kindness become the accepted custom and those who do not display these traits are completely out of fashion.

ACTIVITIES SUGGESTED

1. As a "get-acquainted" idea, each child in the room may be asked in turn to stand, tell his full name, where he lives, where he has gone to school before, what his hobby is, what pets he has, what he likes to do in his spare time, etc. If the children of a new class do not know each other well, it may help to insist that they call each other by name frequently during games on the playground.

2. As another means of becoming better acquainted, each child may be asked to write his name on a slip of paper and drop it into a box. The group may then be divided into two teams. A person on one team may draw a name from the box and endeavor to give some interesting information concerning this person, such as some special skill or talent he possesses, his hobby, what he likes to do on Saturday, his pets, his brothers and sisters, etc. If correct information is given, a point is scored for the team. Otherwise, the other team gets a trial at the same name. This may continue until the name of each member of the class has been drawn and some interesting facts about him have been mentioned.

3. Discuss with the pupils their need for friends all through life and their opportunity to start making friends now. Talk to them about smiling, being cheerful, greeting each other pleasantly, showing little courtesies to all the teachers, the principal, the lunchroom staff, and the janitors, being helpful and considerate at home and in the neighborhood, and expressing friendliness and good feeling toward each other in the classroom, the halls, the lunchroom, and on the street. Make some specific plans for being more friendly toward parents and other visitors who come to the school.

4. Read or tell a good story which will illustrate the value of friendship.

5. To keep the idea of being friendly constantly before the children a different quotation or reminder may be written on the blackboard each morning. Examples:

> Everyone smiles at ———————— School.
> Have you made anybody happy today?
> The only way to have a friend is to be one.
> Helping someone else is the secret of happiness.
> We help ourselves when we help others.
> Whatever you dislike in another person, take care to correct in yourself.
> A willing helper does not wait until he is asked.
> Grumblers never work, and workers never grumble.
> Happy pupils make a happy school.
> Have you done anything today that would make people like you better?
> Politeness is to do and say
> The kindest thing in the kindest way.
> Smile!

6. During the time that the friendship project is under way, the room may be decorated with pictures of smiling faces and of persons doing kind deeds for each other. In the upper grades a bulletin board committee may be appointed to take care of this. The younger children may make line drawings to illustrate friendly and unfriendly acts, using smiling and grouchy faces in contrast.

7. Hold a class discussion concerning the traits and the actions which will attract friends and those that will drive them away. Then ask each

child to check on himself for a week by keeping a running list of the kind acts he has done for others.

8. Have the boys and girls draw up a list of the social behavior traits which they think can be expected at their age, mimeograph the list, and send it home asking that parents check the traits which they observe in their child and return it to school.

9. Ask the children to make a list of some of the things which kind, friendly people do

    a. At home
    b. At school
    c. In the neighborhood

10. Have each child write a paragraph describing the friendliest person in the class and telling what it is about this person that makes everybody like him. This may be done with or without using the name of the person described.

11. Ask each child to keep a complete list of all the kind and friendly acts seen in and around the school and also a list of unkind and unfriendly acts. This list should be kept for a week and discussed at the next guidance period.

12. Each child may be asked to draw a picture to illustrate "How I Can Be a Kind Friend."

13. For use with the younger children, compose some short sentences which describe pleasing or disagreeable characteristics of children in your own class. (Example: "There is a boy in our class who always smiles and says 'Good morning' when he comes into the room.") If the children think this is a person they would like for a friend, they should draw a smiling face with upturned mouth. But if a sentence describes a person who would not be a desirable friend, the answer should be indicated by a sad face with downturned mouth.

14. Children in the lower grades who cannot write well may indicate their opinions of certain personal characteristics by coloring "balloons." For instance, if a child likes a person who does what the first statement says, he should color the first balloon red; if he does not like him, he should color it black.

Takes turns with toys.
Pushes and shoves when going to the
    lunchroom or playground.
Tattles a great deal.
Always plays fair.
Is willing to share with others.
Says kind things to others.
Is always polite.
Teases and picks at younger children.
Is especially kind to new pupils.
Will not play unless he can have his own way.

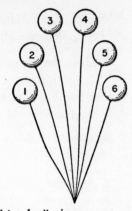

15. The younger children may observe a "friendship day" about once a week. On this day each child who wishes to do so may choose a friend for the day. He may sit by the friend, walk with him, play with him, and try to do something nice for him. This activity helps little children to know their group members and to work and play better together.

16. Start a "kind words campaign." Make the children conscious of the importance of saying only kind things about others. If a pupil is heard making an unkind remark about any other pupil, he should be reminded of the campaign. Special mention may be made of those who have not been heard saying anything unkind about others during the week.

17. Help the children plan a campaign to *do* nice things for others—for those whom they do not particularly like as well as for their special friends. This may take the form of a game in which each child draws the name of some other child in the room. During the week the one who draws the name is to be a "secret friend" of the one whose name he has drawn and to do something kind for him each day. If the children prefer it that way, better results may be obtained by having boys' names drawn by boys; and girls' names, by girls.

18. Ask your pupils how they think the class should welcome and treat a new pupil. Allow them to make a blackboard list of friendly actions which they would like to adopt as their pattern of class behavior toward newcomers.

19. In connection with a language lesson have each child write a paragraph describing the way he imagines he would feel if he were left out of everything which the other boys and girls do; if he were never asked to

take part in their games; if nobody ever talked to him before or after school; if nobody ever wanted to sit by him in the lunchroom; if he were always the last one to be chosen when teams were made up; and if he had not a single friend at school.

20. Suggest that the children dramatize some different ways of being friendly or kind

a. To a new pupil entering the class.

b. To a child who usually walks home from school alone.

c. To a boy or girl who has been teased about being fat, skinny, freckled, or bowlegged.

d. To a blind person waiting to cross the street.

e. To an old person carrying several heavy bundles.

f. To a small child being bullied by a large boy.

g. To the bully—because he is the one who really needs a friend (see Chap. 8).

21. Explain to the children how each of us needs to belong to a group and to have friends. Tell them that sometimes a boy resorts to pulling the girls' hair, putting his feet in the aisle to trip those who pass, throwing paper wads, and doing numerous other things which will attract attention to himself because he needs more success and recognition or because he is lonely and wants friends. Ask the class to be on the lookout for such children and to think of ways of befriending them and making them happier. The personality and the disposition of the attention getter are likely to improve when he realizes that he can be noticed without having to perform silly antics.

22. Ask the children to describe a person who is happy, to draw or cut out pictures of happy people, and to demonstrate the posture, the walk, and the expression of a happy person. They may illustrate unhappiness in the same way. Then ask them to watch for children who show evidences of being lonely, unhappy, and friendless, and to make a special effort to be friendly to them.

23. You may find it beneficial to have private conferences with some of the children. If you think it wise, show a particular child a sociometric chart of the class (without names, of course), explaining how he is rated by his classmates. The unpopular child may be given some specific pointers for improving his status. The popular one may be asked to do some definite things for the neglected children who would like to have him for a friend.

24. Suggest that the children compose a "friendship song" to be the theme song of the class.

25. Suggest that the children play a game of collecting smiles. Tell them to count the times during the day that they can do or say something so pleasant, kind, or friendly that it will bring a smile to someone's face.

26. The following films are appropriate for use with this lesson:

How Friendly Are You? (for intermediate grades and junior high school), 16 mm., sound, 10 min., Coronet Films, Chicago, 1951. This picture presents some of the values of being friendly and encourages the broadening of one's range of friends through generosity, consideration, and a sincere interest in other people.

The Fun of Making Friends (for kindergarten, primary, and intermediate grades), 16 mm., sound, 10 min., Coronet Films, Chicago, 1951. This film helps teachers of young children guide them to a realization of what friends are and how easy it is to be friendly.

The Outsider, Discussion Problems in Group Living Series (for grades 5 to 9), 16 mm., sound, 11 min., Young America Films, Inc., New York, 1951. This film presents the problem of a girl who feels rejected by the group and leaves the situation open for class discussion.

FOLLOW-UP

This concentrated effort to encourage friendliness should not be just a flash in the pan. Even after this project has been completed and the next one started, the idea of being friendly should be kept constantly before the children. They need to be reminded again and again and to be commended when they remember to be considerate of the feelings of others.

BIBLIOGRAPHY

BARUCH, DOROTHY, W. W. BAUER, WILLIAM S. GRAY, GLADYS G. JENKINS, ELIZABETH R. MONTGOMERY, and HELEN SHACTER: Health and Personal Development Series, Scott, Foresman and Company, Chicago:

Happy Days (grade 1), 1948
Good Times with Our Friends (grade 1), 1948
Three Friends (grade 2), 1948

Five in the Family (grade 3), 1947
The Girl Next Door (grade 4), 1948
You (grade 5), 1948
You and Others (grade 6), 1949
You're Growing Up (grade 7), 1950
Into Your Teens (grade 8), 1951

BULLIS, H. EDMUND: *Human Relations in the Classroom,* The Delaware State Society for Mental Hygiene, Wilmington, Del., 1948, Course II, pp. 186–192.

FEDDER, RUTH: *A Girl Grows Up,* McGraw-Hill Book Company, Inc., New York, 1948, Chap. 5.

JENKINS, GLADYS GARDNER, HELEN SHACTER, and WILLIAM W. BAUER: *These Are Your Children,* Scott, Foresman and Company, Chicago, 1949, pp. 90–92.

JENNINGS, HELEN HALL: *Sociometry in Group Relations,* American Council on Education, Washington, D.C., 1948.

JERSILD, ARTHUR T.: *Child Psychology,* Prentice-Hall, Inc., New York, 1947, Chaps. V, VI.

Staff of the Division on Child Development and Teacher Personnel, Commission on Teacher Education: *Helping Teachers Understand Children,* American Council on Education, Washington, D.C., 1945, Chaps. IX, X.

THORPE, LOUIS P.: *Child Psychology and Development,* The Ronald Press Company, New York, 1946, Chap. 13.

CHAPTER 5

Encouraging Wise Use
of Leisure Time

Aims of This Lesson:
   To discover the interests and aptitudes of pupils.
   To encourage children to use their leisure time to advantage.
   To contribute to the mental health of children by helping them to develop worth-while interests which will take them out of themselves.

A great deal can be learned about a child by finding out what he does during his leisure. The way in which he uses his spare time is often the key to his unmet needs. It is also an indication of his home background, of the interests of his parents, and of his own aptitudes and ambitions.

The way children spend their leisure determines to a certain degree the kind of adults they will become. Youngsters who have nothing more interesting to do with their spare time than to hang around the corner drugstore, stand on the street, or tease the neighbors' children often fall into habits of idleness. They may grow into adults who do not know what to do with their leisure and who must depend upon amusement parks, movies, night clubs, or some other form of paid entertainment for their good times. If they face an evening without plans for such entertainment, they begin to wonder how they can "kill" the time.

Boys and girls who find absorbing ways to spend their leisure while they are young usually have interesting hobbies when they are older. They generally grow into adults who realize the value of time, who know how to find pleasant release from their daily work, who are not bored with their own company, and who have a basis for making friendships with congenial

64

people of similar interests. Future vocations may even develop as the result of childhood interests.

Many well-meaning parents are unable to suggest worth-while activities for boys and girls at different stages of growth. Frequently the leisure time of their children is not directed or supervised in any way.

All one summer from morning until night two children, ages five and eight, were observed playing in their front yard. Although they were of average and above average intelligence, their play seemed to have no plan or purpose. They appeared restless and spent hours upon hours just tearing around. They ran, jumped, rolled on the grass, pulled leaves and twigs from the trees, shouted, called to passers-by, and darted into the street to annoy motorists. They never played ball, jumped rope, skated, played house, or engaged in any of the other activities that children of the same age usually enjoy. Apparently they did not help with any small tasks about the home. Surely, with a little parental direction, these children could have used the time more advantageously. No one will deny that it is the right of childhood to enjoy ample opportunity for play and wholesome recreation. However, much of the free time of boys and girls is frittered away when it could be directed into constructive channels.

Teachers sometimes consider leisure-time activities as altogether outside their realm. They feel no responsibility for what a child does on his out-of-school time. Actually, most children have as many hours of free time each day as they have hours in school. During this time it is possible for them to acquire bad habits and undesirable attitudes which may carry over into school life. Because of her special training in extracurricular activities and because her influence is one of the strongest in a child's life, the teacher is in a position to do a great deal toward creating wholesome attitudes concerning the use of leisure. This can be accomplished not only through planned lessons and group activities but by casual remarks and subtle hints to individuals.

Though teachers cannot control the use of children's time after school hours, they can arouse their interest in suitable group games that can be carried on at home and in the neighborhood. They can casually suggest to those children who read well or who tell interesting stories that they entertain the younger children at home or next door in this way. They can do their bit to encourage boys and girls to learn to set the table, make the beds, cook, sew, administer first aid, use tools, make repairs, and do many other helpful things. School children of all ages should realize the importance of participating in the activities of the home and of taking the responsibility for doing some particular tasks.

One teacher always asks children who seem lonely and unhappy and those who are newcomers in a community about their church affiliation. If it is found that they attend no church, she asks some other children in the same neighborhood and with the same church preferences to take them to religious and social functions. Sometimes shy, withdrawing children who need more social contacts can be helped a great deal by membership in the boy scouts, girl scouts, YMCA, YWCA, or a community welfare or recreation center. A word of encouragement from the teacher or a definite arrangement to go with some other child may be all that is necessary to give them a start.

Children should not be given the impression that they must necessarily be busy at all times. Rest and relaxation are also necessary to a well-rounded life. Boys and girls need some time in which they can think, plan, and dream alone without being supervised or hurried. They should have opportunities to explore and enjoy their everyday surroundings. Life means much more to those who recognize and appreciate the beauty of the flowers, the birds, the clouds, the sunset, and other wonders of nature.

It is well for children who have special talents to spend a reasonable portion of their leisure in developing them. When the teacher notices that a youngster is gifted in some line, she may find out whether or not he is being given private lessons. If the parents are unable to provide such lessons, some individual, group, or organization may be interested in helping. At least, the matter should be brought to the attention of the principal, the music director, or some other person who can advise the child and his parents.

Lessons in addition to schoolwork are fine for children who really want them. However, in order to gratify their own ambitions, parents often impose training in music, art, dramatics, dancing, or public speaking upon children who are not physically and emotionally able to stand the strain. Youngsters should not be so pushed that every minute of their time is filled with lessons, practicing, and studying. School alone is a full-time job for many.

Teachers start many a young person on the road to finding an enjoyable pastime or even a lifework by recognizing and developing a potential ability. Because most children like to do things with their hands, they can readily be interested in hobbies. Older children may have several absorbing interests at the same time. It is expected that children will change their hobbies frequently because certain ones have an appeal only at certain ages.

But although it takes different forms as the child passes through various stages of growth, a basic interest created in childhood often continues through life. A great deal can be learned about the interests and the aptitudes of a child by observing the pattern and the trend of his hobbies.

In trying to help create hobbies for children who have no particular interest, several points should be kept in view. Hobbies are for pleasure and enjoyment. A person does not choose photography as his hobby if making pictures has no special appeal for him. What is fun to one may be work to another. Suggest to a child a hobby that is suitable to his age and stage of development. It should be one that will require no more time and money than he can afford to spend on it. To be worth while, a hobby should be more than busy-work; it should bring out the child's initiative and resourcefulness and cause him to do something creative; or it should contribute in some way to his physical, mental, social, or emotional development.

A child may become interested in a hobby because of the zeal some member of his family has for it. On the other hand, his interest may be killed by the family's lack of patience and understanding of his hobby. Because enthusiasm is heightened and family ties are made stronger by common interests, it is a good idea for the teacher to suggest to boys and girls that they try to start some project in which mother, father, brother, or sister can participate.

Both adults and children are interested in gardening, swimming, camping, ice skating, roller skating, fishing, hunting, riding horseback, dancing, archery, playing musical instruments, playing Ping-pong, playing checkers, raising rabbits, pigeons, cats, dogs, and fish, learning magic tricks, using a chemistry set, and making and decorating pottery.

Some other things that both old and young members of a family may enjoy doing together are studying the stars, making toys from wood, metal, spools, and clothespins, making kites, jewelry, paper flowers, puzzles, Christmas cards, scrapbooks, puppets and marionettes, and articles from plexiglass, painting and decorating bottles for vases, binding books, drawing with crayons and charcoal, painting with water colors, oils, and finger paints, carving wood, soap, and leather, modeling clay and wax, cooking, weaving, sewing, knitting, and hooking rugs.

Practically all young persons like to make collections. At a very early age boys and girls begin to collect rocks, sticks, strings, and odds and ends of all kinds. By the time they are about eight years old they usually start to make real collections of such things as match cases, playing cards, and bottle tops. Some of the things which older children most often collect are autographs, photographs, wild flowers, leaves, insects, butterflies, stamps, coins, rocks, seashells, old glass, Indian relics, arrowheads, comic books, mystery stories, newspaper clippings, phonograph records, cartoons, puzzles, dolls, guns, miniature whatnots, toy animals, model airplanes, model ships, and model trains.

Many collections are kept in a careless, slipshod fashion. After the teacher finds out what a child is collecting, she can help him plan some systematic way of grouping, mounting, labeling, or preserving his treasures. Perhaps a collection may need to be put in special boxes, folders, scrapbooks, or albums. A child who writes poetry may be encouraged to bind his verses in attractive little booklets. A girl who cooks may be helped in starting a file for her recipes.

Teachers not only make leisure hours more enjoyable for children but they also contribute to their mental health when they help them to develop worth-while interests. Shy, fearful, withdrawing children can often be helped by an absorbing hobby which causes them to forget themselves and to participate with other children in a common interest. Daydreaming about an outside activity can sometimes be eliminated by allowing the dream to become a reality. A boy who constantly gazes at the ceiling and thinks about how model airplanes can be made to fly needs more opportunity to work on, not dream about, model planes.

Many a difficult pupil has been won by a teacher who showed an interest in his hobby and who made him feel like a real person because he knew more about some one thing than anyone else in the group—perhaps even more than the teacher. A child who is never able to excel in his schoolwork may experience a feeling of real success and importance by being allowed to bring into the classroom and to explain or demonstrate some outside accomplishment.

Jack was a quiet, slow-learning boy who sat without any show of animation in spite of the teacher's desperate efforts to interest him. A private interview with the boy revealed that he liked to draw and to make things with his hands. But on the occasions when he had taken some of his handwork home to his mother, she had criticized the imperfections in it and had invariably ended by saying, "Your brother Billy always did much better work than this." She had admired and used the articles which the older boy had made for her but now she rejected Jack's offerings. He began taking any handwork made at school to a kindly neighbor. After a while he completely lost interest in any class participation. He said that neither of his parents was interested in his progress. When he showed them his monthly report card, they merely glanced at it, saying, "I don't see why you can't do as well as Billy did when he was your age. Now he is in the university and is going to make something of himself. But look at you!"

Billy's interest in photography had fascinated Jack. But the younger boy was not allowed to touch any of the equipment or even to watch while the pictures were being developed and printed. Jack was made to do all the odd jobs about the house while Billy studied uninterrupted. However, he was never trusted to buy the groceries or to run an errand that required the least initiative or responsibility. When the teacher phoned to ask the mother for an appointment, she was greeted with, "Oh, that's the school. I have been expecting you to call about Jack. We are so ashamed of him. He never does anything right. Now, his brother Billy . . ." The teacher tried to explain to the mother Jack's feeling of rejection and his justifiable jealousy of his brother. She asked the college brother to pay more attention to him and to let him in on some of the interesting things he was doing.

One day the teacher mentioned that she would like to have a name plate for her desk. A day or two later Jack brought to school a beautiful name plate with an intricate design burned in wood. It had obviously taken many hours of painstaking work. The teacher proudly showed it around the school. Jack was asked to make similar plates for the desks of the principal, visiting teacher, health counselor, guidance counselor, and others. With a great deal of pride he worked out different designs for each one. Seeing his own creations displayed and admired, Jack immediately began to experience the feeling of approval which he so much needed. He was taught to operate the motion-picture projector and to do other responsible jobs about the school. Because he had artistic ability, he was asked to make posters and do decorative work of all kinds. Not only had this boy found school life more fun, but his classwork showed miraculous improvement. Strangely enough, he proved not to be nearly so dull as the teacher and his parents had thought him to be.

In this case, as in many others, a teacher's understanding and sympathy for a child's outside interests helped to untangle some badly mixed up emotions.

ACTIVITIES SUGGESTED

1. An approach may be made by asking the class to sit quietly without speaking or moving while the hands of the clock move a space of five minutes. The children will thus be impressed with the length of five minutes of time. Talk to them about the importance of using their time well and the

folly of wasting many short periods of time throughout the day. Emphasize the value of doing tasks quickly and well both at home and at school. Some boys and girls have less leisure time to enjoy because they dawdle over necessary jobs and then have to stay after school or do more homework in the evening to make up for their dallying.

2. Ask each pupil to make an estimate of the amount of time he spends in various activities from the time he leaves school in the afternoon until he goes to bed. The activities may be grouped into (a) going home, (b) playing, (c) helping mother, (d) eating, (e) getting ready for bed, (f) other activities, and (g) time wasted. Talk about the many useful and interesting things that could be done in those minutes when one does not know what to do with one's time and whines to mother, "What can I do now?"

3. As a means of finding out how children use their leisure, each member of the class may be asked to keep a complete diary of Saturday and Sunday experiences or to tell in detail how the last week end was spent.

4. Talk to the children about the importance of being able to do a great many things, such as cooking, sewing, weaving, knitting, using hand tools, playing a musical instrument, and playing games.

5. Suggest that a committee make an attractive bulletin board display of pictures showing children enjoying hobbies or worth-while activities. These may be grouped into hobbies of making, doing, learning, collecting, helping, and earning, and headed by some such caption as, "How do you spend your leisure time? Try some of these ways."

Or the bulletin board may carry companion pictures or clippings showing a child enjoying a hobby and an older person participating in a similar activity or engaging in an occupation to which this hobby might lead. The purpose is to show the trend of a hobby throughout a lifetime.

Some of the children may be interested in making posters about their own hobbies. The best ones may be displayed in the hall so that other classes can enjoy them.

6. Ask each child to fill out a slip giving the following information:

My hobby————————————————————————

What I like most to do in my leisure time————————————

————————————————————————————————

What I would like to learn to do————————————————

Someone in this class who has an interesting hobby——————

His hobby———————————————————————————
My name———————————————————————————

From this information it will be possible to discover the interests of some of the children and to arrange a program of demonstrations and talks given by the children concerning their hobbies. Each child should be given a chance to have an appreciative audience when he shows his hobby. Perhaps if one child has a hobby which someone else would like to adopt, the two can get together. If several children enjoy the same hobby, they may plan a group demonstration. If there are not enough real hobbies to make the lesson interesting, some of the pupils may find and present information about the ones they think they would enjoy.

Make an effort to include every child in this activity. One who apparently does nothing special with his spare time may be able to juggle, whistle, or use a Yo-yo unusually well. Let this child demonstrate to the class any accomplishment that will give him a feeling of being a part of the program.

7. Very young children may be asked to bring some of their treasures to show to their classmates. These may include any of the many odd little items that appeal to small children. Some of them may bring rocks, shells, spools, a tool, a toy, or a book. A special "treasure shelf" or "treasure chest" may be used for arranging a display.

8. For a language lesson have the children write or tell about someone whom they know who has an unusual hobby or who does something interesting or profitable in his spare time. Perhaps some of these people may be invited to visit the class and talk to the pupils.

9. Help the children make a list of things which boys and girls of the age of your group can do in spare time, grouping them as follows:

Collecting	———————	———————	———————
Creating	———————	———————	———————
Helping	———————	———————	———————
Playing	———————	———————	———————
Learning	———————	———————	———————
Enjoying	———————	———————	———————
Earning	———————	———————	———————

10. Teach the children some interesting form of handcraft which you yourself may like to do. Sometimes it is possible to get a parent or other in-

terested person in the neighborhood to come to school and show the children how to do some appropriate kind of handwork.

11. Talk to the children about the fun that can come from finding pretty leaves, rocks, and wild flowers, recognizing different kinds of birds, trees, and plants, discovering outlines of objects when looking at the clouds, and learning the stories of the constellations. At this point the teacher may use some of the phonograph records which reproduce various bird calls, show motion pictures on nature, and plan some interesting walks or field trips.

12. Discuss with the children of the upper grades the possibility of earning money during their spare time. Help them to think of skills which they may acquire and to enumerate job possibilities in their own neighborhood, such as taking care of children, raising rabbits, pigeons, white mice, or chickens; making birdhouses; running errands; and taking care of lawns.

13. As a means of recording personal data that can be used for guidance purposes, it is suggested that the following inventories be used in the upper grades:

> HILDRETH, GERTRUDE: *Personality and Interest Inventory*, Elementary Form (for grades 4 through 8), Teachers College, Columbia University, New York, 1936. This inventory provides for information concerning the child's spare-time activity preferences, interest in sports and games, reading tastes and habits, school subject preferences, together with his own evaluation of his personality characteristics.

> WITTY, PAUL, and ANNE COOMER: *Teacher's and Clinicians' Child Study Record*, Form VI, Northwestern University Psycho-Educational Clinic, Evanston, Ill., 1948. This report of pupil interests and activities consists of four parts: the interest inventory, the book list, the play inventory, and the evaluation guide.

FOLLOW-UP

Having once created an interest, try to keep it alive and growing. From time to time, ask individuals about their hobbies. Let the children know that you are interested in what they are doing.

Continue to bring outside interests into the classroom by suggesting to various children that they use their hobbies as a basis for language lessons, reports, paragraph writing, and storytelling. Many lessons and units can be made vital, attractive, and interesting through the use of hobbies. By knowing the special abilities of the members of a class, it is possible to make use of their various skills in producing a play, planning a picnic, making exhibits, and conducting other group activities.

BIBLIOGRAPHY

BULLIS, H. EDMUND, and EMILY E. O'MALLEY: *Human Relations in the Classroom,* The Delaware State Society for Mental Hygiene, Wilmington, Del., 1947, Course I, pp. 195–199.

GRAY, MADELINE, and ROBERT C. URBAN: *Bright Idea Book,* E. P. Dutton & Co., Inc., New York, 1942.

LETTON, MILDRED CELIA: *Your Child's Leisure Time.* Bureau of Publications, Teachers College, Columbia University, New York, 1949.

MATHIEWS, FRANKLIN K.: *The Boy Scouts Book of Hobbies for Fathers and Sons,* Boy Scouts of America, New York, 1942.

MENNINGER, WILLIAM C.: *Enjoying Leisure Time,* Science Research Associates, Inc., Chicago, 1948. Pamphlet.

PARKHILL, MARTHA, and DOROTHY SPAETH: *It's Fun to Make Things,* A. S. Barnes and Company, New York, 1941.

VERRILL, A. HYATT: *Young Collector's Handbook,* Robert M. McBride & Company, New York, 1948.

CHAPTER 6

Studying Aggressive Behavior

Aims of This Lesson:

To learn to differentiate between aggressiveness which creates and that which destroys.

To try to find the underlying causes of children's defiant, rebellious, and antagonistic behavior.

To help children progress from infantile to mature ways of managing their emotions.

Whether to develop or to subdue aggressiveness in children is a problem of all parents and teachers. Although aggressive behavior is sometimes desirable and sometimes undesirable, it is a common error of adults to think of it only in its negative sense. When it takes the form of ambition, initiative, enterprise, and self-confidence, it is to be cultivated and promoted. When, on the other hand, it manifests itself in hostility, resentment, and hatred, it needs to be brought under control. All children experience aggressive feelings at some time. The turn these feelings take depends largely on the understanding and the training techniques employed by parents and teachers.

The mild, quiet, pleasing child who does not fight, quarrel, or talk out of turn is likely to have the approval and the admiration of his elders but he may be totally lacking in the qualities which will make him a leader of his own generation. In all probability, the bold, talkative, bossy, persistent one who frequently takes initiative without permission and sometimes resists authority will develop a stronger, more dynamic personality. Although the children who display aggressive traits may be frowned upon and rebuked by the teacher, they are often the most popular and influential members of the group. All too often the enthusiasm of these potential leaders is destroyed by the bungling of well-meaning adults.

Aggression is a natural, instinctive trait which is necessary, to a certain degree, in order for youngsters to hold their own among their peers and eventually to achieve independence from their elders. As children grow older it is natural for them to strive for an increasing amount of freedom and to struggle against the many thwarting experiences which they are sure to meet. If they are always prevented from asserting themselves, they either become passive and submissive or resentful and hostile in nature. The wise teacher tries to understand children's aggressive actions and to determine whether they are the result of positive impulses which should be encouraged and guided or whether they are due to negative feelings which need to be released or controlled.

The roots of aggression are often to be found in early home life. A child's hostility may have been aroused by an overprotective or dominating mother, by a fear that his parents do not love him, by the arrival of a new baby in the home, by a jealous feeling that another child in the family is the favored one, or by a general sense of insecurity. Chronic rebellion is often caused by adults who are too strict and demanding in their control. Tension and nervousness in children are sometimes clear reflections of the worries and anxieties of parents. For this reason, it is often necessary to study the home environment and to change the attitudes of the parents before the child can be helped. When a youngster shows off in class, fights, or attempts to run away because he feels that he is not wanted at home, the teacher should not add to his sense of rejection by scolding and disapproval but should try to build up his self-esteem by giving him some extra attention and consideration. When hostile behavior is caused by unfairness or pressure at home, the wise teacher will not increase the child's resentment against authority by further curbing his actions but will try to relax the pressure at school and to make opportunities for him to use initiative and to assume responsibility.

The atmosphere of the classroom itself frequently creates rebellion and antagonism. Teachers who are too strict in their discipline are sure to generate tensions in pupils. A reasonable degree of order and freedom from confusion is essential to good work. However, children are always happier, more responsive, more agreeable, and more susceptible to learning when teachers control them by using good humor and friendliness rather than by making them feel guilty and fearful.

A child who pushes, shoves, kicks, and fights may be indicating to the world that he is desperate for friends. He may act as he does because he feels frustrated by his unpopularity, because he is attempting to retaliate for real or imagined slights, or because he wants to demonstrate his strength to the other children. When a lonely child mistreats his associates in a frantic effort to gain their attention, he should not be punished for his behavior but should be shown a better way to attract and win friends.

There is always an underlying reason when children seem compelled to strike out against every person around them. Because they do not know why they feel out of sorts, they cannot combat the direct cause of their dissatisfaction but they can try to protect themselves from further hurts by being defiant and hard to live with. Although teachers cannot allow aggressive behavior to run rampant, they recognize the rights of children to have strong emotions and to build up feelings of power within themselves. They realize that those who are constantly fighting, quarreling, grabbing, pulling, shoving, hitting, teasing, and destroying property need help and guidance in finding some more acceptable ways to release their mean feelings.

A fourth-grade girl was constantly being reported for fighting with the other children on the way to and from school. Both boys and girls told how she threw rocks, pulled hair, and tripped, scratched, pinched, and fought them at the slightest provocation. When questioned about it, the girl wept bitterly and said that none of the children liked her. Although she did not realize it, this little girl was not fighting at any particular individual or at any special slight which had been shown her, but she was striking out against all the circumstances of her life. Because she had a harelip and was physically unattractive, her family felt ashamed of her and kept her in the background as much as possible. Her mother was employed and reached home each evening just in time for dinner. After school the child returned to a dismal rear upstairs apartment where she was required to clean the rooms, wash the breakfast dishes, and prepare the food for the evening meal. There was no time, opportunity, or place for her to play or to enjoy the companionship of other children. When this condition became known, it was a challenge to the teacher to make school life happier for this child and to arrange for her to participate in some out-of-school activities. One day when the girl was absent, the teacher explained her self-consciousness, hurt feelings, and violent reactions to the other children. Together they made plans for showing her more consideration and friendliness.

Although fighting among children should not be condoned, it cannot be eliminated simply by punishing or trying to place blame. Instead, the problem must be approached indirectly by studying the background of the belligerents and trying to discover the cause of their hostile feelings. Some children resort to fighting as a means of feeling important and secure in their own right. Some fight because this is the only way they have learned to compete successfully with friends of their own age. Some try to solve all their differences by force because of the examples they have always seen at home. Fighting and other forms of hostility are more prevalent among children who are under the constant arbitrary rule of adults.

Youngsters need help in formulating a code of their own with regard to fighting. They are quite naturally confused by the standards of adults who tell them not to start a fight but to strike back if they are struck. They cannot be taught self-assurance simply by being told that they must stand up for their rights. Parents and teachers have to be constantly on the alert to help children progress from the stage of snatching, hitting, and kicking to the stage when they have enough self-control and command of language to settle their disputes peacefully. Youngsters can be taught that it is fairer and more fun to compromise or to arbitrate than to fight. However, there are times when, for the sake of a child's mental health, he needs to feel that he is able, if need be, to meet other children on their own terms.

One sixth-grade boy was overweight, rather awkward, and disinclined to enter into the games of his more aggressive classmates. He found compensation in making a good school record, which caused his adversaries to feel inferior in the classroom. They dubbed him a sissy and a crybaby and waited around the corner to gang up on him each afternoon after school. This boy's father had died when he was an infant and he had been brought up by an anxious, possessive, overprotective mother, who had taught him that it was wrong to fight. This boy became so frightened that he would not go to school unless his mother accompanied him and went again in the afternoon to walk home with him. Finally the boy reached the point of being so tense and nervous over the situation that he was unable to concentrate on his lessons, to eat properly, or to sleep soundly.

Then the mother appealed to the principal, who realized that some conflict is indispensable to the development of personality and that occasionally it is necessary to encourage a child to protect himself. He explained to the boy that, when it is possible, arbitration is a better solution, but that sometimes the only way is to fight. So, keeping their plan a secret, the principal and the boy agreed to meet in the basement each afternoon after school for a brief lesson in boxing. This was a remarkable tonic for the boy's self-confidence and self-assertiveness. He was no longer afraid of the boys. In fact, he began to look forward to the time when he could test his new skill.

Later, when he proved himself a match for any boy who wanted to put on boxing gloves and fight with him, he gained the respect and the friendship of the fellows. His chief worry was eliminated and once again he could bend his efforts toward his studies.

Some children express anger, envy, jealousy, disappointment, revenge, or other unhappy or unfriendly feelings by willfully destroying property. Although they must be held responsible for their acts and made to repair, replace, or pay for the damaged property, they cannot be cured by punishment. Extreme destructiveness in children is a symptom of serious emotional disturbance which calls for thoughtful investigation, study, and treatment. The sly, cowardly boy who deliberately breaks windows and street lamps, throws mud against buildings, tears down fences, and damages property, in general is usually a neglected and unloved child who has no close, warm relationships with either family or friends and who feels hateful and rebellious toward everybody and everything. He may generate a feeling of animosity toward the school and a desire to destroy its property if he has an unsympathetic teacher, if he is unable to find his place in the group, or if he feels that he is being unjustly treated by any of the school personnel. A youngster who cannot win the esteem of his fellows by excelling in any of the things that are important to them sometimes tries to prove his toughness by joining a gang of young vandals. Unless such a child is helped to get his emotions straightened out and is given some real opportunity to gain approval and to make friendships, his feelings of hatred and destructiveness are sure to increase.

Because Charlie's conduct had been unsatisfactory, he was not allowed to make model airplanes with the group. He felt so resentful that he broke into the building that night and destroyed the work of the other boys. When his guilt was discovered, he seemed to revel in the unfavorable attention that he received as a result. Reprimands and punishment only added adult recognition to his achievement. He had the satisfaction of knowing, too, that if he could not enter an airplane in the contest, neither could the other boys.

Many of the activities which are so disturbing to adults are not acts of intentional destruction, disobedience, or disorderliness, but are characteristic behavior of certain stages of development. When teachers feel the urge to suppress children who are not acting as grownups do, they should remember that some types of behavior are natural steps in achieving maturity. Too much opposition or interference from adults only tends to prolong these phases of growth. Teachers need to make a study of the normal behavior of children at various stages. When they know what to expect of the youngsters in their classes, they will realize that it is wise to allow them freedom to play at war games and to go through all the other normal stages of releasing their aggressive feelings.

Refusing to conform to social customs, rebelling at school rules and regulations, and meeting all problems with some kind of aggressive behavior are a child's ways of expressing his bothers. Such actions are a challenge to the teacher to find out what there is in his background or environment that is causing the trouble. When a child is consistently noisy, irritating, or belligerent, he is usually fighting against circumstances that have gone wrong in his life. A sympathetic teacher will not think of him in terms of being bad and will not blame him for the way he feels. Instead, she will accept his behavior as a natural reaction under the circumstances and will help him to find a more satisfying way of meeting his problem. It is difficult to feel kindly toward a child when he is defiant and belligerent, but this is the time when he is most in need of kindness.

Some teachers find it hard to cope with behavior problems without using force. They punish every action which they feel is intended as a threat to their authority. A teacher's reaction to aggressive behavior is greatly affected by her own physical well-being and her emotional state of mind at the particular time. If her needs for success, recognition, a secure and happy home life, and satisfactory social relationships have not been met, she is likely to have aggressive feelings of her own which need to be expressed. The teacher should see to it that her mental health is good so that she may be able to accept without shock or show of emotion the attacking, aggressive behavior of children in her classroom.

It is impossible to control the violent instincts of children simply by applying strict methods of discipline. Instead of getting the hostile feelings out, scolding, criticism, sarcasm, and prohibitions only increase the antagonism and make it more difficult than ever to eradicate. Slapping a child, keeping him after school, imposing extra work on him, shaming him, ridiculing him before the class, requiring a public apology, or embarrassing him and wounding his pride in some other way may relieve the teacher's own state of tension and frustration but it is almost certain to aggravate the behavior problem. Although such measures may bring temporary quiet and order, they are likely to generate more rebellion and defiance and to set in motion a whole chain of attacks and counterattacks between teacher and pupil.

Aggressiveness can be managed better when the feelings that caused it are taken into consideration. By studying the child's records, talking with his previous teachers, visiting in his home, and watching him on the playground and in the lunchroom, it is usually possible for the alert teacher to find out some of the reasons for his behavior. Then the problem may be helped by seeing to it that some pressure is relieved, by seeking the cooperation of parents, or simply by giving the child more opportunities to get his feelings out in the open. When, however, the case is too complicated for the teacher to handle, she should endeavor to get professional help. A child should not be allowed to become delinquent before a psychiatrist or a psychologist is consulted.

Aggression that is not gotten out of the system in early years is often stored up only to come out later in life in the form of resentments, intolerant attitudes, hatreds, and prejudices which may be entirely unrelated to the original antagonistic feeling. Most of the neurotic difficulties and the immaturities of adults are the direct result of unsolved emotional disturbances and childish feelings of hostility which were not released in early life. The outlet which some grownups formerly found by shrieking, hitting, banging their heads, and spitting may still be sought through swearing, refusing to talk, and purposely offending others. Children who are constantly provoked to anger and are not allowed to vent their emotions are actually being given practice in the kind of antagonistic behavior which will later turn them into quarrelsome and domineering home members, overbearing employers, or troublemaking employees.

It is natural for all persons to have hostile feelings at some time. The harm lies in repressing these feelings and hiding them in the subconscious. When undesirable emotions can be expressed honestly, they seem less important and tend to disappear. A child is fortunate indeed when he has a parent or a teacher with whom he can share all of his fantasies, fears, conflicts, guilts, and belligerent and destructive impulses, knowing that she will not condemn, blame, or punish him or even think less of him because of his thoughts. Every child who has an emotional problem should have an opportunity to have a private talk with a teacher who will let him know that she understands how he feels, who will listen sympathetically without taking any personal offense at what he says, and who will not make him feel afraid or guilty even though she cannot sanction his badness.

When having a personal interview with a belligerent child, it is no use asking him why he behaves as he does, because he does not know. Although he realizes that his behavior does not meet with the approval of others, he also realizes that he cannot help acting as he does. He understands nothing about basic physical and emotional causes for his actions. The teacher should not chide or lecture the offender but should remain in the background as much as possible, simply encouraging the child to say anything he feels like saying, assuring him that she understands his feelings in the matter, and gradually leading him to see his behavior as others see it. Just by talking, the child will get release from his angry, hostile, or guilty feelings and he may unconsciously give the teacher a clue to his troubles.

One of the most valuable things a teacher can do for the cause of mental health is to help children analyze, study, and understand their own feelings. This can be done impersonally through the use of posters, motion pictures, stories, and group discussions concerning the way emotions spread and affect the dispositions of others, things that can be done to prevent ill feelings from arising, and differences between infantile and mature ways of handling frustrations. It is good practice for children to learn to settle their disputes amicably, to consider the opinion of the group in adjusting certain individual problems, and to vote on issues that are important to all. Even a group of kindergarten children can be gathered around in an informal circle where they can think and talk freely about their bothers and their feelings and reactions toward adults and other children. Group guidance is well worth while even though it must be done at the expense of an occasional arithmetic or geography lesson. Subject-matter requirements should never take precedence over the emotional needs of children.

Younger children often get release from their unpleasant emotions by playing them out with dolls. As they grow older they can learn to work off some of their aggressive feelings by writing or painting about the way they feel. The music and dancing lessons, clubs, and other adult-sponsored activities in which so many children participate give them very little time to let off steam in a safe way by yelling, digging, climbing, and jumping. Youngsters need many opportunities at school to use tools, to sing, to play active outdoor games, to pound on modeling clay, and to express their feelings through puppets, rhymes, and dramatics.

When children have been accustomed to being suppressed and punished for aggressive behavior, they may be surprised to find a teacher who accepts and understands their feelings. When they are first allowed to express themselves freely, they may appear to take undue advantage of the situation by getting out a great deal of pent-up emotion, including some old hurts of long standing. But after a while, when all these stored up feelings have been released, their displays of negativism, rebellion, and hostility are likely to show a marked decrease.

It is true that some children who have suffered severe early deprivations continue to show aggression for long periods of time. Those who have been tested and definitely diagnosed as psychopathic personalities do not respond to the release treatment or to group therapy. Such children are self-centered, disorderly, disturbing, and destructive. They apparently experience no anxiety or guilt concerning their behavior and feel no need to be accepted socially. Their chief enjoyment in belonging to a group is the satisfaction they get from disrupting it. Since psychopathic personalities are lacking in the capacity for personal and group relationships, the faculty for moral judgment, and regard for social rules and regulations, they usually respond most successfully to treatment in an institution where there is an authoritarian environment.

ACTIVITIES SUGGESTED

No subtle probing activities are needed to discover the children who always meet their problems with some kind of aggressive behavior. These youngsters cannot and will not be ignored. In dealing with them the chief problem is to devise ways of letting them admit and drain off some of their bitterness and resentment. Focus on feelings. Be constantly on the alert for opportunities to foster good feelings toward parents, classmates, and teachers.

1. Draw the children of any age group into an informal circle and encourage them to talk about things that trouble them. When they find that many of their worries are common to others, they will talk frankly and freely about them.

Conflict with authority is one of the most frequent causes of frustration in elementary school children. Feeling that adults are unjust and unreasonable in their demands, youngsters often have an intense urge to assert their own wills. If you can create an atmosphere in which they will talk freely, you will find that many of them are concerned about relationships with parents. Help them to try to see the parental viewpoint. When parents appear impatient and unsympathetic, they may be tired, worried, and overworked, and they may feel that the children do not understand and do not help enough. Perhaps they act as they do because of things that happened in their early lives and now they are treating their children as they were treated when they were young.

Ask the children to mention typical situations in which parents or teachers impose restrictions that seem unfair. Plan a "panel discussion" in which certain pupils assume the roles of parents, children, teachers, or other characters and give their opinions on various questions.

2. Youngsters have a right to understand their own feelings and the causes back of them. Explain to them some of the emotional reasons for fighting, destructiveness, and quarreling. Tell them how some problems can be helped more by the cooperation of the group than by the teacher herself. Show how the children who have a habit of fighting may not actually be fighting a particular individual but may be striking at the world in general because they feel unwanted and unloved and they need friends. Explain how boys and girls should try to understand their unhappy classmates, to be more friendly to them, and to try to make them feel that they really belong.

3. Keep a "bother box" at a convenient place in the room and suggest that the children drop into this box anonymous accounts of the things that disturb and annoy them. Or ask each child to keep a small "book of troubles" in which he enters in his own way his hurts and bad feelings. Or invite the children to write letters to you about their problems and drop them in a "mailbox" in the room.

Boys and girls get a certain amount of relief from tension just by writing out their bothers. But the manner in which the activity is suggested to them, the feeling they have toward the teacher, and the way in which the problems are handled determine the actual benefit derived. It is important that the writing out of bothers be followed by quiet, private, informal talks with the teacher or by group discussions of problems that are of mutual concern. If you have the confidence and good will of your pupils, they will feel free to discuss their troubles with you, knowing that you will not scold or preach but will lend a sympathetic ear and will permit them to talk until they see their own problems more clearly.

4. Allow children to release their feelings through dramatization. The defiant, rebellious, belligerent ones need opportunities to play at being in authority, at being powerful, and at being admired. Plan the dramatizations so that these children may have roles in which they can talk big and authoritatively. They usually like to play the parts of army officers, policemen, traffic directors, FBI agents, airplane pilots, and teachers. Being able to mystify others with magic tricks gives some children a feeling of supremacy which they need.

5. Ask each child to write or tell a story or draw a picture about anybody or anything that he dislikes, that bothers him, or that he feels unkindly about.

6. Watch the aggressive children in your classes. Try to find suitable outlets for those who have leadership possibilities. Be alert to the needs of the ones who want to push, shove, fight, and destroy, and provide safe ways for them to vent their feelings. Singing, playing active games, boxing, building, finger painting, easel painting, and clay modeling are excellent ways of working off energy.

7. Encourage the boys and girls to get rid of any old resentments by discussing questions similar to the following:

a. What are some of the things that often hurt you and made you angry when you were a very small child?

b. Do you ever remember feeling a strong hatred for anyone? Whom? When?

c. Do you remember a punishment which you thought was unfair (like being locked in a dark closet or being sent to bed without your supper)?

d. Do you recall having your feelings hurt by a teacher?

8. Talk to the youngsters about good ways of adjusting their disputes peacefully. By carefully leading the discussion it is possible to get them to see how their arguments over possessions, rights, and viewpoints can be settled without fighting. Consider with them the possibilities of getting along together by taking turns, sharing, obeying the rules of fair play, compromising, and seeking the opinions and advice of others. Suggest that they watch for and report to the class on any good ways to settle disputes which they observe from time to time. Also ask them to report on the lost time, the hard feelings, and the injuries to persons or property resulting from disputes which are not settled peacefully.

9. Make the children conscious of the kind of behavior that is normal for their age level. Explain how older boys and girls who are emotionally disturbed may act like preschool children. Get the pupils to list some of the mature and some of the immature actions which they observe every day among persons of their own age. Inaugurate an Act Your Age Campaign in which everyone will be made to realize the importance of managing his strong feelings in as mature a manner as possible. Ask each person to be responsible for a poem, an essay, a poster, a drawing, a motto, a skit, or some other creative effort to illustrate ways of acting or not acting one's age.

10. Although you are well aware of the aggressive children in your class, you may gain a better insight into their problems by finding out about their

behavior at home and in the neighborhood. A check list similar to the one below may be sent home to be filled out by parents:

To the parents:
We are trying to help children learn to manage some of their aggressive tendencies. If your child has any definite behavior problems which you feel should be worked on before they affect his personality or become fixed habits, will you please check them? Any others may be added at the end of the list.

Fights
Quarrels
Teases maliciously
Bullies younger children
Pushes and shoves
Grabs and pulls
Kicks and hits
Bites and scratches
Tries to appear tough and hard-boiled
Is bossy and officious
Has temper tantrums
Destroys property
Pouts and sulks

Parent's signature ————————

11. The following films are very effective for use with this lesson:

Act Your Age (for junior and senior high schools), 16 mm., sound, 13½ min., Coronet Films, Chicago, 1949. This picture shows examples of temper, weeping, and other common types of infantile reactions as they continue into adolescence. It offers a method of self-evaluation to help overcome the social handicaps that come with inability to grow up.

Other People's Property, Discussion Problems in Group Living Series (for grades 5 to 9), 16 mm., sound, 11 min., Young America Films, Inc., New York, 1951. This film presents a situation in which a boy becomes angry because he is kept after school and tries to get revenge. It offers no ready-made solution but leaves a problem to be discussed by students.

Problem Children (for adults), 16 mm., sound, 20 min., Ohio Division of Mental Hygiene, Columbus, 1947. This story of two school boys shows how the school can help both the shy, withdrawn child and the aggressive, antisocial one.

Ways to Settle Disputes (for primary and intermediate grades), 16 mm., sound, 10 min., Coronet Films, Chicago, 1950. This film suggests compromise as one of the simple ways to prevent and settle disagreements. Other ways are presented as a guide for students to follow while maintaining a cooperative attitude on the part of both parties.

FOLLOW-UP

Make a chart containing the names of children in your class who are quarrelsome, belligerent, negativistic, defiant, and destructive, the treatment which you have applied in each case, and the results obtained. Check this chart from time to time and consider the progress you are making. Be sure to commend the children who have found satisfactory ways of handling their emotional problems.

BIBLIOGRAPHY

ATKIN, EDITH LESSER: *Aggressiveness in Children,* The Child Study Association of America, New York, 1950. Pamphlet.

BARUCH, DOROTHY W.: *Parents Can Be People,* Appleton-Century-Crofts, Inc., New York, 1944, Chaps. 7, 14.

BRECKENRIDGE, MARIAN E., and E. LEE VINCENT: *Child Development,* W. B. Saunders Company, Philadelphia, 1949, pp. 452–458.

GESELL, ARNOLD, and FRANCES L. ILG: *The Child from Five to Ten,* Harper & Brothers, New York, 1946, pp. 159–217, 326–391.

KORNER, ANNELIESE FRIEDSAM: *Some Aspects of Hostility in Young Children,* Grune and Stratton, New York, 1949.

RATHS, LOUIS E.: *An Application to Education of the Needs Theory,* Louis E. Raths, Bronxville, N.Y., 1949. Pamphlet.

CHAPTER 7

Handling Angry Feelings

Aims of This Lesson:

To find the hidden causes of temper tantrums and other violent emotional outbursts in individual children.

To help children to release, not to store up, angry feelings.

To encourage boys and girls to learn to handle their aggressive feelings in acceptable ways that will not injure or antagonize others.

Anger is an emotion with which every teacher has to deal at some time or other. It may manifest itself in the form of temper tantrums in very young children and even in preadolescents who have allowed fits of ill temper to become an established habit. As children grow older they usually cease to fall on the floor, kick, scream, and hold their breath, but they often show the same feelings by crying, hitting, stamping their feet, slamming doors, throwing objects, arguing, calling names, and attempting to hurt the feelings of others. Some persons express their anger by boasting, making sarcastic remarks, blustering, or trying to appear tough. Others sulk, pout, decline food, fail to speak, refuse to play, or simply withdraw from the group. By watching children in the classroom, in the lunchroom, and on the playground, the teacher can easily detect those who are attempting to hide violent emotions as well as those who are plainly displaying them. Both groups need help.

When a child shows some form of uncontrolled anger, the teacher should be on the alert for the cause. It is vitally important that the problems of young children be studied and analyzed while the source of the trouble is still near the surface, where it can be plainly recognized. As persons grow older, it becomes increasingly difficult to understand their behavior either because they attempt to cover up their real feelings or because the origin of the feelings has been lost in some long-forgotten experience of early childhood.

Children's displays of temper are often brought on by fatigue, hunger, insufficient sleep, lack of exercise, or other physical cause. A child is more susceptible to attacks of extreme anger if he has bad tonsils and adenoids, poor teeth, impaired eyesight, defective hearing, or some other physical condition which needs to be corrected.

If a child's emotional outburst is not due to weariness, malnutrition, or illness, the teacher should take another look at the circumstances that seem to have irritated him. When the thing which thwarts the child is not sufficient reason for an explosion, the next step is to try to find the hidden cause of the conflict. It may be a faulty home environment or poor guidance on the part of parents or teachers. It has been found that anger and other types of aggressive behavior are most often present in children who feel deprived of love and affection, who have reason to feel jealous or inadequate, or who are under pressure to do something they are unable or unwilling to do.

Frequent and violent outbursts of anger or spells of sulking and pouting are sometimes due to the hostility which children unconsciously feel toward society in general because it makes unreasonable demands on them. A youngster may finally reach the breaking point when adults constantly subject him to too rigid discipline or put too much pressure upon him to learn faster than he is capable of learning or to act more mature than he actually is. Feelings of anger and frustration can often be traced to a thoughtless parent or teacher who invariably finds fault with a child's creative efforts, tries to impose upon him an adult's way of doing things, or blocks all of his endeavors by telling him not to do this or that. When adults consistently scold, belittle, and stifle children's impulses to assert themselves, they can expect not only temper tantrums but defensiveness, withdrawal, indifference, and other undesirable reactions.

Anger in children is often caused by their inability to handle situations. There are certain things that may cause frustrations at different age levels. For example, a young child may become irritated when he is suddenly interrupted at his work or play and not allowed to finish what he has started. An older child may feel thwarted when he cannot get the pieces of a model airplane together, when he cannot make a kite fly, or when he cannot get a drawing to look like he wants it to.

The way children react to trying situations is often a reflection of the way they have seen their parents act under similar circumstances. Expressions of temper are contagious. Children are quick to imitate adults of their family who are victims of worry, vexations, and tensions and who are prone to strike out at anybody who happens to be in reach when they are in an angry mood. In the same way, they learn self-control by living with parents who can manage their moods. When a child goes into a rage over trivial matters, it is usually not the child himself who is to blame, but the model from whom he copies.

Some children get into a habit of making unpleasant scenes when things do not go to please them. They find that by prolonging a temper tantrum until they have aroused the pity or exhausted the endurance of their parents, they can gain a desired end. Then they deliberately and frequently repeat this action which is always sure to make them the center of attention or excitement.

When a child is often angry, the teacher should try to get at the root of the trouble. It is advisable to find out from parents about the child's behavior at home so that treatment can be adjusted to his particular situation. Different methods must be used to help the youngster who is not well, the one who lives in a home that is emotionally disturbed, the one who feels inferior because of a more gifted brother or sister, the one who vaguely feels that his parents are disappointed in him, and the one who is constantly dominated by other members of the family. By considering his home environment, the teacher can avoid putting too much pressure on a child who may already be pushed or suppressed beyond endurance.

A child may be mild and quiet at school where he feels adequate and secure and yet have temper tantrums at home where he feels that he does not get enough attention, consideration, or love. Or he may show an outburst of rage at the smallest bit of discipline at school because of pent-up anger which he has never dared to express at home. Parents may blame the teacher for such conduct in a child who has always seemed to them to be quiet and even-tempered. They often find it hard to realize that the negativistic and defiant attitudes at school are the direct result of constant repression at home. It is true that the school itself is sometimes to blame for hostile feelings. Children who are seldom antagonistic at home may be rebellious at school because of unjust or unreasonable punishment, because of the pressure of class work that is too difficult, or because of inability to handle social situations with other children.

When children are angry, frustrated, and thwarted, they need to find relief in some way or other from the pressure they feel. But if they try to express their anger directly at the person who caused it, they are usually scolded, punished, and made to feel guilty and uncomfortable. So, instead of attacking the parent, teacher, or classmate who aroused his animosity, a child may whine, cry, tease, fight, bully, or become destructive. He may react by being stubborn and antagonistic toward the group and opposing everything they want to do. If he is not allowed to get his feelings out more directly, he may vent his anger by pulling wings off flies, stoning birds, tormenting cats and dogs, or doing some other act of cruelty toward insects or animals. When his anger is aroused by a sense of inadequacy, the child may even release his feelings by pulling his own hair, biting his fingernails, stumbling and falling purposely, or otherwise hurting himself. He may turn his rage in upon himself by having a temper tantrum. Thus, instead of fighting someone else, he knocks himself out.

It is the belief of modern psychologists that some outlet for feelings of aggression is necessary. But when children are told that it is bad to display temper and are severely punished for fits of anger, they become obsessed with feelings of guilt and fear. They often repress their emotions until the tension becomes unbearable and shows up in some worse form of behavior. If they are forced to suppress all their early hatreds and resentments, they may learn to carry them deep in their souls only to release them with increased strength when they grow up. As adults, they are likely to be spiteful and hostile in their dealings with others, to have violent hatreds and prejudices, to try to crush minority groups, or to storm, rave, and throw and break things in fits of anger. Childish hurts that are forced to lie hidden for years often appear in adulthood as phases of immaturity. Some young persons so completely succeed in covering up all their emotions that they grow up to be uninteresting, lacking in force, and colorless in personality. They may become the kind of adults who are easily led, readily confused, unproductive, indecisive, and unable to act or assert themselves.

Suppression and repression of anger, fear, hate, jealousy, and other emotions are known to be closely related to asthma, arthritis, colitis, stomach ulcers, high blood pressure, heart disease, allergic illnesses, diarrhea, pains in the back, neck, and shoulders, and many other physical ailments. Since the mind and body are inseparable, it is small wonder that somatic ills befall the person who grows up with all his emotions still smoldering within himself and who allows these emotions to explode inside rather than outside his body.

Parents and teachers can do a great deal to forestall outbursts of temper by preventing situations which arouse undesirable emotions. When angry feelings are unavoidable, however, they should not be repressed but should be allowed to run their course. Adults who pride themselves on never allowing a child to "talk back" to them cause many boys and girls to store up feelings that make them rebellious and antagonistic throughout life. Instead of shaming, scolding, and punishing children for their emotional upheavals, an understanding teacher will do everything possible to show them that she sympathizes, that she knows it is normal to have mean feelings sometimes, and that she understands that they have real reasons for being angry. When allowing a child to pour out his feelings, she should be able to say convincingly, "I know you are mad. That's all right. I feel that way myself sometimes." Simply by being assured that his emotions are understood and accepted as natural, an upset child can get his feelings out into the open and be rid of them. More important still, while expressing his present feelings, he may at the same time work off some of his earlier resentments toward an environment that has disturbed him emotionally.

While his mother was employed, one unfortunate child was left with a demanding, domineering nursemaid who constantly nagged, scolded, and threatened him. This small child was frustrated and blocked at every turn. Because he was not permitted to pit his fury against the direct cause of his trouble, he became antagonistic toward the world in general. His anger mounted with each injustice, and punishment only increased his inner turmoil. During the night he screamed, cried, and gritted his teeth in his sleep. His interest in blocks, balls, and wagons was replaced by a passion for playing with battle axes, swords, spears, daggers, and guns. He spent his time chopping and mutilating imaginary victims. When the nursemaid was discharged and the mother gave up her job and remained at home, the pressure from the outside was relaxed. But the hostility which had been repressed was still there.

Realizing that something must be done to get the rebellious feeling out of his system, this little boy's mother was glad when he suggested that they play a game in which she would be a witch and he would attempt to capture her. For about a year the child found his greatest satisfaction in pretending that he was torturing the witch, chopping off her head, and throwing her into a dungeon. As time went on, however, the game was played less violently and less frequently. The night terrors and other signs of tension disappeared. But it took much longer to uproot the feelings than it had taken to implant them and the scars remained. The child continued to hold a feeling of intense and unreasonable animosity toward any hired per-

son who came to the house and to become extremely upset at the thought of
being left alone with a sitter.

Displays of temper are a necessary means of emotional release for young
children who have not yet learned more socialized ways of expressing their
feelings. But complete lack of control is a sign of immaturity in older boys
and girls. Emotional stability must be achieved by a slow, gradual process,
not by severe discipline or by repression of all hostile behavior. Step by step
children can be taught that there are more acceptable ways of meeting
difficult situations than by storming, sulking, or crying. Finally they may
come to realize how foolish it is to nag, tease, argue, and refuse to cooperate when there are so many more satisfying ways of getting along with
friends and of gaining a point with parents or teachers.

Children should be encouraged to explain frankly but calmly to their
classmates or family exactly how they feel about a slight or an injustice.
They should be urged to express their opinions freely and openly during
class and committee meetings. When they have learned the value of releasing their own feelings and of talking over situations which have aroused
their anger, they will recognize the right of others to do the same thing and
will be willing to listen while their friends air their grievances. Children
also need practice in considering the opinions and respecting the viewpoints
of others and in effecting satisfactory compromises.

Although youngsters should be assured that their defiant feelings are
accepted and their expressions of anger are tolerated, they cannot be allowed
to let themselves go to the extent of injuring others, hurting themselves,
or damaging property. Anger is a perfectly normal and natural emotion
but, if allowed to run wild, it can be very harmful. Everything possible
should be done to prevent angry behavior from becoming a habit.

A child who is subject to temper tantrums needs all the help he can get
to outgrow a habit which may otherwise be a great handicap to him in
later life. It is useless to try to reason with a child who is having a fit of
anger. The best thing to do is to let him get his violent feelings out of his
system. The teacher should leave the child alone and ignore the tantrum
if possible, try to give him a graceful way out of the situation, and then
treat him as if nothing had happened. She should not lose her own temper,
demand an apology, penalize or punish the child, or allow him to gain any
satisfaction or gratify any desire by means of the tantrum. If the outburst
lasts very long, it is sometimes wise to remove the child from the room
until he has recovered. Afterward, the teacher should try to discover the
need that was being expressed by the fit of temper and to avoid the frus-

trating situation that was the immediate cause of it. Tantrums are frequently an indication that a child is under pressure and needs more independence or that he needs more attention, interest, and affection. Sometimes he simply needs to have his ego built up. In the latter case, the teacher can help immeasurably by praising him and giving him a reputation to live up to.

Children should be taught to seek other ways of releasing their feelings than by becoming unpleasant and disagreeable to those about them. Some persons rid themselves of unhappy moods by playing a musical instrument, singing, painting, drawing, writing out their feelings, or getting busy at something that requires physical activity. Others find that it helps to beat a drum, drive nails, punch a bag, or bat a ball. Sweeping, walking, digging in the garden, raking leaves, and shoveling snow are a few of the many safe and useful ways to reduce anger.

In childhood, social adjustment is made difficult and the efficiency of ordinary learning is greatly impaired by the power of angry and hostile emotions, particularly if they are suppressed. In the adult world, promotions are missed, friends are lost, and life becomes unpleasant for the person who makes a scene every time he fails to get what he wants. The person who is so lacking in self-control that his moods and reactions cannot be depended upon and who is so sensitive and touchy that he is likely to be offended at any unexpected or insignificant thing cannot be very popular with his associates. One of the most important things, therefore, that a teacher can do to ensure the happiness and success of her pupils is to help them learn to manage their moods and control their emotions.

ACTIVITIES SUGGESTED

The activities used in connection with this lesson should be selected according to the needs of the individual members of the group and should be altered to suit any special problems which may need attention.

1. As a language lesson assignment ask the children to write, tell, or dictate to you some thoughts on the subject of "Things That Make Me Angry" or "Some of the Big Worries of Boys (or Girls) My Age." By analyzing and studying these reports, the teacher should gain an insight into the problems of at least some of the children. It will be helpful in many cases to have personal interviews with these children. Merely by talking to an interested listener they may be able to release their feelings and to work out solutions to some of their difficulties.

2. You may discover some of the emotional needs of your pupils by having each child in the class keep over a period of several days a list of the times he becomes angry, the reasons for his anger, the persons involved, and the way he meets the situation. These may be confidential accounts which are only for the teacher's use or they may be discussed in class, depending upon the wishes of the children. In either case, ask the boys and girls to reflect on the circumstances which caused hard feelings and to decide whether their anger was justifiable.

3. Keep a list of the times that various children come into conflict with you or with the other children, together with comments on how the situation is handled, and the results. Ask some of the parents to keep similar lists concerning conflicts at home. Use these lists as a basis for a class discussion of acceptable and unacceptable ways of settling differences.

4. Ask each child to sit quietly and thoughtfully for a period of five minutes while he asks himself if his friends are frequently angry at him or if he has recently lost any friends. If so, he should check on himself. Is he irritable, cross, or easily angered because he is tired, worried, or sick? Does he always want to have his own way at any cost? Is he unusually sensitive and touchy? Help children to learn to look at themselves objectively, to consider how their behavior affects others, and then to try to work on themselves to improve their weaknesses.

5. Suggest that each child in the class secretly choose some person whom he does not like very well and toward whom he often has angry feelings. Describe the satisfaction he can experience if he will try to change this person from a disagreeable adversary into a friend by applying the principle of the Golden Rule, by saying complimentary instead of cutting things to him, by trying to find opportunities to build up his ego, and by making him feel appreciated.

6. Suggest to the pupils that they make a bulletin-board display of magazine and newspaper pictures of persons who are out of sorts. Call attention to the facial expressions and the gestures of those who are experiencing anger. Talk with the children about the effect which one's hostile emotions have on one's looks, health, personality, and good times, as well as the effect on the dispositions of others.

7. The younger children may be provided with housekeeping materials and indestructible dolls with which to play out home situations. If a child

has indicated that it makes him angry to have his parents go out in the evening and leave him at home, to have an older brother enjoy privileges that are denied him, to have his mother give all her attention to the sick baby, or to be made to go to bed earlier than the children next door, he may be able to release his feelings by enacting such scenes with dolls or puppets.

Good examples of ways in which parents and teachers can use dramatizations in helping young children with their social relationship problems, in ridding them of undesirable feelings, and in preparing them to meet new situations may be found in Rosemary Lippitt's *Psychodrama in the Home,* Beacon House, Inc., New York, 1947.

8. Set up some imaginary situations which will provide problems similar to the ones the children in your class may be facing. Then ask a number of different children to tell how they would handle each problem. Or the situations may be dramatized, being careful to select the characters so that each child will play a part with which he has difficulty in real life. Children in the audience should be encouraged to comment on the portrayals of the various characters. Examples:

a. There is a Saturday matinee which you especially want to attend. You have been standing in line for an hour to get your ticket. When it is announced that only a few seats are left and you realize that you will probably be the last one admitted, two boys push ahead of you in line.

b. The family overslept this morning, so you were late getting started to school. As you were collecting your books, you found that your little sister had scribbled on the homework with which you had taken such pains last night. Just as you reached the corner you realized that you had forgotten your lunch money and had to return for it. Thus you missed the bus and reached school too late to take part in an assembly program for which you had practiced. When you tripped, fell against a desk, and broke your new wrist watch, all because another pupil had carelessly left his books in the aisle, it was almost more than you could stand.

9. The children's answers to the following and other similar questions will give you an insight into their own reactions to thwarting situations and may also furnish clues to some of their home problems. Examples:

a. One little girl did not want to carry an umbrella to school because she thought that the other girls would not be taking umbrellas. Her mother insisted, however. The girl slammed the door and left the house without saying good-by. What do you suppose she was thinking as she walked to school that morning?

b. A mother and father went out of town for a week and left the children in care of their grandmother. During this time, the children were not allowed some of their usual privileges. Because the grandmother would not permit one of the boys to go to a neighbor's home after dinner, he went to bed early and lay awake for a long time. What do you suppose he was thinking?

10. Have the entire class or an appointed committee help to prepare a questionnaire concerning angry feelings. As they answer these questions about themselves, the children will become more conscious of their own feelings. By noting the questionnaires which show a high percentage of positive answers, the teacher will be able to recognize some of the cases which need help. The following questions are merely suggested. Others should be added to meet the special requirements of a particular group.

a. Do you get mad when somebody plays a joke on you?

b. Do you storm and rave when you cannot have what you want?

c. Do you often cry when you do not get your own way?

d. When your team is not winning or when your friends will not play the way you want to play, do you quit and go home?

e. Do you get mad because you cannot have a new bicycle or a new dress just when you want it?

f. Do you become angry if someone criticizes your work?

g. Do you sometimes feel hurt because your parents seem to do more for another child in the family than for you?

11. Talk to the children about the necessity of getting rid of any mean feelings that they may have. Allow them to enumerate harmless but effective ways they have discovered for venting their anger. Then suggest other methods that may occur to you. Tell how it often helps just to take a piece of paper and start writing about why one feels angry. Some persons release their hostile feelings by drawing what they feel or by working out their emotions with finger paints. Explain to the children that they will get the same release from hitting an inanimate object as from hitting a person and they will not have to suffer feelings of regret about it later. Provide a rag doll or a punching bag and have it understood with the children that they are to use it when they feel like striking out at someone. A hammer and

nails, a mallet and board, a drum to beat, darts to throw at a target, or a ball to kick will serve the same purpose.

FOLLOW-UP

Keep anecdotal records of the angry outbursts of various children. By studying these from time to time it will be possible to see which children are suppressing their feelings of aggression to the breaking point, which ones need more help in self-control, and which ones are beginning to show new problems. Be sure to see that the children who are making progress in managing their emotions are recognized and commended.

BIBLIOGRAPHY

BRECKENRIDGE, MARIAN E., and E. LEE VINCENT: Child Development, W. B. Saunders Company, Philadelphia, 1949, pp. 452–456.

RATHS, LOUIS E.: An Application to Education of the Needs Theory, Louis E. Raths, Bronxville, N.Y., 1949.

SORENSON, HERBERT, and MARGUERITE MALM: Psychology for Living, McGraw-Hill Book Company, Inc., New York, 1948, pp. 181–186.

CHAPTER 8

Dealing with Bullies

Aims of This Lesson:

To study cases of bullying, teasing, and cruelty and to investigate the under-lying causes.

To make some definite plan for meeting the particular needs of each child who shows symptoms of bullying.

To create a school atmosphere that is conducive to children's working with, not against, each other.

It is sometimes necessary for children to fight in order to protect their rights and to be accepted and respected by their peers. Occasional fighting among children is normal and should not be a matter of great concern to adults. But the habitual quarreling, fighting, and bullying of overaggressive children is a serious school and neighborhood problem which calls for thoughtful and judicious treatment by the teacher.

The bully may be a larger boy who constantly annoys the younger or smaller children. Or he may be an undersized child who tries to make up for his smallness by appearing very loud, tough, and hard-boiled. In either case, he is an overbearing fellow who swaggers, shouts, bosses, and pushes others around. In a showdown, he often refuses to fight even with a smaller child. If he is forced into a fight, he resorts to biting, scratching, kicking, and other unfair tactics. The bully likes to think that everybody is afraid of him. He takes delight in frightening timid children, appropriating their belongings, picking on girls, and dictating what games are to be played and how.

Some children enjoy the sense of power that comes from being able to make others suffer or feel helpless and blocked. They seem to be constantly jerking chairs from under other children, pulling their hair, tripping them as they walk, pinching them, pulling their ears, stepping on their feet, bending their fingers back, pushing them off the sidewalk, and doing many other annoying little tricks. Sometimes the same feelings of frustration which cause this type of behavior manifest themselves in cruelty to animals, birds, and insects.

In the same category with the bully is the boy or girl who torments others by malicious teasing. Instead of inflicting physical pain, the teaser hurts the feelings of his playmates by constantly making unkind remarks about them, calling them offensive nicknames, and poking fun at them. When he finds a child who is sensitive about his size, his features, his hair, his clothes, or his speech, he takes special pleasure in calling attention to these points. He may get a feeling of superiority and prestige by teasing another person about his ability, his personal habits, his family, or his background. Children who are easy marks for teasing are always lacking in self-confidence. The things about which they can be teased indicate the characteristics that make them feel different from the other children. The teacher can use these vulnerable spots in sensitive children as clues to their difficulties.

Because the bully is repelling and annoying in his behavior, he does not attract the sympathy and patience which he so much needs. Teachers are naturally prone to reprimand and punish him and to indulge and console his victims. Actually, the bully himself is the one who is most in need of understanding and help. Excessive teasing and acts of cruelty are expressions of deprivations, tensions, or problems in his own life which call for thoughtful study and investigation rather than for hasty punishment. When a teacher observes these symptoms in a child, she should make an effort to discover the contributory causes of the trouble.

When a child bullies others who are smaller or weaker than he is, it is almost always an indication that he himself is being bullied by parents, teachers, brothers, sisters, or older playmates. Because he is unable to strike back at the person who is repressing him, he "takes it out" on younger children or those who are less likely to defend themselves. In this way he displaces his feeling of helplessness with one of strength.

If the reason for the bully's behavior is not apparent in school, the teacher should try to find a clue by getting in touch with the parents. It may be that the child's home life is being made intolerable by a dictatorial grandparent or an officious servant. An anxious or overprotective mother may be depriving him of all self-assertiveness. Perhaps the young bully is imitating the domineering and superior attitude of an overaggressive father or some older·boy whom he admires. Because he is constantly bullied by older brothers and sisters, he may find relief in tormenting other children as he is being tormented. Sometimes the child gets a more direct satisfaction by teasing the person who is dominating him.

A youngster who comes from a home where each member is vying for leadership often feels that in every situation somebody must be the boss and give the orders. Because he has had no opportunity to be the one in charge, he reacts either by becoming very submissive or by attempting to bring his playmates under his control. Perhaps he has been taught to fight for his rights and "not to take anything off of" others. After learning more about the child's relations with his family, the teacher may be able to analyze the problem. Then, by tactfully explaining the situation and suggesting some practical remedial measures, it is often possible to work out a satisfactory solution with the parents.

Teachers themselves sometimes unwittingly foster bullying. Because children so readily reflect the feelings and attitudes of their elders, they become antagonistic, boisterous, and harsh under the influence of one who is impatient, critical, sarcastic, and faultfinding. A child has no recourse when an overaggressive teacher constantly scolds, nags, threatens, and directs in a "Do as I say and ask no questions" manner. He can only wait until playtime and vent his feelings of resentment and rebellion on someone smaller or more helpless than himself. Such feelings, however, are conspicuously absent among pupils whose teacher is calm, cheerful, friendly, and firm; who has regard for the children's feelings and viewpoints; and who knows how to handle their conflicts in such a way that they learn to like, respect, and appreciate each other.

Sometimes the bully is suffering from a sense of general insecurity. In addition to feeling unloved at home and rejected by his teacher, he may also realize that he is unpopular among the children at school or in the neighborhood. Although he really wants friends, he unknowingly drives them away by mistreating them. Because he craves recognition and attention, he asserts himself by playing a strong-man role, by acting tough and cruel, or by teasing perpetually. Having been hurt so often, he feels that the whole world is against him and he is constantly on guard ready to strike before he is struck. Thinking that the bully is their natural enemy and not realizing that he would really like to have them as companions, the children retaliate by being unkind to him. This vicious circle continues until an understanding adult intervenes and shows the bully how to cooperate with his classmates instead of intimidating and antagonizing them.

A bossy, officious attitude in a child is sometimes mistaken for leadership ability. A real leader works with other children and gets their willing cooperation without trying to promote his own selfish interests or to exalt his ego. A bully, on the other hand, is interested only in gaining a feeling of superiority by bending others to his will. One of his greatest needs is to experience the satisfaction that comes from working with, not against, other children. An understanding teacher can help by placing the over-aggressive child in numerous situations that require cooperativeness and fair play. Membership in the YMCA, the boy scouts, the girl scouts, or some church club which offers recreational outlets is usually good for the child who does not get along well with others.

The bully is frequently a slow learner. This is not due to any particular relation between bullying and dullness but rather to the fact that slow children who have been retarded often act the bully in order to cover up their feelings of inadequacy or inferiority. A child who knows that his classmates learn more quickly than he, that they always outstrip him in games, and that they are superior to him in many other respects must find some way to excel. At least, he can experience some satisfaction by lording it over smaller children. Putting on an act of fearlessness and superiority helps to keep up his spirit.

The teacher can turn this child in the right direction by helping him to acquire the feeling of importance and worth that he so much needs. A small beginning can be made simply by calling attention to some desirable trait that he may display. It is sometimes difficult to find even one thing that can be sincerely and genuinely commended. But a defeated child will respond favorably even to so small a thing as being told that he is a very good listener, that his posture is unusually good, or that he whistles exceptionally well. Amazingly, one word of praise opens the way for others. After the bully has once been recognized for something worth while or has experienced some kind of success, he can drop the pretense and become an acceptable person in his own right.

The bully feels afraid, inferior, insecure, and inadequate, but makes a desperate effort to appear quite the opposite. Therefore, he can be helped only by being made to feel secure, adequate, and appreciated. He should be studied for any potential ability that can be developed. If he can learn to do any one thing exceptionally well, he will have one of the first requisites for winning the admiration of his peers. The teacher can set a good example for the other children by showing that she, for one, accepts the rejected bully and appreciates any of his good qualities.

Alvin was the youngest of five children. His mother was dead and his sister kept house for the family. His three older brothers, who had been incorrigible while in school and who had since been in a great deal of trouble with the police, teased and bullied Alvin unmercifully. The father, a hard-working and respectable man, had become very rigid in his discipline lest this child follow in his brothers' footsteps.

This frail, sullen, slow-learning child was a bully of the worst sort. With a scowl and a sneer on his face, he pitted himself against the rest of the school. He tripped the children in the halls, tipped over their trays in the lunchroom, destroyed their property, and defied the teachers. He was so hostile and unpleasant that he had not a single friend among the children. The teachers were unable to reach or interest him in any way. Apparently his only purpose in coming to school was to disrupt the classes and torture the smaller children.

In a quiet talk with the boy it was found that he was an expert bowler, that he had won several medals in competition with men, and that he spent much of his leisure at the bowling alley. This information was just what the teacher needed to help her make a miserable little boy feel important. She helped him find interesting reading matter in his field and suggested that he give his long-deferred book review on the subject of bowling. She asked him to bowl with her and give her some pointers on improving her technique.

Although Alvin did not suddenly stage a complete rightabout-face, it was gratifying to notice that he gradually became more sociable. He began to smile, to participate in group discussions, and to be less belligerent toward the children. The fact that his prowess in one line had been recognized and appreciated gave him courage to take part in other sports in which he was not so capable. Best of all, he now felt that he had a place of his own to maintain, that he could do something his classmates could not do, and that he no longer needed to emulate his brothers. His change of attitude toward school made it easier to work on his basic difficulties at home. When the situation was fully explained to the father, he was glad to be less severe in disciplining Alvin and to concentrate his efforts on getting the older brothers to cooperate.

Because of the arrogant nature of the bully, the teacher is often tempted to suppress him and beat him down. She is right in feeling that she should deal with him firmly. But no amount of punishment, moralizing, or preachment will have any lasting effect. It is a mistake, too, to think that the bully can be conquered by getting a larger boy to fight him or by encouraging the smaller children to gang up on him. The bully is by nature a coward. When he is defeated by those whom he is trying to dominate, he only becomes more afraid, and the problem is accentuated. Bullying and malicious teasing are symptoms of some real need in the life of the child. The best remedy is to find and treat some of the contributing causes.

If a child is punished and stopped from bullying without having anything done to change the factors in his environment which are causing the problem, he will be no better off than he was before. His fundamental trouble will still bother him and he will have to find release through some other form of behavior. For this reason, his aggressive behavior should not be curbed until a worth-while outlet for his feelings can be substituted. To be sure, the bully should not be allowed to endanger the safety, the freedom, and the rights of the other children.

If nothing is done to help bullies while they are young, they will grow up to become disagreeable autocrats who expect everyone to take orders from them without question. The teacher has an opportunity to make life more tolerable for these children and, incidentally, for all those who cross their paths both while in school and in later years.

ACTIVITIES SUGGESTED

The activities should be so planned that they will reach the particular pupils in your class who are given to bullying. Use any activities which you think will be effective in making bullies feel secure and self-sufficient. The ones mentioned here are merely suggestive.

1. The teacher is usually well aware of the identity of the bullies in her class. But because some tendencies toward bullying are evident only on the playground or on the way to and from school, it may be enlightening to get the children's point of view. To this end, a questionnaire similar to the one below may be filled out by the older children and answered in the form of a "whisper test" by the younger ones. The questions may be answered with names of any number of children, with their own names, or left blank. Assure the pupils that their answers will not be made known and that the information will be used only to help those who really need help.

    a. Who always insists upon deciding what and how to play?

    b. Whom do you refuse to have on your neighborhood football team (or other group) because he is too bossy?

c. Who is constantly doing mean little tricks to make smaller children cry?

d. Who is always trying to cause trouble but refuses to fight when his bluff is called?

e. What girl makes children unhappy by teasing them?

f. What large boy constantly picks on girls and smaller boys?

g. Who is especially cruel to animals and birds?

h. Who appears to be tough and hard-boiled?

i. Who acts as if he does not want any friends?

j. Who kicks, scratches, bites, and takes unfair advantage in a fight?

k. Who is considered the "big bully" in your neighborhood?

2. The way in which young children play with pets or treat animals, birds, and insects is sometimes an indication of attitudes which they have toward people. As a method of discovering bullying tendencies which have not yet been noticed by the teacher, questions similar to the following may be asked:

a. What pets do you have at home?

b. Who takes care of them?

c. What do you do when you find a bird's nest or a cocoon?

d. Have you ever had any fun with a stray dog. How?

e. What do you do when you find a stray kitten?

f. Do you ever feed wild squirrels? Throw rocks at them?

3. Through an informal group discussion get the children to mention all the characteristics which they have observed in a bully. Find out their opinions of the reasons for a child's becoming a bully. Tell them that the persons whom they know as bullies are not actually the hard, tough characters they appear to be but that they are really weak individuals who are trying to build up their courage and self-esteem by bossing others around. Explain that some boys and girls are afraid, they feel that they are not so good in studies or in games, they are bullied at home, or they think that nobody likes them. They must make up for these feelings by "taking it out" on somebody and so they are cruel and hateful to younger or smaller children. They really want friends but do not know how to go about being friendly. Ask for specific suggestions of kindnesses that may be extended to these children.

One group of small children gathered around their teacher for this type of discussion gave the following possible reasons for a child's becoming a bully:

"Maybe the daddy is a bully."

"Maybe the child sees others showing off and thinks it is smart."

"Parents may mistreat the child."

"Maybe his parents whip him too much."

"Maybe older brothers tease him."

"Maybe he sees shows he should not see."

"Maybe the parents do not take the trouble to teach the child the right thing."

"Perhaps his mother never asks him in a nice way to do something."

It is interesting to note that the class bullies often disclose their own reasons for bullying through these suppositions.

4. Tell some stories about bullies you may have known, gearing the stories to the age level and the needs of your group. Then ask questions concerning the needs of the bully in the story and the ways in which these needs could be met. Example:

Nobody liked Elmer. When he came out to play, most of the children on the street went home. And it was no wonder. If a child happened to be eating an apple, Elmer would grab it away from him and either eat it or throw it away. If he had a new toy, Elmer would snatch it from him and begin to take it apart. He twisted the smaller children's arms, pulled their caps over their eyes, and did everything he could think of to interrupt their play. All of this came to an end, however, when David, Elmer's big brother, came on the scene. David picked on his younger brother constantly and beat him at the very slightest provocation.

Elmer was just as unkind to the children at school as to those in his neighborhood. He had no friends and was never chosen until last when the group was divided into teams for games. This was partly because he was slow and awkward and not at all good at sports.

Elmer's classwork, too, was very poor. Often when he thought the teacher was not looking he took out his knife and a bit of wood and proceeded to finish a piece of carving which he had started. His wood carving was excellent but few people got a chance to see it. His mother was a very painstaking housekeeper who did not like to have the place cluttered with Elmer's miniature birds, dogs, and cats. She nagged at him constantly about getting shavings on the floor. David took delight in destroying any of the carvings that he could get his hands on.

As you may guess, Elmer was very unhappy. At home, at school, and in the neighborhood, he felt that he was not liked or appreciated.

a. What do you think caused Elmer to become a bully?
b. What things were lacking in his life?
c. What do you think could be done to help this boy?
d. If you were one of his classmates, what would you do?

5. Ask the children to describe the actions of some bullies they have known without mentioning the identities of the persons. Tell them to give their opinions as to why the children became bullies and what might have been done to help them.

6. Hold a group discussion on the characteristics of real leadership. Do this with a view to helping the children see that a leader is not one who can bring others to submission, but that he is one who cooperates and has the ability to get along well with others. In order to make the activity more meaningful, the discussion may lead into a consideration of the characteristics which would qualify certain persons in the group to become class officers. Talk about how some students are leaders even though they are never elected officers.

7. If it is at all possible to do so, place a bully in a position of responsibility, preferably where he can be of service to someone who is weaker than he. One bully was helped by being given complete charge of getting a little spastic child to and from a taxicab before and after school each day. He was very dependable and extremely careful and gentle with the child. He had found a way of feeling strong and important and no longer needed to get this feeling by picking on weaker children.

8. If it seems advisable, take into your confidence two or three friendly, reliable children from the group. In a private conference explain to them the problems of one or more of the bullies in the class and ask their cooperation in being friendly to these children, inviting them to play on their teams, and in other ways showing a kindly spirit toward them.

9. If properly presented, dramatizations showing a larger child teasing smaller ones, some causes back of the trouble, and kindnesses shown the bully by his classmates may be effective. However, such an activity must be supervised and previewed. Otherwise, the emphasis is likely to be placed on the teasing rather than on the cure.

10. Group discussions may be introduced by two films of the Discussion Problems in Group Living Series (for grades 5 to 9), produced by Young America Films, Inc., New York, 1951. *The Bully* and *The Other Fellow's Feelings* (which focuses on the subject of ridiculing and teasing), 16 mm., sound, 11 min. each, are designed to challenge students to think about the problems presented, to express their opinions, and to work out their own solutions.

FOLLOW-UP

It will be helpful to the teacher to keep in her room a file containing brief case studies of the problems being studied. In this file there should be a card for each bully in the class, giving an estimate of his desires and unmet needs, comments on the attempts that have been made to fulfill these desires and to meet these needs, and evidences of any results that have been obtained. This file should be checked from time to time as a reminder of the objectives to be reached and the progress made in each case.

BIBLIOGRAPHY

BAUER, W. W.: *Stop Annoying Your Children,* Bobbs-Merrill Company, Indianapolis, 1947, pp. 74–80.

HURLOCK, ELIZABETH B.: *Child Growth and Development,* McGraw-Hill Book Company, Inc., New York, 1949, pp. 285–289.

WOLF, ANNA W. M.: *The Parents' Manual,* Simon and Schuster, Inc., New York, 1947, pp. 132–136.

CHAPTER 9

Attacking the Problem
of Dishonesty

Aims of This Lesson:
  To develop a sense of fair play that will curtail dishonesty and encourage pupils to report cases that need treatment.
  To detect in the children any marked tendencies to steal, lie, or cheat.
  To try to uncover and solve the emotional problems that cause dishonesty.

What teacher has not been confronted with the question of what to do about stealing, lying, cheating, and untruthful boasting among children?

When personal belongings of the pupils begin to disappear and small amounts of money are frequently missing from the teacher's desk, it is time to try to detect the thief. By carefully watching their spending habits and observing any unusual behavior among the children, the teacher is sometimes able to spot the guilty one. Often, however, the identity of the culprit remains a mystery.

When stealing occurs, more than one child usually knows about it. But the youngsters' code of honor prevents them from squealing. Nobody likes a tattletale who delights in running to the teacher with disparaging stories about others. But children should be taught the difference between petty tattling and reporting an incident that might cause serious harm to someone. If they should see a burglar breaking into a neighbor's home, they would surely call the police. They are just as much obligated to report to the teacher when a classmate has been robbed. Naturally, they will do this more readily if they can be certain of the fairness and justice of the teacher. When

108

children have reason to feel that the teacher is on their side and is really a friend to all of them, they realize that she is not looking for reasons to punish them but that she genuinely wants to help those who are in trouble.

If his friend should break an arm on the playground, a child would hasten to report the accident to the teacher and enlist her help. He needs to understand that when the friend resorts to stealing, he is badly mixed up and is even more in need of help than if he had a broken arm. The best thing he can do is to tell a kind and sympathetic teacher who can help to keep his friend from becoming involved in more serious trouble.

After a child has been found guilty of stealing, the main issue usually becomes one of trying to apply punishment suitable to the crime. Too often the child is openly condemned and labeled a thief by his teacher and ostracized by his classmates. He gets a reputation which he cannot live down and which may lead to some other form of maladjustment. Severe punishment is seldom effective. It frequently serves only as a challenge to the child to make other attempts to outwit the teacher or the law. The offender should not be publicly disgraced but should be corrected in private and given an opportunity to return the stolen article or to pay for it if it cannot be replaced.

The impulse to hoard is quite prevalent among young children. This accounts for the fact that at some time or other most of them will take a piece of money, a pencil, a colored crayon, a pair of scissors, an apple, a piece of candy, or any other item that may be attractive to them. By patient supervision and by having quantities of supplies within easy reach of all so that no child needs to take from another, the teacher can help youngsters to pass through this phase. By the time a child is about nine years of age he should have developed a social conscience. Stealing after this age is a more serious matter and calls for careful investigation and study.

A single stealing episode does not mean that a child is doomed to a career of dishonesty. Having once learned to steal, however, he may easily acquire the habit and soon become a hardened thief. For this reason, it is extremely important that each case be handled wisely.

A child who steals usually has some lack in his life which causes him to be emotionally disturbed. If the disturbance is great enough, he may need the service of a psychiatrist. In most cases, however, a little timely help from an understanding teacher is sufficient. By observing the type of thing which a child takes, the teacher may get a clue to his real needs or desires. After studying his background and trying to analyze the underlying trouble, the problem can usually be solved by providing ways in which the child can satisfy his wants legitimately, by showing him how to make friends, by arousing his interest in new experiences, or by giving him a great deal of affection.

Sometimes the cause for stealing is so obvious that it can be seen through at once. An undernourished, shabbily dressed child may succumb to temptation because of a desire to look like the other children. Sometimes a child steals toys, candy, school supplies, and other small items because he feels that he must have the things his classmates have. An older girl may take cosmetics, hosiery, and jewelry for the same reason. Children often have an unusual craving for some one thing which they have always been deprived of. Their standard of values may have been distorted until they overestimate the worth of the item.

One child formed the habit of pilfering an orange, a banana, or an apple from a fruit stand on the way to school. She was one of thirteen children living with their parents in a small, four-room house. Her father's earnings were very meager. The little girl confessed that she was tantalized by the sight of so much fresh fruit and could not resist satisfying her hunger. When her teacher understood the situation she saw to it that the much-needed fruit was frequently made available from various sources. She also brought the girl in contact with an old lady who needed someone to go to the grocery and run other errands for her in the afternoons. When the child could earn the extra money which her father had been unable to provide, there was no further need for stealing.

Children who have an uncontrollable desire for money must be taught that material possessions are not the key to happiness—that good health, a happy home, and friends are more important. These children must also learn not to feel resentful, envious, or discriminated against when their parents cannot satisfy their every whim. All boys and girls can no more expect to have the same amount of spending money than all parents can expect to have the same incomes.

When children are constantly thrown with others who have more money than they, they sometimes steal in order to keep up with the crowd. They would rather be dishonest than to lose face by being unable to compete with their associates. If such a child never has any money of his own, the teacher may help by suggesting to the parents that they give him a regular, definite allowance consistent with his need and with the family's standard of living. Even a small allowance saves the child from the embarrassment of having to ask for each nickel as it is used. It helps him to learn the value of money and to find satisfaction in saving and in spending to the best advantage.

Stealing is not always the result of a need for material things. Often it is prompted by feelings of insecurity, loneliness, and unhappiness. This is the type of problem which should be of most concern to teachers. When a child steals trivial, worthless articles that he neither wants nor needs, it is usually because of an intense resentment toward someone, a feeling of being rejected by his parents, a fear of being disliked by his teacher or classmates, or some repressed impulse of which the child is totally unconscious. In some instances, stealing may even be the result of a guilt feeling over some other misdeed. By stealing, being caught, and punished, the person gets vicarious relief from a guilt that he feels over some greater offense.

One case of stealing was due to a boy's efforts to free himself from domineering parents. Dick was the only son of a banker and had always enjoyed the comforts of life. He was handsomely dressed but he was never allowed to select any of his clothes. He had innumerable toys but he was not permitted to take any of them out of his room. He had plenty of books but they were always of his parents' choosing. His mother would not let him play where he might get dirty or have guests who were likely to disorder her house.

As Dick grew older he began to steal money from his relatives and friends. He forged checks and stole automobiles. He took long trips and spent money lavishly and foolishly. The parents felt that they had been very careful in bringing up this boy and were at a loss to know why he should turn out so badly. Because of their secure economic position, they were especially puzzled about the stealing. It was hard for them to realize that they were the direct cause of the trouble. Their son needed freedom and the privilege of spending money, making decisions, and doing things without always having to get their consent.

A child who is poor, unattractive, or unable to excel either in classwork or in sports may have an intense desire to gain some sort of prestige among his fellows. He may be so hungry for friends or for the approval of his classmates that he will steal in order to have money to spend on his would-be friends. Such children need to be taught how to understand people and to win friends. It is tragic to let them go through life thinking that love and friendship can be bought with favors and gifts.

A lonely, pathetic little boy began to bring his teacher gifts which he was not financially able to have purchased. She was perplexed until she recognized one gift, a fountain pen, as belonging to another teacher. Upon investigation it was found that the boy's father was in the penitentiary, his mother worked away from home, and his older brother had no time to be bothered with him. Since he had no friends among the children at school, he was attempting to gain the affection and esteem of his teacher. When the teacher realized this and gave him the special interest and attention he craved, he no longer felt the urge to steal.

Children who are physically handicapped, who come from broken homes, who have very few interesting experiences, or who feel inferior because of some other lack in their lives sometimes resort to stealing. In this way they try to find adventure or some satisfaction which will compensate for the loss they feel.

Before stealing actually occurs, some preventive measures should be taken. Of course, it is not enough for the teacher to present a lesson on honesty or to preach about the immoral nature of stealing. She must be constantly on the alert for occasions to teach respect for property rights, to put the children in positions of trust, to demonstrate to them that they can trust each other, and to commend them for honesty and fairness.

Most children respect fair play. They realize that if one person steals, everyone has an equal right to steal. They must learn that our social scheme of property rights requires the cooperation of everyone and that the one who fails to cooperate is the loser. They need to be well grounded in the importance of taking care of their own property and of keeping hands off things that do not belong to them. Few children want to steal after they have experienced the satisfaction that comes from being strictly honest in their dealings with their fellows.

The form of dishonesty most frequently found in the classroom is cheating. The fact that a child cheats in school does not mean that he is naturally untrustworthy. It is often an indication that the work is too difficult and that he is not keeping up with his class. Children who copy, cheat on tests, get parents or friends to do their homework, or change their report cards usually do so because they are incapable of succeeding in any other way. They are afraid of failure, punishment, or humiliation if their grades are poor. It may be that the parents, the teacher, or the child himself is trying to hold to an impossible standard.

The best scholars rarely find it necessary to cheat. Sometimes, however, even good students resort to copying from each other when lessons are long, dull, and uninteresting. One child does the homework for all, and the others have more time for play. When this happens, it is possible that the assignments contain too much drill work or that they are not sufficiently challenging to the brighter pupils.

If cheating is prevalent in a class, it may be remedied in part by requiring no more or less than the pupils are able to do. Teachers should not put too high a premium on grades and correct answers, but place the emphasis on understanding. Teachers should help any overambitious parents to adjust their standards to the capacities of their children. There is less temptation to cheat if children are sometimes given an opportunity to work together legitimately on committees or group assignments. They must understand, of course, that at other times when they are doing individual tasks, the work must be strictly their own.

Lying is another form of dishonesty which is often indulged in by children. It is understood that childish inaccuracies and misinterpretations are not considered falsehoods. Small children soon learn to get attention from grownups by telling imagined stories. They often become so absorbed in the products of their own imagination that they have difficulty in distinguishing between fact and fancy. They need to be reminded each time that their stories are not true but "just pretend." Teachers should notice the trends in the tall tales told by young children. Exaggerations that have to do with being big, being independent, having many friends, or being liked may really be reflections of unmet needs.

Children who are untruthful are usually victims of emotional disturbances of some kind. Those who feel neglected, unwanted, or inferior may tell lies which build up their self-esteem. Those who are jealous of brothers, sisters, or playmates may tattle or tell lies which show their longing to hurt or outdo the ones of whom they are jealous.

Boasting, too, is usually an effort to cover up a feeling of inferiority or defeat. Because a child is lacking in self-confidence, he may assume an attitude of superiority and try to impress the teacher or the other children by overrating his abilities. He may brag that he is the best baseball player in the school, that his father can whip any other child's father, or that he has many possessions at home that the other children do not have. Talk with the boastful child to find the possible reason for his feeling of inferiority. It may be that he is seeking the admiration of others, that he is trying to hide his poor home environment, that he needs encouragement in his schoolwork, or that he craves love and companionship. Try to build up his self-respect by recognizing his abilities and praising him whenever possible. He will not need to boast and appear conceited if he can feel that he is successful in something and that he is socially accepted.

A child's code of honor is made up largely from his daily contacts with adults. Children easily catch a spirit of honesty and fair play from parents who are truthful and upright in all their dealings with their fellow men. On the other hand, they just as readily follow the example of parents who lie about their children's ages in order to avoid paying full fare, who have children answer the doorbell and say that they are not at home, who refuse invitations by giving untrue excuses, who frequently and obviously resort to telling "white lies," who use gross exaggerations in order to make entertaining conversation, who fail to correct an error in a bill when it is in their own favor, and who write false excuses for their children's absence from school.

A teacher can do a great deal to offset these impressions by letting the children see honesty and sincerity in operation every day. Pupils are impressed by the fact that a teacher consistently keeps her promises to them, that she tells the truth without embellishment, and that she is honest enough to say "I don't know" and "I was wrong" rather than try to conceal an error or a lack of information.

If a child is given to telling untruths, observe him carefully for traces of fear. Does he seem to be afraid of parental disapproval? Is he afraid of punishment? Unreasonable punishment at home or at school often makes children shrink from telling the truth. They come to realize that no matter what they have done, the truth brings punishment while a well-told falsehood brings release from blame. Children respond to fair treatment and will usually tell the truth if they are not driven to lying by the fear of severe punishment.

In dealing with all problems of stealing, cheating, and lying it is well to remember that hasty punishments which are aimed at the immediate offense can never correct the trouble. They may even increase the child's maladjustment by driving him to find some other solution to his emotional problem. Treatment should be directed at the underlying causes—if it is possible to discover them. In the meantime, chiding will do no good; love and understanding may work wonders.

ACTIVITIES SUGGESTED

Use only the activities which are most suitable for your particular group. In many cases it will be advisable to make revisions and additions so that the activities will be more meaningful for a certain child or group of children who especially need help in the matter of being honest.

1. Plan to observe "honesty week," during which you recognize, emphasize, and discuss honesty every day. Praise all honest acts of individuals to the class. For example, if a child returns money or an article he has found, stop whatever you are doing and comment to the class about his honesty.

2. Place on the teacher's desk a "borrow box" containing crayons, pencils, erasers, and other small articles which children sometimes take from each other. Let the children know that they are free to use the materials they need from this box.

3. Making an effort not to appear preachy, explain to the class some of the reasons why children steal, lie, and cheat. Tell an illustrative story geared to the age level and the needs of your own group.

4. Without allowing them to call names, ask the pupils to have in mind some child whom they think of as being dishonest. Then, still keeping the identity of the person secret, ask that they answer questions similar to the following:

   a. Why do you think this person takes things that do not belong to him?
   b. Can it be because he really needs the money or the articles he steals?
   c. Is it, perhaps, just for adventure?
   d. Do you suppose he wants friendship and takes money to buy candy or other treats for his friends?
   e. Do you think he gets any real pleasure from using the money or the articles that he steals?

5. Ask each child who will do so to write or tell about a time when he lied, cheated, or boasted falsely, explaining why he did it, what happened as a result, how he felt about it at the time, and how he feels about it now.

6. Hold class discussions on the following questions:

   a. Do you know anybody who feels that he must win every game he plays even if he has to cheat and take unfair advantage? Why do you suppose that winning is so important to such a person?
   b. What do you think of the code of some children who think that they must defend and protect their friends when they steal, cheat, or play unfairly? Can you recall a story or a movie about a person who found his brother, son, or best friend guilty of a crime and had the courage to turn him over to the authorities?
   c. A school boy notified the police when he saw a thief stealing a tire from an automobile. Would you consider this boy a good citizen?

The same boy knew the identity of the pupil who had been stealing books, pencils, and other items from the lockers and classrooms. He informed the principal, who had been unable to stop the thefts. In this case, would you also consider him a good citizen?

d. Do you think that a person is a very good friend to you if he steals or destroys property and then expects you to lie or cover up for him? He would let you be dishonest in order to save himself from punishment. Why doesn't he have the courage to take his own medicine?

e. Have you seen boys and girls steal fruit or flowers from neighbors' yards? Is it fair to have fun and adventure at the expense of another person's property?

f. When people steal it is because they need something which they do not have. The thing they steal is not always exactly the thing they need but it may give them some comfort or help to take the place of the thing they lack. List some of the needs which sometimes cause boys and girls to steal.

g. What amount do you think is a reasonable weekly allowance for a person of your age? Should this include lunches, school supplies, and other necessities? What factors should be considered in determining a fair amount for an allowance? Why may the amount of your allowance be different from that of your friends? What are some odd jobs which boys and girls of your age can do to earn spending money?

h. Do you think it is all right for a person to take things he needs if he has no money? Is it all right to steal from a person who has much more than you have?

7. Let the pupils work out a "code of honor" for their class. This should be carefully worded, neatly lettered, and placed in a conspicuous place in the room so that it will be constantly before the children. The contents of the code should come from the pupils themselves. It will probably include such ideas as:

I will not cheat.
I will keep the rules and play fair.
I will be honest in my work as well as in my play.
I will tell the truth at all times.
I will try to help my friends to be honest.

8. Gather the group about you in an informal circle and encourage the pupils to express their views on cheating, trying to decide what causes the practice and what can be done to curb it.

Children who talk freely may say that *teachers* foster cheating by making the work too difficult, by urging slow students to work harder than they are able, and by scolding them for low marks until they feel that they must copy from others in order to keep up. If this idea is advanced, perhaps your standards are too high or your assignments are not planned according to the needs and abilities of the children.

By encouraging the children to talk about *parents'* reactions to the reports taken home, it may be possible to get additional light on the standards that parents have set for their children. Talk about the meaning of marks, the desirability of making as good a school record as possible, and the futility of cheating just to get a good report card. Help the pupils to understand the importance of improving their own rating without feeling defeated or inferior if they cannot equal or surpass the other children. Each person has his own peculiar strengths and weaknesses. One who excels in arithmetic may be very awkward in the gym class. Children should be taught to respect the ability of their classmates without being envious or being tempted to cheat in order to rival them.

See that the discussion leads to the responsibility of the *child* for being on his honor at all times. Explain that teachers do not watch a class during a test just for the purpose of catching cheaters but to protect students who do not want to cheat and who may be put on the spot by their classmates if they do not. Help the children to understand the difference between working cooperatively on a project and cheating.

9. Suggest that the children prepare some little skits in which they illustrate how a person may get into difficulties and embarrassing situations by telling falsehoods. Examples:

  a. Just to tease a little girl, a boy slipped a package from her desk and hid it. When she reported to the teacher the loss of her costume for the PTA program to be given that evening, the boy was too frightened to admit that he knew anything about it. A number of persons were inconvenienced that night and the boy's untruthfulness was discovered when the package was seen in his locker the next day.

  b. One child refused to lend her roller skates to a careless friend, saying that she was going to the skating rink that evening and would be using them herself. Instead, she went to a movie where she met the friend and was faced with the problem of explaining why she did not go skating.

10. Perhaps you may want to use a film with this lesson. *How Honest Are You?* (for intermediate grades and junior high school), 16 mm., sound, 13 min., Coronet Films, Chicago, 1951, deals with some of the deeper aspects of honesty and suggests ways in which a person may apply the test of honesty to his thoughts and actions.

> *Angry Boy* (for adults), 16 mm., sound, 33 min., Affiliated Film Producers, Inc., New York, 1951, may be used by groups of teachers or parents. This is the story of a boy who reacts against emotional difficulties at home and at school by stealing.
>
> *Cheating,* Discussion Problems in Group Living Series (for grades 5 to 9), 16 mm., sound, 11 min., Young America Films, Inc., New York, 1951, gives students an insight into a life problem and brings it out into the open for discussion, without suggesting a ready-made solution.

11. Talk to the children about the importance of being sincere and genuine in their dealings with each other. Discuss social lies and ways of avoiding them. Explain that it is sometimes kind to withhold some of the truth, but it is not necessary to tell deliberate lies. Plan some tactful but truthful things that one might say instead of saying:

"I like your new dress" (when you do not like it at all).

"I'm sorry you can't be on our team" (when you are not sorry).

"I had a wonderful time at your party" (when you did not have a good time).

12. If you think it will be helpful, make opportunities to give those children who seldom have a chance to handle money the jobs of counting the milk money, the ticket money, or the Red Cross contributions at school. One child who had been found stealing was allowed to have charge of the piggy bank, to hold it when the children had money to drop in, and to count and report to the class the amount they had saved. He loved this responsibility and no longer tried to take money out of the bank as he had formerly done.

Children who seldom have the experience of handling money of their own will profit by being allowed to go shopping with the teacher for supplies for the room, to spend money the class has earned or saved, or to buy food for a party or picnic.

FOLLOW-UP

If any of the children have in the past been guilty of stealing, lying, or cheating, show them that they are not marked for life by trusting them and giving them a chance to prove their honesty.

BIBLIOGRAPHY

BAUER, W. W.: *Stop Annoying Your Children,* Bobbs-Merrill Company, Indianapolis, 1947, Chaps. VI, VII.

BEVERLY, BERT I.: *A Psychology of Growth,* Whittlesey House, McGraw-Hill Book Company, Inc., New York, 1947, pp. 142–146.

JENKINS, GLADYS GARDNER, HELEN SHACTER, and WILLIAM BAUER: *These Are Your Children,* Scott, Foresman & Company, Chicago, 1949, pp. 77–79.

WOLF, ANNA W. M.: *The Parents' Manual,* Simon and Schuster, Inc., New York, 1947, pp. 60–67.

CHAPTER 10

Controlling Jealous Feelings

Aims of This Lesson:
  To understand the most common causes and effects of jealousy in children.
  To trace feelings of jealousy which have arisen in early childhood and to try to find antidotes for them.
  To help young persons to release, not to suppress, their jealous emotions.
  To avoid arousing jealousy at school.

Jealousy, which is one of the most common types of maladjustment in children, can be found at the root of many classroom behavior problems. Youngsters who are uncertain of their standing with parents, friends, or teachers are sure, sooner or later, to release their emotions in some undesirable way. Many fights, temper tantrums, and angry outbursts are brought on by jealousy. Selfishness, self-consciousness, unfriendliness, fear, or self-pity can often be traced directly to a child's inability to hold his place in the family or the school group. Daydreaming, lying, and tattling are often indicators of jealous feelings that have originated in early life.

Childhood jealousy, if uncontrolled, can become a powerful habit which may eventually cause real damage to personality. Even complex physical disorders may be caused by jealousy. Many a sick headache is induced by inability to compete with a rival. Stuttering and speech defects often develop as the result of tension that comes from being displaced as the favored member of a family.

Although jealousy appears to be most prevalent in the preschool years and again in adolescence, there are inevitable outbreaks of envy and rivalry among children of all age levels. Boys and girls tend to transfer to their school companions jealousies which have been engendered among members

120

of their families. Teachers must find ways to solve the resulting emotional disturbances before these children can be expected to get along harmoniously with each other.

One of the most frequent causes of jealousy in young children is the arrival of a new baby in the family. No matter how well a child has been prepared for the event, he is bound to feel that the newcomer is a rival for his parents' affection and that he can no longer be the center of attention in his home. When a youngster announces that he has a baby brother or sister, the teacher should use the information as her cue to give the child a little more love and attention and to exercise patience if he starts to bite, kick, scratch, or pinch others as a release for his feelings. Although jealousy usually manifests itself in a direct attack on the rival or on the parents, there may also be an indirect reaction toward playmates and others outside the family.

When a child becomes unusually hostile, moody, sensitive, or withdrawn after the advent of a new baby, the teacher should talk to the mother and try to make some suggestions for easing the situation. Parents may need to be reminded that the older child requires a great deal of extra love and assurance that he is needed in the family. It is especially important that the mother give him some undivided time for reading, storytelling, or playing just as she did when he was the only child or the youngest one. This cannot be done effectively while she is washing dishes, ironing, darning, or holding the baby in one arm, but at a time set aside exclusively for the older child. Although this plan may at first seem impracticable to the mother, it is certain to pay dividends. To be sure, the idea of appeasing the older child should not be overdone to the extent of making him feel that the newcomer is of little importance in comparison to himself. Each member of the family needs to realize that he is valued, loved, and accepted for himself and that there is room in the home for all. When an older child gets enough affection to satisfy his own need, and when he understands that his mother gives more time to the baby because of his utter helplessness and not because she loves him more, he will have little reason to be jealous.

Because he is afraid of parental disapproval if he demonstrates any sign of jealousy, a child may hide his dislike for a new brother or sister by appearing to be exceptionally affectionate and attentive. This attitude often covers up the guilt and shame which he really feels because of his hatred toward the baby or his resentment toward the parents for giving the newcomer so much attention. Even when it is not apparent, there is always a spark of jealousy in the child who must learn to share his parents. The silent, preoccupied youngster who suppresses his hostile emotions in order to please his parents or teachers may be more in need of help than the outspoken one who openly expresses his rebellion. Children who are hushed up and not allowed to communicate their honest feelings may store up hatreds which will smolder for years. However, such feelings are sure to come to the surface later in life in the form of undesirable behavior or unpleasant personality traits.

Jealousy, like fear and anger, is an emotion that needs to be released. One of the best things that a teacher can do for a jealous child is to help him unload his burden and relieve his tension by talking. If the child knows that the teacher is sympathetic and that she will not upbraid him for his feelings, he will be glad to have an opportunity to tell her about his bothers. She can usually put him at ease and get him to start talking simply by saying, "I know that it makes you feel mad to have another child getting some of the love and attention that you want for yourself alone. Tell me all about it." The teacher who understands that it is normal and healthy for children to have intense feelings and who is willing to listen while they pour out their grievances can do a great deal toward helping them to work out their inevitable problems of rivalry.

It is not uncommon for jealousy to result when younger children feel that older ones are allowed more than a fair share of privileges or when able-bodied children resent the parental attention given to the sick or physically handicapped ones. Jealousy is very likely to occur when one child in a family is brighter, more talented, or better looking than another. This is especially true when the younger child outshines the older. One who is frequently placed in an unfavorable light by comparison with a more gifted or more lovable sibling is sure to feel resentment either toward the rival or toward the one who makes the comparison. A parent or teacher can do a child no greater injustice than to say to him, "Why can't you be as polite as your little sister?" or "Aren't you ashamed to do such sloppy work? Your brother is always so neat and accurate." It is small wonder that such remarks frequently lead to covert rivalry or create aggressive feelings which result in constant fighting, quarreling, and other forms of open hostility.

Adverse comparisons with classmates or playmates not only cause hatreds toward the favored children but an abhorrence for the very traits that adults wish to cultivate. One little girl was repeatedly told, "If you do not take care of your lovely dolls, we are going to take them next door and give them to Susan. She always puts her toys away. Hurry and get into bed now or we shall give your pretty new bed to Susan. She never frets about going to sleep." Needless to say, this child developed a thorough dislike for her little neighbor and for the perfect habits which she seemed to represent. Instead of copying the desirable manners, she embarrassed her parents by making a violent attack on Susan at every opportunity.

Thoughtlessness of adults is responsible for much of the jealousy among children. Sometimes their emotional involvement and their nearness to the problem prevent parents from realizing how much favoritism they show in their relationships with children. A tactful teacher can often point out to them some factors in their family relations which are causing jealousy to flourish. For example, parents sometimes foster unwholesome feelings by forcing an older child to share his toys or to be responsible for the constant care of a younger one of whom he is jealous. Because of the appeal to his vanity, a parent may allow one jealous child to lavish so much affection on him and to take so much of his time that the child crowds out the other members of the family. Some mothers and fathers reward jealous behavior by pampering a child every time he shows that he is envious of his brothers or sisters. Although the jealous child should get his fair share of attention and should have his self-confidence boosted at every opportunity, he should not be allowed to feel that he is being rewarded when he shows resentment toward other children. Certainly he should not be permitted to attract attention or to get what he wants simply by displaying excessive jealousy. A habit will not be long continued unless it brings some kind of satisfaction.

The jealous child is not the only one whose mental health needs attention. The favored one, who arouses the envy of other children, should also be considered. As he guards his key position in the family circle, he is almost certain to become smug and overbearing in nature. Because he is accustomed to getting more than his share of affection at home, he is likely to expect and demand an undue amount of attention and recognition from others outside the family. If he fails to get it, he may resort to undesirable ways of attracting attention.

Some families in which there is a decided preference for one child over another have sought to solve the problem by attempting to appear absolutely impartial. They treat the children exactly alike, giving to each the very same material possessions and providing identical opportunities for each. This is not a satisfactory solution. The child understands the feelings of his parents regardless of the seeming fairness. No two children have precisely the same requirements. They can be treated with equal consideration only when the special needs of each child are met. The methods required to satisfy children of entirely different temperaments, abilities, and interests must necessarily be quite different.

The only grandson of a doting couple was obviously more loved and admired than his older stepsister. When these children came to visit, the grandfather made a great effort to hide his partiality by treating them exactly alike. His daily surprises invariably consisted of two identical guns, trucks, wagons, or other definitely masculine toys. The trips he planned always included the girl but were obviously planned to suit the interests of a young boy. After graduation from high school, the girl hoped to take a secretarial course in a business school but the grandfather, who still wanted to demonstrate his fairness, insisted upon sending her to the same expensive college that her brother chose to attend. In his effort to conceal his favoritism, the grandfather only succeeded in emphasizing it.

Jealous behavior may spring from various causes. Sometimes it is copied from the bad example of parents or other members of the family. It is not unusual to find a child with jealous tendencies if his parents are jealous of each other. There is certain to be an undesirable effect on the child when one parent holds a grudge because the other gives too much time or attention to his or her own relatives or when the father feels resentful of the time the mother must give to a new baby. Children are sure to sense the jealousy which parents feel toward grandparents, neighbors, teachers, or even toward friends whom the children particularly admire, in whom they confide a great deal, or with whom they spend much of their time.

Many cases of jealousy are directly traceable to the marital status of the parents. When a stepfather or stepmother replaces a devoted parent and deprives the child of some of the affection and attention which he has been accustomed to receiving from the other parent, a trying situation usually results. When there are stepchildren, the problem is even more complicated. An adopted child in the home with a natural son or daughter is another rather common cause for jealousy in a family. Any home condition which causes real or imagined favoritism or rejection of a child is sure to generate unhappiness, dissatisfaction, and unrest. Unless measures are taken to assure the child that his rightful place in the home has not been threatened, symptoms of jealousy and rivalry are likely to appear sooner or later.

The emotional problems of a child are sometimes due to the possessiveness of a parent who has been disappointed in marriage or who has lost a mate by death or divorce. Because the parent looks to him as his only source of companionship and affection, the child may be so completely possessed and smothered that he can have no outside interests and can cultivate no friends of his own age. Some young persons refuse to accept the responsibility of filling this need in a parent's life. Others, rather than rebel and suffer consequent feelings of guilt and remorse, give in to the situation and allow themselves to be changed into withdrawing, unhappy, neurotic individuals.

A popular, attractive sixth-grader was the only son of a physician. When his father died suddenly, his mother shut herself off from all social contacts and clung to the boy as her only source of comfort. This boy, who had been a happy, outgoing individual, became quiet and moody. The other children soon learned that it was useless to ask him to play ball or to go on hikes with them after school for he would always say that he could not leave his mother. The teacher noticed that instead of leading the class as he had previously done, the boy began to daydream and to lose interest in schoolwork. It was not until she was able to interest the mother in helping with health examinations at school and later in devoting a generous amount of her time to various fields of welfare work in which her husband had been interested that the boy was again free to pursue his own life without a sense of guilt and disloyalty to his mother.

A feeling of insecurity is at the root of most jealousy. A child is jealous when he feels uncertain of his place in the family. A husband is jealous when he is not sure of his ability to hold the interest and affection of his wife. Adolescents often experience a feeling of insecurity when they are doubtful of their capacity to handle social situations and to compete with their rivals in attracting friends. A great deal of jealousy can be prevented or eliminated by helping young persons to feel secure and adequate in their environment. When a teacher realizes that a child feels uncertain of his place in the affections of his family, she may be able to make suggestions or provide pertinent reading matter for the parents. If he needs a better relationship with his classmates, she may find a way to give him some pointers on cultivating the friendships he desires.

Sometimes children are envious because others have material possessions that they would like to own. They may suffer from feelings of self-pity at the thought that other children are better off financially, that they have nicer clothes, more friends, or a better scholastic standing. Their feelings of jealousy may be so intense that, in order to boost their own ego, they belittle the accomplishments of other children, ridicule their ambitions, and try to put obstacles in their way. Unless they can be helped while they are still young to keep their wants in line with their ability to satisfy them, they are sure to grow into unhappy, dissatisfied adults. Children who have a deep sense of being deprived can be encouraged to look forward to the time when they can provide more adequately for their own needs.

Children who feel unloved often have an intense desire for popularity. Because they cannot compete successfully for a fair share of affection or attention at home, they make a great effort to excel in scholarship or athletics, to be chosen for leading roles in school performances, to be elected to class offices, and to be included in all social activities. They seem to get their values mixed and to try to make up for a lack of love with an excess of sociability. On the other hand, instead of expressing itself in exaggerated rivalry, intense jealousy sometimes takes the opposite turn and causes a young person to withdraw altogether from competition and to become completely indifferent to schoolwork, athletics, and social life.

Because Wayne had always been a quiet, retiring boy who had caused no trouble, it was a shock to his parents when as an adolescent he began to play truant from school, to refuse to do his homework assignments, and to walk out of the house and slam the door when he was reprimanded by his father or mother. He began to stay away from school a great deal because of pretended illness. Much to the chagrin of his parents, he became involved in several cases of petty theft.

When this boy was finally taken to a psychological clinic, he revealed his intense hatred for his youngest brother, aged three, who was a hopeless cripple and required a great deal of care and attention from his parents. There were six children in this family. At the birth of each successive child, Wayne had seemed to be pushed further from his parents. As he had felt more and more neglected and unnoticed, as his material wants had increased and there had been less money to meet them, and as he had had to give up more school and social activities to help with the additional work at home, a growing resentment had burned within him. The family was extremely religious and the children had been taught that it was sinful not to love, cherish, and help each other. Because Wayne felt guilty about his jealousy, he had buried his hatred and ill will within himself only to have it come to the surface in adolescence when the handicapped baby had taken a greater share of the family's time, money, and love than he could bear.

After the parents realized the tension that this boy was feeling, they relaxed their demands on him and gave him more of their time; the father hunted, fished, bowled, and went to basketball games with him; the mother rearranged the basement for the use of his friends; and they both gave more attention to the boy's progress at school. After the jealousy had been brought into the open and faced squarely, it was no longer an insurmountable problem.

In the treatment of this case, Wayne's parents had been warned about the possible effects on other members of the family while giving one child their all-out, concentrated attention. Although they were concerned about healing the breach with the oldest son, they also had to consider the feelings of the younger brothers and sisters. Each child needed some time when he could have the exclusive, undivided time of his parents. It is expedient that parents learn the particular desires, interests, and emotional requirements of each child in the family so that they can give of themselves to each one according to his need. Children are not satisfied with parental love that is always carefully rationed. Only as a child is given enough attention all his own in the way and at the time it is needed will he willingly allow other members of the family the same privilege.

Adults err when they ostracize, shame, and punish a child for hostile behavior that is caused by jealousy. Since jealousy comes from a fear of being disliked, unwanted, or discriminated against, strict disciplinary measures only make the feeling stronger. The best procedure is to reassure the child as much as possible and then to discover and try to change the circumstances in his life that he cannot tolerate any longer.

Just as all children are rivals for the love of their parents, they are all in competition for the affection of the teacher who has any warmth in her nature. In order to avoid arousing or aggravating jealousy, it is necessary for the teacher to give unstintingly of her love wherever and whenever it seems to be most needed. She does not have to be afraid that she is unfair to the other children when she bestows an extra amount of affection on the ones who seem to be constantly striving for all the recognition they can get or on the ones who have reached the point of withdrawing from every form of competition. The teacher should never allow any child, no matter how annoying and unlovable he may be, to feel that he is disliked or rejected by her. She should be generous enough with her understanding and love to make up, in a measure, for the warmth and affection which some children fail to get at home.

A sympathetic teacher who accepts a child's feelings without criticizing or preaching can usually get him to release his pent-up emotions. If a child does not talk readily, it may be easier for him to let his feelings out through playing with dolls or puppets, through dramatizing or telling stories, or through drawing or painting. But if he has turned all his jealousy inside until he is unable to get it out of his system in any way and until he does not even realize what is bothering him, he should be referred to a psychiatrist for professional help before his trouble becomes even more deep-seated.

ACTIVITIES SUGGESTED

The activities for this lesson should be planned with the purpose of discovering the children who have intense feelings of jealousy, of helping them to get these feelings out of their systems, of making them feel more secure in the group at school, and of helping them to acquire some of the social skills which may make them more acceptable to others.

1. Make occasions to engage the younger children in conversation about their families and to get them to dramatize home situations. From chance remarks about parents, brothers, sisters, and new babies, you will be able to sense feelings of envy and jealousy in some of the children. Talk to the parents of each child who shows evidence of unhealthy emotions and suggest possible ways of treating these feelings.

2. Attempt to find out how the boys and girls get along with other children in their homes. This cannot be done by direct questioning because children seldom admit that they are jealous, resentful, or scornful. Ask each one to describe some of the accomplishments and talents of his brothers, sisters, or cousins. From the inflections of their voices and the expressions on their faces, it will be possible to distinguish between admiration and jealousy. The following subjects are suggested:

"What I like most about my brother (or sister)."
"Things my brother (or sister) and I enjoy doing together."
"Some special privileges my brother (or sister) is allowed."
"How my brother (or sister) helps at home."
"My brother's (or sister's) hobby."
"My brother's (or sister's) favorite radio or television program."
"The sports my brother (or sister) likes most."
"Why I am proud of my brother (or sister)."

3. Talk with the children about the desirability of being the oldest, the middle, the youngest, or the only child in the family. Help them to see that there are advantages and disadvantages in each status and that there is no real reason to be jealous of the child who happens to be in any of these positions. It is quite common for younger children to feel that the older ones

have more privileges. The older children usually think that the younger ones get more attention from their parents and have fewer duties and responsibilities in the home. They need to understand that parents have their reasons for giving certain members of the family more time and attention than others. It sometimes helps to be reminded that mothers must necessarily give more time and care to completely helpless babies and to frail, sick, or crippled children than to independent, strong, healthy ones. This certainly does not mean that they love these children more.

4. Hold an informal discussion concerning the symptoms of jealousy which the children sometimes recognize in other persons. For example, if a brother or sister consistently destroys property belonging to another member of the family, it may be an indication that he is jealous. Ask the pupils to enumerate possible causes for such jealous feelings. They may have observed that jealousy is apparently aroused over material possessions, good looks, school grades, friends, parents' love, or teacher's favor. Talk with them about the effects of jealousy both on the person who is envious and on the one who is unjustly treated because he has something that others want. Suggest that they try to make jealous friends or relatives feel that they are liked and respected rather than disliked or envied. Brothers and sisters do not naturally love and admire each other simply because they happened to be born into the same family. Love must be earned.

5. Encourage the children to talk about the brother-sister or the parent-child relations that are most satisfying and the ones that are most annoying to them. By carefully steering the discussion it is possible to help the pupils get some insight into the reasons for these situations and the things they can do to improve them. Writing or talking, either privately or in a group, will give them opportunities to release their emotions.

6. It may give you a clue to some of the jealousies of the children in your class if you have them fill out a chart similar to the following:

Name	What this person has that I would like to own	Name	What I have that this person wants

7. The following companion filmstrips produced by Young America Films, Inc., New York, in 1949, can be used effectively with this lesson:

David and His Family (for kindergarten and primary grades) shows how a kindergarten boy is affected by the arrival of a new baby brother and how he adjusts to the situation in his activities at home and at school.

David's Bad Day is based on Else McKean's book by the same name, published by Shady Hill Press, New York, in 1949. This filmstrip, which is intended for the use of parents and teachers, deals with the jealousies and frustrations aroused in a four-year-old boy by the arrival of a new baby in the home. It shows how emotional outbursts at school are traced to the difficulty at home and how the parents help the child to make an adjustment.

The following films may be shown to groups of parents, teachers, or prospective teachers:

Human Beginnings (for elementary school children and adults), 16 mm., sound, 22 min., Eddie Albert Productions, Hollywood, Calif., 1950. This film is designed to help boys and girls feel emotionally secure with a baby brother or sister.

Feelings of Depression (for adults), 16 mm., sound, 30 min., National Film Board of Canada, New York, 1950. This is a psychological film which gives the case history of a sensitive, despondent, insecure adult whose trouble stems from jealous feelings toward a younger brother.

FOLLOW-UP

Continue to be on the alert for symptoms of jealousy. Learn to think of this emotion as a normal reaction which should be discussed openly and not as a wicked feeling that should be suppressed. Be especially conscious of the outstanding problems of jealous behavior and, from time to time, check on the progress you are making with these cases. In so far as possible, eliminate all classroom situations which are likely to arouse jealousy.

BIBLIOGRAPHY

BARUCH, DOROTHY W.: *Parents Can Be People,* Appleton-Century-Crofts, Inc., New York, 1944, Chap. 7.

BAUER, W. W.: *Stop Annoying Your Children,* Bobbs-Merrill Company, Indianapolis, 1947, Chap. IX.

BLACK, IRMA SIMONTON: *Off to a Good Start,* Harcourt, Brace and Company, Inc., New York, 1946, pp. 79–87.

NEISSER, EDITH G.: *Children in the Family: Rivals and Friends,* Bureau of Publications, Teachers College, Columbia University, New York, 1951. Pamphlet.

ULLMANN, FRANCES: *Getting Along with Brothers and Sisters,* Science Research Associates, Inc., Chicago, 1950. Pamphlet.

CHAPTER 11

Heeding the Attention Seeker

Aims of This Lesson:

To learn to look upon class show-offs as children who are in need of help and understanding.

To provide wholesome ways in which attention seekers can gain legitimate recognition.

Even the most self-controlled and long-suffering teacher is likely to lose patience with the continuous antics of the show-off. In almost every class there is at least one youngster who misbehaves when the teacher is out of the room, says silly things to get a laugh from the other children, purposely trips when he walks across the room, makes unnecessary noises, and does numerous other things of a similar nature. He makes faces, throws paper wads, scrapes his feet on the floor, giggles at inopportune times, and refuses to conform to class routines and assignments. He may even call attention to himself by temper tantrums, an undue display of fear, or some unusual manner of dress. No matter what method he uses, he never relaxes in his effort to distract the children from their work and to draw all eyes to himself.

On the playground, too, the attention seekers can be seen continually shouting, screaming, and engaging in all types of restless, aimless, and boisterous behavior. They make constant bids for attention and approval by such remarks as, "Look at me!" "Watch how far I can throw a ball," and "See how high I can jump."

Very young children are naturally self-centered and it is expected that they will sometimes whine, cry, cling to the teacher, and in other ways demand a great deal of attention. But this tendency should be outgrown.

132

Older children who constantly strive to usurp the attention of everyone around them show marks of immaturity which, if not treated, are likely to become more pronounced and more obnoxious as they grow older.

It is natural for the teacher to feel that a child's clownish behavior is a personal affront and an indication that he is showing his dislike by trying to annoy her. Her first impulse may be to suppress him, to remove him from the room, or to use sarcasm in dealing with him. In desperation she may have him stand in the hall while the others recite, send him to the principal's office, keep him after school, or embarrass him before his classmates. A child who is so unlovely may seem to deserve any or all of these punishments. But such methods can be no more than momentarily effective.

Attention-getting behavior is not a case for preaching, moralizing, punishing, and embarrassing. It does no good to tell a child to stop being silly or to exact a promise from him that he will improve. He knows that his actions are not looked upon with favor and he would like to do something about it. But until his longing for attention is satisfied in some other way, he cannot seem to refrain from showing off. His effort to gain the center of the stage at school is his way of indicating that something is wrong in his life. The teacher should be glad, at least, that this child is giving a warning of his need for help and is not developing a more serious problem by withdrawing into a shell.

When a child is constantly trying to attract attention, there may be a combination of reasons. The tendency to show off is often the result of too little or too much attention at home. It may be due to the child's desire to cover up a deficiency in scholarship, a feeling that he is different from others, or a fear that he is not liked by his classmates. It may mean that he needs more social skills, more opportunities to be in command, or more chances to succeed and to feel important. In order to know what type of treatment will be most effective in each case, it is necessary to study the child's background and find out the underlying cause of his trouble. This involves talking to the child, watching his behavior, checking with his parents, and perhaps visiting in his home.

If the show-off is a child who has long been the center of an admiring group of adults at home, he is probably striving to be the most important figure at school as well. Finding that actions which amuse and delight his family do not get the same results at school, he has to devise new methods of attracting attention. Naturally, he will continue to use only the ones that prove to be successful.

A little wholesome neglect is sometimes good for the self-centered young-ster. Whenever possible, it is wise to ignore the clowning of a spoiled, over-indulged child who persists in disrupting the class in order to get the atten-tion to which he is accustomed at home. Although it is necessary to use firmness with such a child, it is a mistake to humiliate him. He has a crying need for recognition which must be satisfied in some way. He should be allowed to get attention and praise through teamwork, cooperation, and the proper use of any talent or ability which he may possess. Working on group projects usually makes him realize that others also have rights and that the limelight must be shared. At the same time, however, he can retain his feeling of importance by knowing that his contribution is needed by the group.

The tendency to show off is more often the result of an unhappy home life in which the child has been starved for praise and affection. Because he is one of many children, he may be unnoticed, neglected, or pushed aside too much. If he is of a different temperament than his parents, they may not understand him or may never be pleased with what he does. Whether it is justified or not, there may be the feeling that another child in the family is preferred to him. A child may feel insecure because his parents are in-consistent in their love or their discipline, severely punishing and criticizing at one time and pampering and condoning at another. Parents who are worried and preoccupied are likely to pay less attention to a child and, un-consciously, to give him the impression that they are not interested in him. A broken home, constant discord, or emotional instability of parents may cause a child to feel uncertain of his place in the family. Since his need for attention is not being met at home, he often seeks to satisfy it at school by making his classmates laugh or his teacher scold.

When a child shows off and makes himself ridiculous in school, it is usually an indication that somebody who is important to him does not love him or notice him enough. The warmth and friendliness of his teacher will go a long way toward making up for the attention and love he is missing elsewhere. An extra smile, a pleasant look, and a genuine interest in his well-being may be just what he needs to assure him that the teacher really likes him and that he does not need to attract her attention by acting silly.

Children who feel inferior because they cannot keep up with the class in academic work very frequently try to satisfy their need for recognition by bragging, feigning indifference, or showing off. It is impossible for the slow learners to sit quietly by and watch the others succeed. They become restless and impatient; they must do something that will cause the teacher to notice them, too. Even unfavorable attention is preferable to no attention at all. In order to inflate their own ego, these children often wisecrack and belittle the efforts of their classmates.

Some teachers encourage other members of the class to shame and deride these unfortunate children for their undesirable behavior and scholarship. Sometimes they even display samples of their poor work for the others to criticize. This technique not only tends to increase the slow children's feelings of inferiority, but it develops in the young critics the undesirable trait of glorying in the mistakes of others. A childhood habit of looking for others' faults and enjoying their misfortunes may persist until it makes a person bitter and unsympathetic in later life.

The child who shows off because he is not doing well in his work needs attention and praise, not belittling and sarcasm. The teacher should observe this child carefully to find out the classes in which he always acts up, the ones in which he contributes most and disturbs least, and the occasions when he appears to get some satisfaction without being silly. By becoming cognizant of his strong points, it is possible to play up his abilities and to find ways in which he can become at least moderately successful. When a child can excel in one subject, he sometimes gets enough satisfaction and recognition to make up for his feeling of inadequacy in other fields. If he cannot achieve in any area, he will be forced to show off most of the time. A little private tutoring may do a world of good. If the teacher cannot help the pupil after school, she may tell the parents how they can work with him or suggest a special teacher or an older child in the neighborhood who could give him individual instruction.

Attention-getting behavior can often be forestalled simply by showing an interest in a child's hobby or by asking him to bring a prized possession for the other children to see. The boy who brought his homing pigeons to school, the one who invited his teacher to his home to see his collection of Indian relics, and the one who made display cases for the seashells which he presented to the class furnished their teachers with opportunities to make them feel important and useful. Anything that a child brings to school or any constructive ideas that he advances can generally be used in some way. If it relieves his intense longing for legitimate recognition, it makes no difference how farfetched the relation to the curriculum happens to be.

The child who is tormented by the knowledge that he is different from other children will do almost anything to relieve his feelings of inferiority. If he senses that others shun him because of his race, his speech, his clothes, the social or economic status of his family, or any peculiar feature or trait, he is likely to have an inner urge to do rude, annoying things that call attention to himself. Both the child with an apparent deformity which cannot be corrected and the one with a minor physical defect which is hardly noticeable to others may allow their real and imaginary disfigurements to assume tragic proportions in their lives. They need to be taught to see these imperfections in their proper perspective, without being overpowered and made bitter and spiteful by them. When worried, disturbed children are most irritating, they are most in need of understanding and genuine friendship. The teacher who wins their confidence can usually help them, in time, to see that most deviations do not matter so much as they think.

When the show-off has no reason to feel inferior and does not appear to be neglected or overindulged at home, his trouble may be that he does not get along well with others of his own age. It is pathetic to see a child want the good will of his comrades so much that he is willing to pay for it by being punished for their misdeeds. Sometimes he tries to win the favor of the bad boys in the class by acting silly and bringing down the wrath of the teacher upon himself. He may be so eager for the attention and friendship of other children that he will allow himself to be used as a scapegoat for his fellows and will do any foolish or risky thing that he is told to do. A timid youngster who is constantly teased and annoyed by his associates often tries to meet the situation by clowning. In this way he furnishes amusement for the other children in the classroom in order to escape being fought, ridiculed, and tormented by them outside of school.

The child who resorts to clowning because of his need for friends should not be punished by being deprived of playing with other children, removed from the group, or caused to miss some special treat with the class. His trouble is that he needs more love and more social contacts. Harsh discipline, isolation, and severe criticism will only add to his unhappiness.

Although clowning is the most frequently used, there are many other devices for gaining attention. Some children assume an air of helplessness and awkwardness as a means of getting adults to wait on them. Simply by appearing unable to do anything for themselves, they get constant care and service from their elders. Instead of becoming increasingly independent, they become more helpless as they grow older.

It is not uncommon for children to feign illness as a means of attracting attention to themselves. By pretending to be sick, a child may be excused from obligations at school and may get the attention of the doctor, the school nurse, the teacher, and the children. He may also be able to get special consideration and comfort from his mother, who may usually be too busy to spend much time with him. If injuries seem to cause special concern on the part of parents, it is no wonder that a much-neglected or harshly treated child will frequently fall down, get his head banged or his finger mashed, and come screaming for consolation.

Some bright children have found that they get more attention from parents and teachers by appearing dull. The special tutoring which they receive satisfies a need for attention. There are many variations of the story about the brilliant child who did not learn to read at school in spite of the efforts of regular and special teachers. It was discovered that the half hour when his mother read to him each day was the only time which she devoted exclusively to him. He was afraid that he might lose this special attention if he learned to read for himself. His difficulty disappeared only after his mother agreed to stop reading to him and to give him more of her time in other ways.

A child who needs attention will soon learn what type of behavior is most likely to bring the desired results. If his attempts to get into the limelight at school cause the teacher to become excited and to scold, threaten, and punish, he has been successful and will repeat his actions again and again. He will undergo any harsh treatment rather than be overlooked. If his antics are ignored, however, he will try other tactics. When he finds that good work and good behavior are the things that cause the teacher to focus the spotlight on him, he will concentrate on these ways of gaining attention. Legitimately earned approval is much more satisfying than the dubious notice that comes from irritating the teacher.

Charles was a constant source of trouble to the sixth-grade teacher. Although he was one of the brightest children in the room, he apparently could not read, insisted that he did not understand the vocabulary in the books, and claimed not to remember anything that he had been told. The teacher found it almost impossible to ignore his idleness and his distracting behavior. She was disturbed by his incessant requests to sharpen his pencil, to get a drink, to borrow paper, to open and close the windows, and to have explanations repeated.

During several quiet interviews after school, the teacher gave this boy ample time to talk over his bothers. She learned that he was the youngest of three sons, that his father had died when Charles was a baby, and that his mother had been employed since that time. Charles felt that he was a special burden because his mother had often remarked that he was "the only one of her children who had ever given her any trouble." Several of his former teachers, too, had called him "the worst boy in the class." Since he felt so worthless and since his older brothers teased and bullied him so unmercifully, he had often considered running away from home.

The teacher realized that this was a case for sympathetic treatment and understanding. Without being too obvious, she got Charles to take the responsibility for several jobs in the classroom; she gave him some private tutoring in reading; and she visited with his mother and brothers and suggested that they stop nagging, criticizing, and teasing the boy and try giving him more of their time and interest. It was gratifying to see this boy respond to warmth and friendliness and to the praise which naturally came as a result of his improvement in attitude and work.

Intellectually, the teacher may know exactly how the attention seeker should be handled. She may be fully aware that the best form of treatment is to keep him busy, to change activities frequently enough to whet his interest, and to give him an opportunity for real achievement. Emotionally, however, she may find it difficult to give him the love and consideration he craves. The child's behavior may be so disgusting to her that she wants to leave him alone, to be sarcastic with him, or to mete out some fitting punishment. But when she begins to study his background and to analyze the reasons for his actions, she is likely to feel more kindly toward him. She may be sure that the child who uses unpleasant behavior as a way of demanding attention has found someone in his life who has succumbed to this device. It is not his fault that he has continued to use a method that has proved satisfactory in helping him to be noticed or to get his own way.

Reformation of the show-off is a challenge to the teacher. She should not become discouraged, however, if progress is slow. An attention getter has usually formed the habit of acting as he does over a long period of time. It cannot be expected that he will change his pattern of behavior until he has found and adopted some more desirable way of getting recognition.

ACTIVITIES SUGGESTED

Although the tendency to show off requires individual treatment, group activities can help all the children to understand the needs which some of them may be expressing by constant clowning. By using stories, games, and questionnaires, you may discover abilities and skills of the attention getters which can be used to help them gain legitimate approval. Then concentrate on your young show-offs. Select activities which will fit their peculiar needs and which will give them a chance to be genuinely accepted and appreciated by the others in the group.

1. For your own use make a chart containing the names of the most obvious attention seekers in your class. Keep the record for a week, making a mark each time the child is silly, loud, or obviously playing to the grandstand. By studying this chart, you may be able to find the situations in which he feels adequate and the particular times when he must build himself up by attracting attention. Example:

Child's Name	Attention-getting Situations				
	Reading	Arithmetic	Music	Art	Playground
Dorothy			//	/////	///
Martha					/////
Paul	////	////			
Sam	/////	////	////	////	
Tom		///////			

2. Ask each child to write or tell about What I Can Do Best, What I Most Enjoy Doing, or My Most Prized Possession. From this source you may get information about interests, skills, or hobbies that can be given some special emphasis. If you find that an attention getter has an interesting collection, unusual souvenirs from trips, or possessions which the other children could profit by seeing, ask him to bring them to school. Use this as a means of giving the child some of the attention he needs and craves.

3. Initiate a "personality of the day" feature in your room. As a language assignment present a list of names of class members (being sure that the attention getters are included), and ask each pupil to choose the name of one child whom he knows well and to write a complimentary account of this child's good points, his talents, his accomplishments, and his hobbies. By posting a different description each day in a prominent place in the room, the current "personality" may be given a feeling of importance and worth. The information thus furnished by the child's classmates may also give you some clues on which to work.

4. As a help in finding out what is troubling the attention getters, have each child in the class list his bothers as follows:

My greatest bothers at home:

_____

_____

My greatest bothers at school:

_____

_____

My greatest bothers on the playground:

_____

_____

If the children have the right feeling toward the teacher and if they are assured that their answers are to be held in confidence and used only as a help in understanding their problems, they are likely to be honest and frank. The answers of those children who constantly act silly or boisterous may give you some ideas about why they act as they do.

5. Talk with the group about how most people have a desire to improve either in their work, in games, or in some skill. Explain that if you could know just what each one in your class would like to do better, you might arrange for some other person who is especially proficient in that line to help him. Tell them that it is possible, too, for them to make many of their own wishes come true. Ask the older children to fill out a form like the one below; allow the younger ones to take turns whispering their wishes to you.

I would like to do better in these subjects:

_____

_____

I would like to be more like these persons:

_____

_____

I wish that I could learn to do these things:

_____

_____

I wish that these persons in my family could spend more time with me:

_____

_____

I wish these persons would be friends with me:

_____

_____

You may be able to make some of the wishes come true by doing a little private coaching, by giving the children some definite hints about winning friends, or by talking with parents and other persons who may be directly responsible for the attention-getting behavior.

6. Plan a game of charades in which individuals or groups act out something that they have always wished they could be or could do well and the others guess what is being represented. Good actors may be given the first opportunities to perform so that the children will get the idea. Then, without being too obvious, see that the attention getters have a chance to participate. From this game, you may be able to get a few clues to needs or desires. By devising ways of making some of the wishes come true, you may automatically eliminate some clowning and showing off.

7. Allow the children to present a variety show in which each attention getter is sure to have a part of some kind. Whistling, whittling, asking riddles, operating the record player, teaching the class a new game, doing a magic trick, dancing, playing the harmonica, showing a collection of rocks or fossils, singing, or doing anything else that will bring the participant genuine approval, not ridicule, is desirable. If a child is timid about performing before the class, he may prepare the settings, take care of sound effects, or assist in some other way. His contribution should be properly recognized and acknowledged, however.

8. Talk with the group about the possible causes of attention-getting behavior. Explain that the child who is always trying to get the center of the stage has a special need either for friends or for achievement. Ask the pupils to describe some of the ways in which they have seen children try to get attention on the playground, in the lunchroom, in the halls, in the classroom, on the street, and at home. Discuss the needs which these children may be expressing and some of the things their classmates can do to help them.

9. Wage a campaign for self-control. Just before dismissal each afternoon take a few minutes to look back over the happenings of the day. Mention examples of especially commendable behavior which you have noticed. Without scolding or preaching, endeavor to get the children to review instances of misbehavior, silliness, or clowning which have been disturbing to the class. One kindergarten child referred to undesirable actions and unpleasant feelings as "scratches on the day." The children in his class started each morning with "a new pink day without any scratches" and

made an effort to reach the end of the day with as little unhappiness and as few "scratches" as possible.

10. Find occasions before and after school and at recess to have private talks with individual attention getters. Do not criticize an offender or try to get him to promise to do better. Through friendly conversation about things that interest him, you will be able to find out whether he seeks attention because he is so accustomed to being the center of things at home; because he has had so little affection from his family; because he feels inferior, inadequate, or different; or because he is timid and unpopular and uses this means of getting the attention and approval of other children. Simply by being an interested listener, you may learn a great deal. Afterward, you may be able to find subtle ways of helping. Perhaps the very fact that you are especially friendly to a child may reduce his need to demand your constant attention in the classroom.

FOLLOW-UP

Cases of clowning and showing off cannot be dismissed and regarded as permanently cured simply because they have once been observed and treated. The cause of the trouble sometimes recurs and the symptoms return. Teachers need to be continually on the alert for attention-getting behavior, which is a broad hint to them that something is lacking in a child's life.

BIBLIOGRAPHY

Hymes, James L., Jr.: *A Pound of Prevention* (How Teachers Can Meet the Emotional Needs of Young Children), New York State Committee on Mental Hygiene, New York, 1947. Pamphlet.
————: *Teacher Listen, The Children Speak,* New York State Committee on Mental Hygiene, New York, 1949. Pamphlet.

CHAPTER 12

Understanding the Shy, Withdrawing Child

Aims of This Lesson:

To focus attention on the timid, sensitive, withdrawing children in the class.

To look for the underlying difficulties which have caused these children to shrink from social contacts.

To help withdrawing children to learn ways of releasing their feelings instead of hiding them.

To use techniques which will enable unhappily introverted pupils to become more outgoing in nature.

Children who meet thwarting or unpleasant experiences with temper tantrums, fighting, or defiance cannot long be ignored. They express their rebellious feelings by disrupting class routine and using various devices that are irritating and frustrating to the teacher. Because they resort to these methods of relieving their tensions and protecting themselves from hurts and disappointments, they are labeled as "bad" and are subjected to thoughtful observation and treatment.

Actually, the aggressive children who have found ways of releasing their own emotions by disobeying, interrupting, and showing off are far less in need of help than are the shy, timid ones who prefer to remain inconspicuous and unnoticed. It is natural for the teacher to look with approval at the quiet, respectful, cooperative children who create no disorder and to be more concerned about the noisy, impudent, obstreperous ones. But every teacher should endeavor to give some time and thought to the emotional

143

problems of the solitary, sensitive, shrinking children. These youngsters probably have underlying personality difficulties which are causing them to pull away into a shell and to be overlooked by the busy teacher.

Children with marked withdrawing tendencies usually bottle their emotions inside themselves until they finally have to release them in some way. Their withdrawal from disagreeable situations may show itself in the form of fear, anxiety, daydreaming, nightmares, hysteria, sulkiness, or depression. These timid, unsocial persons are really in danger of personality breakdown or mental illness in later life. Unless something is done for them while they are young, they may eventually find ways of shutting out all their difficulties by drinking, by becoming drug addicts, or even by suicide. A large percentage of the patients in mental hospitals are victims of complete withdrawal from reality.

Because of a feeling of insecurity or inadequacy, because of inability to compete physically with other children, or because of a lack of friends, a youngster may make a desperate effort to compensate by excessive studiousness and model behavior. The adult recognition which he receives, as a result of his perfection, only intensifies his problem. While basking in the teacher's favor, he usually forfeits the admiration and companionship of his classmates. Since one of the greatest needs of children is to be accepted and liked by their contemporaries, it is much more important to their happiness that they adjust well to other children than that they meet adult standards of behavior prematurely. Unfortunately, parents and teachers often encourage withdrawing behavior because it makes discipline easy.

It is true that many children are naturally quiet and retiring. They prefer sedentary activities and are perfectly satisfied with their own company. These youngsters do not need to be forced into active participation or to have their happy way of living changed.

Some boys and girls find a satisfactory way of escape from emotional problems through creative and imaginative pursuits. They spend many hours contentedly reading, studying, experimenting, building, painting, or writing. Those who have the necessary intelligence and perseverance may later become scientists, research workers, writers, or inventors.

Although some introverted children are able to make a satisfactory adjustment through scholastic achievement, many others are weak in their studies. They daydream or sleep in class. They shrink from competition with other children and withdraw still further within themselves because they feel inferior and inadequate. No matter how well these quiet, retiring children may be able to cover their feelings, they are usually unhappy and very much in need of help from sympathetic and understanding teachers.

The sensitive, withdrawing children in a class have certain identifying characteristics. Most of them never volunteer to recite, although they may hand in all written work. They rarely voice an opinion or advance an idea. They prefer to study, work, and play alone. They stand around on the fringe watching the others play but seldom being chosen or taking any part in games and physical activities. They do not often quarrel, fight, or defend themselves, but back away when other children bother them. They sometimes escape from the realities of life by forgetfulness or by placing the blame for their actions on others.

Most withdrawing children show nervous symptoms. They often have poor sleeping habits and are subject to spells of irritability, headaches, and indigestion. They may bite their nails, suck their fingers, twist their clothing, pull at their hair, stutter, squirm, and fidget. Such mannerisms seem to have a soothing effect by giving them something to do with their hands. Adults should not try to take away from nervous children any of their little comforting devices unless they can substitute some more substantial props.

After watching the children closely and focusing upon the ones who are shy and ill at ease, the teacher should find out all she can about their backgrounds, their home life, their school records, and the way they spend their time out of school. She will need to learn what it is in each child's life that has pushed him to the wall. It is difficult to help him come out of his shell without discovering what caused him to withdraw in the first place.

Sometimes a child appears shy and aloof because he has a physical defect or abnormality which makes him self-conscious or because he is lacking in the strength and energy to compete with strong, vigorous children. If the teacher is not sure that a withdrawing child is physically well, she may talk with the parents about having some obvious disability corrected or may arrange for the child to have a thorough physical examination. More food, a properly balanced diet, extra vitamins, less excitement, or more rest may be all a child needs to enable him to meet others on their own level.

It is extremely important to school children to feel that they do not differ in any way from their associates. A child who has recently moved into the community from another locality may shrink from others because he knows that his speech, clothing, or mannerisms are different. An understanding teacher can do much to make a new pupil realize that such differences are inconsequential or to help him conform to local customs. A girl who is self-conscious because of an unattractive appearance usually appreciates tactful suggestions from an interested teacher. Some subtle hints about cleanliness, styles of dress, and color combinations may be all that she needs to start her on the road to better grooming and more poise and self-assurance.

Home life has a great deal to do with mental health. A child may be sensitive or depressed because he feels that his parents do not love him enough, that they prefer another child in the family, or that his associates reject him. He may be timid, fearful, and cringing because of restraints imposed upon him by his environment. Upon looking into the situation, the teacher may find that the child has little chance for success at home, that he is nagged, scolded, ridiculed, and dominated, that he sees examples of emotional immaturity in his parents, that he is treated so inconsistently that he never knows what to expect, or that he is not capable of doing all that is demanded of him.

For a long time a child may suppress his real feelings and give expression only to those feelings which he is sure will meet with approval. Then when the pent-up emotions can no longer be hidden, they may suddenly be released in an outburst of uncontrollable laughing or crying which has little apparent cause. Such hysterical behavior is a common symptom of a withdrawing personality.

One of the most frequent causes of withdrawing tendencies in children is parental overprotection that is continued long after the child should have developed some independence. Some mothers enjoy the feeling that children need them and they do everything they can to make themselves absolutely necessary to their happiness and comfort. Thus, unconsciously, they delay the process of growing up by trying to keep their children helpless as long as possible.

A seventh-grade boy of more than average ability lived in a world of dreams and was quite oblivious to his surroundings. It was almost impossible for his teachers to interest him in any type of classroom procedure. He never had his materials and he constantly left his homework at home or in his locker. His mother followed him to school almost every morning, bringing his lunch, his raincoat, his library books, or his notebook. She told the teachers how this child would not take any responsibility for his personal belongings or obligations, how he would forget instructions when he was sent on an errand, how he would fail to come to meals when called, and how he would frequently lock himself in his room and sulk for hours.

In an effort to provide companionship for this only child, the mother invited a boy from an orphanage to spend a year in her home. She planned every minute of the day for the two boys, providing music lessons for them, taking them on interesting trips, and helping them with their homework in the evening. The boys had no time which was free of her excessive and smothering attention. This overprotective, oversolicitous mother managed all their activities so that the visiting boy would play a minor role and remember his duty to entertain her son. The guest became so rebellious and the son became so dependent, withdrawn, and dreamy that there seemed to be no help for them in the same environment. As a solution, the orphan was returned to the institution and the son was enrolled in a private school in a distant state.

Fear is often the basis for a child's withdrawal into himself. Although a timid youngster may do well in written work and in noncompetitive activities, he may refrain from speaking up in class even when he knows the answers lest he make an error. Fear of competition sometimes causes a child to stay away from school, to avoid companions, and gradually to withdraw from many social contacts. The child who is afraid to tell his parents that he made a poor grade on a test, the one who does not have the courage to tell the teacher that he lost her borrowed book, and the one who will not invite his friends to his home because he is ashamed of it are storing up feelings of guilt, fear, and inferiority which are sure to have undesirable effects.

It is not unusual for children to find that they can avoid difficulties by feigning illness and to use this method until it becomes a habit. When a pupil is frequently absent because of a headache, a sore throat, or an upset stomach, the teacher should watch the record carefully to see whether the absences usually occur on days when there is a test, an oral report, or some other special assignment from which he is trying to run away. Fear and worry can actually induce illness and the victim may suffer as much as if he had an organic ailment. But when a person recovers from real or imagined suffering as soon as the situation which he dreads has passed, it is very likely that he is building up a bad habit of escape.

When a junior high school counselor realized that one boy's schoolwork was suffering as a result of his poor attendance, she made a careful study both of his past records and of his present circumstances. It was found that since kindergarten Judd had had a pattern of spotted absence amounting to from forty to fifty days each year. A conference with the mother revealed that she was a fearful, emotional, withdrawing person who had kept the child at home and pampered him at every slight indication of illness. This attitude had probably been induced by the child's very serious illness at the age of four years and his enforced separation from the mother during his long stay in the hospital.

When Judd was ten years old the family had moved into a new neighborhood, where he had been unable to form friendships. The extended illness of his aged grandfather who lived in the home and the poor arrangement of the house had made it impossible for children to have any freedom there. Judd had spent more and more time alone in his own room, where he tinkered with old guns, a radio, and a chemistry set.

Now, at the age of fifteen, with a speech defect, a withdrawing personality, and no friends, Judd was developing many ailments. He asked to be excused from band practice because of ear and throat trouble, to withdraw from the typing class because of double-jointed fingers, and to be transferred from mechanical drawing because of poor eyesight. He frequently came late to school or asked permission to leave soon after arrival. According to the doctor's statement, there was no physical basis for his constant complaint of nausea.

A close check of the pattern of absence over a period of several weeks showed that when Judd came to school tardy, he always arrived about ten thirty o'clock, just at the close of the history period. If he became ill and had to leave, it was about nine thirty o'clock, just before the history class started. The illness consistently occurred on the days when a test was scheduled, when an oral report was to be given, when a notebook was due, or when some special obligation had to be met. Having failed the history course two years in succession, Judd had built up a fear of this particular subject. His mother's sympathy and support were making it easy for him to establish a habit of illness as a means of escape. After she and Judd were able to see that the problem was emotional, not physical, the situation began to improve.

Fear of the future and a dread of growing up are other evidences of a withdrawing nature. The older child who has temper tantrums when things do not please him, who runs crying to the teacher when he is hurt, or who resorts to baby talk or some other type of infantile behavior is saying by his actions that he is trying to retreat from an unhappy present and to go back to a time when life was more pleasant. This attitude may be caused by the fact that he has been pampered too much, that his parents have encouraged him to remain an infant, or that a younger brother or sister has gotten more than a fair share of attention. A child who is constantly trying to revert to infancy needs to be convinced that the future holds more for him than the past. It may be helpful to give him a succession of goals to reach or events to look forward to in the not too distant future. A child who prefers not to grow up because he has observed or heard so much about the hardships of adulthood needs to see parents, teachers, and other older persons in a happy state of mind.

Unlike the ones who live in the past, some children spend their time dreaming of the future. They meet every rebuke concerning their neglect of present duties by telling how well they intend to work when they reach the next grade or after they leave school. Children who live either in the past or in the future as a means of escaping from a disagreeable or difficult present are very much in need of help.

A sympathetic teacher is often the one who is in the best position to help a timid, unhappy child. By carefully studying his problem and learning the reasons for his difficulty, she can usually find an effective remedy. However, successful treatment often depends more upon the quality of personal relationships than upon the use of any specific techniques. The remedy for withdrawal may be implicit in the warm, friendly, sincere, and interested feeling that the teacher is able to create.

A shy, sensitive child who has retreated because of a lack of friends cannot be forced or reasoned into becoming an extroverted person. It is of no use to tell him how foolish it is to be timid or how important it is to make friends. The best way to help a child to become socially adjusted is to see that he has many opportunities to associate with others who are likely to be good companions for him. By working, playing, and talking with other children, he will learn to understand and cooperate with them, to be sensitive to their wishes, and to contribute to their happiness instead of concentrating on his own wretchedness. Helping children to find specific ways of being of service to each other is much more effective than a great deal of talking about the virtues of friendliness or unselfishness.

A timid, retiring child cannot be thrust into a crowd of more aggressive children and expected to find his place. It is easier for him to participate if he is put in a smaller group at first and gradually absorbed into a larger circle. The personality of the child should somewhat determine the type of group with whom he is expected to work or play. While one extremely self-conscious child will enter into activities only if he can have the support of a leader who is likely to assume all responsibility, another is more likely to compete if he is grouped with other shy children.

The teacher's own attitude toward a sensitive, friendless child can harm or help him immeasurably. By criticizing, belittling, and scolding, she may cause him to become discouraged and to retreat still deeper into himself. But by smiling at him, giving him an affectionate pat and a reassuring look, and by showing him that she likes him, she will cause other children in the group to accept him more readily. Although she should not make her attention too obvious, she can ask the child to run errands, to carry books, and to do other things for her. She can comment on any new possession that he may have, praise him for any good job that he may do, and let him know that she notices him as a person. If the withdrawing child responds to this treatment by developing a "crush" on the teacher, she should not discourage him. She should regard this as evidence that he is developing an outgoing feeling that may lead to his being able to make friends with other children. If she repulses him, he may withdraw still further.

If a child's trouble seems to come from a feeling of inadequacy or inferiority, the teacher should find out whether he has any skill or ability which might be used to make him appear important or successful in the eyes of the other children. Then she can make opportunities for him to compete in games or other activities in which he has a chance to excel. She can encourage him by mentioning to the class something that he has contributed or something that he can do well, by displaying samples of his work where they can be seen, and by planning projects in which he can be sure to participate without embarrassment. If he has no special skill, she can help him to learn how to do something that will give him an advantage or a little prestige among the others. A few lessons in boxing, archery, fencing, weaving, or leather tooling, or even some extra coaching in spelling or arithmetic, are sure to help.

Withdrawing children work better when they are given definite tasks with specific instructions than when they are thrown on their own initiative. Since they are easily discouraged and defeated, they should never be pushed beyond their level of ability or made to work under pressure. It is better for them to be able to excel in a slow group than to be allowed to lag behind in a faster one.

One of the most important things that a teacher can do for a child is to show him how to face, accept, and solve his problems without trying to run away from them. She can help him to experience the satisfaction and relief of squarely confronting unpleasant experiences and confessing faults rather than evading them. She can help him to realize that failures and mistakes are no cause for a person to lose self-respect and to withdraw from his associates but are rather a challenge to try again. At the first sign of emotional disturbance in a child, the teacher should help him to bring his bothers out into the open and come to grips with them instead of driving them back into the subconscious. Just being able to talk a problem over with a friend, a parent, or a teacher releases tension and helps to place in its proper perspective a situation which might otherwise become greatly magnified in the mind.

Work with parents is of paramount importance in overcoming withdrawing behavior. By helping members of the family to understand the child's reasons for acting as he does, the teacher may prevail on them to lighten their demands on the child, to express more affection for him, or to give him more chances to feel necessary and important in the home. She may be able to explain to a possessive mother that when a child is too deeply attached to his parents, he looks to them for companionship and fails to form other social contacts. This situation can be helped not by withdrawing any attention or affection but by bringing the child into pleasant association with a few persons of his own age and then by helping him gradually to increase his circle of friends.

Parents sometimes need to be reminded that the behavior of the withdrawing child cannot be dismissed by saying that he has an inferiority complex, that he is nervous, or that he has always been of a retiring disposition. When they realize that there is a real cause for the tension and that the cause is often found in the home environment, they are usually glad to cooperate with the school in removing that cause.

Teachers need to remember, too, that a child's withdrawing tendencies often have their origin in the classroom. It is possible for feelings to be so deeply wounded by the sarcasm of a thoughtless teacher that they remain hurt and sensitive throughout life.

ACTIVITIES SUGGESTED

The children who most need this project are the ones who are least likely to take part in any form of activity. They should not be forced to talk or made to feel embarassed if they do not participate.

The group activities are suggested for the purpose of helping the teacher to study the withdrawing pupils, to discover possible reasons for their tendencies, and to build them up to the place where they can face life instead of running from it. Although the activities should be selected especially for the benefit of the shy, timid children in the class, they should be so well planned and presented that these children will not become more withdrawn by feeling that they are being singled out for treatment.

1. As a means of deciding which children need most of your attention during this project, notice each one in the classroom, on the playground, in

the lunchroom, and before and after school. Then, after carefully thinking over your observations, answer the following questions concerning the pupils in your class. The ones whose names frequently appear in the answers are likely to be the ones who have given up the struggle to adjust to people.

    a. Which ones are chronic daydreamers?

    b. Which ones never volunteer in class, never take part in open discussions, and seldom give oral reports or take the lead in any activity?

    c. Which ones are always chosen last in games, stand around while the others play, or keep to themselves while others congregate in intimate little groups?

    d. Which ones walk to and from school alone, sit alone in the cafeteria, or read while others chat?

    e. Which ones bite their fingernails, twist their hair, chew on their pencils, suck their fingers, or have other nervous mannerisms?

2. As another means of discovering the shy, sensitive, nervous, withdrawn children, make an attempt to get pupil opinions. Ask the children to answer a questionnaire similar to the one below, giving as many or as few names as they choose. In presenting this activity, make it understood that the information is strictly confidential and that it is being used only to help you discover children who may be unhappy or who may need some help. Explain that the answers can hurt no one.

    a. Which of the children in this class never seem to want to enter into your games, but stand back and look on most of the time?

    b. Which of your classmates seem to prefer walking or riding to school alone and seldom join a group?

    c. Which of the children in your neighborhood do not usually come out to play with the other children and never invite them to their homes?

    d. Which children never offer to help with anything that a group is planning or doing?

    e. Which ones get their feelings hurt very easily and cry, sulk, or pout a great deal?

    f. Which ones are constantly being teased by others?

3. Urge all the children in your class to answer the following questions honestly and frankly, explaining that you are taking a poll of the feelings of the group on certain matters so that you can plan some activities accordingly. Let the pupils know that nobody will be embarrassed by having the

answers revealed. The questions should be answered "yes" or "no" or with plus or minus signs. A high percentage of positive answers is likely to indicate a marked degree of introversion.

a. Do you often feel that you are left out of things at school or at home?

b. Do you worry about things you have done and said that you would like to change?

c. Do you think that other people say unkind things about you when your back is turned?

d. Do you often have your feelings hurt?

e. Are a great many people unfriendly to you?

f. Do you feel that you make a poorer showing than the other children in the classroom and on the playground?

g. Do people often say that you are queer or different?

h. Do you have the feeling that nobody understands you?

i. Do you sometimes think that people are making fun of you?

j. Do you have a habit of biting your fingernails?

k. Do you often worry about your schoolwork or about failing?

l. Do you often find your mind wandering to many other things when you are supposed to be studying?

m. Do you worry about little mistakes you have made?

n. Do you find it hard to talk to new pupils?

o. Do you always prefer to let someone else be the leader in games?

p. Do you frequently feel sad for no particular reason?

q. Do you often feel that you would like to stay at home instead of going to school?

r. Do you usually find it hard to stand before the class and tell a story or give a report?

s. Do you worry a great deal about terrible things that might happen to you or to members of your family?

t. Do you sometimes wish that you could take part in more things with other children and have more fun than you now have?

4. Some personality tests are helpful in obtaining definite evidence of extroversion or introversion. The scores from these tests can often be used to advantage in conferences with parents, teachers, and guidance workers. The following are suggested:

California Test of Personality (Primary Form, grades 1 to 3; Elementary, grades 4 to 6; Intermediate, grades 7 to 8), California Test

Bureau, Los Angeles, 1942. If this test has been given before, the scores on the sections concerning Withdrawing Tendencies and Nervous Symptoms will be useful at this time.

Aspects of Personality (for grades 4 to 9), by Rudolf Pintner and Others, World Book Company, Yonkers, N.Y., 1937. This test deals with Ascendency and Submission, Introversion and Extroversion, and Emotional Adjustment.

5. Allow the children to express their feelings through the medium of poems, stories, drawings, or scribbles. Encourage them to put on paper without regard for perfection or details any bothers, hurt feelings, or resentments that they may be storing up. Merely instruct them to write, draw, or paint about the way they feel toward some other person. Then suggest that each child tell you about his drawing or write its interpretation if he is willing to do so. You may not actually get at the cause of all withdrawing behavior in this way, but, at least, you will furnish the children with some means of releasing their feelings. This is usually the most effective treatment that can be given, anyway. Explain that many people become shy, sensitive, lonely, and unhappy because they have kept hurt feelings bottled up within themselves and that it is a good plan to prevent such a misfortune to oneself by making it a habit to use some harmless way of releasing unpleasant feelings.

6. Plan an informal group discussion based on questions similar to the ones suggested below. The grade level and the withdrawing problems of the particular group will determine the trend which the discussion takes.

a. Have you ever pretended you were sick in order to get out of doing something you did not want to do? Have you played tired or busy with homework when there were dishes to be washed or a lawn to be mowed? Do you know anybody who frequently has headaches or pains in the stomach just at a time when there is something unpleasant to be done? What do you think of this as a way of escape from duty?

b. Have you ever known a person to break a window, cheat on a test, or steal something and then suffer from a guilty feeling and a fear that he would be found out? Even if his misdeed is never discovered, his conscience continues to haunt him. What is a good remedy for feelings of guilt and fear?

c. Have you ever felt like running away? Why? Do you know anybody who has actually left home when things were not going to suit him?

What was this person really trying to get away from? What might have been a better solution?

d. What are some of the excuses which boys and girls frequently offer for their low grades in school? Do you think they would feel happier and less guilty if they faced the situation squarely instead of trying to shift the blame?

e. When you have had the urge to speak to a new pupil, to enter a game with a group, or to volunteer to tell the class something interesting, have you sometimes hesitated and let the opportunity pass because you did not quite have the courage to do what you wanted to do? How might you overcome this tendency?

7. Talk informally with the older children about the characteristics of extroversion and introversion. Make the point that although extroverts are usually thought of as persons who are friendly, cheerful, happy, good-natured and self-confident, who are willing to talk before groups, and who can take the initiative and assume the leadership of projects, yet they sometimes have the tendency to bully, to fight, to attract unfavorable attention, and to be bossy and antagonistic. Although introverts are often self-conscious, shy, sensitive, unhappy, lonely, and given to daydreaming, yet they are frequently better students because they are able to work alone and to concentrate for long periods. It may be encouraging to timid children to hear stories of the work done by inventors, research workers, scientists, artists, and authors as a result of their willingness to withdraw from others and work alone. In giving these examples, be sure to emphasize the fact that the accomplishments of these persons are due not to timidity and constant daydreaming but to habits of studiousness and deep thinking. Also make it clear that although one may be a thinking introvert, it is possible for him to be a social extrovert who is extremely friendly and outgoing in his relations with other people. Help the children to see that there are desirable and undesirable factors in each type of personality. It is not the purpose of this lesson to try to change introverts into extroverts but to help boys and girls to overcome habits which are likely to make them unhappy or unattractive.

8. Keep constantly in mind the children in your class who are especially shy and withdrawn. See that each one of them is called upon to do something that he can do well and for which he can be recognized and praised. Perhaps the one who writes or letters beautifully may be asked to put announcements on the blackboard; the one who is handy with tools may be

asked to do necessary repair jobs; and the one who enjoys library assignments may be asked to do extra research for the class. Be sure to give these children every possible chance to become important and to know that they are appreciated in the sight of their classmates.

Do not make shy children feel conspicuous by giving them individual speaking parts in a program. Avoid calling on them in a discussion until their self-confidence has been built up but be sure to give them every opportunity to participate when they volunteer. Trying to force them into the limelight only increases their trouble. Instead of singling them out for attention, draw them gradually into group activities such as dances, songs, skits, and games. Make an effort to interest the parents of bashful children in promoting trips to summer camps, membership in such organizations as the boy scouts and the girl scouts, overnight visits with relatives or friends, and other out-of-school social activities which help to build up self-confidence.

9. Observe the social relationships and the play activities of the withdrawing children in your class. Point out to these children any behavior which is likely to cause others to dislike them. Show them how to make friendly advances and try to create situations in which they can do little acts of kindness or service for some of their classmates.

10. Hold a free and informal discussion concerning the relief which comes from being able to share one's troubles with another. Ask the children if they ever keep their bothers to themselves. Suggest how much better it is to get worries out into the open by talking them over with a sympathetic friend, teacher, or parent. When a child is unable to make as good grades as the others do, when he is not proud of the kind of work his father does, or when he realizes that his home is not so attractive as it might be, it is much better if he can learn to accept the situation, talk about it, joke about it, and live above it. Encourage the children to find someone in whom they can confide when they feel hurt, mistreated, or confused. Let them know, not just by telling them but by being genuinely friendly and warm, that you are one person to whom they can always come without feeling that they are going to hear a sermon or be condemned to punishment.

11. Plan some specific help for the withdrawing children who are continually being blocked and frustrated by teasing. The recipient of constant teasing is often lacking in self-confidence and is generally different in some way from the group. Whether it is a peculiar mannerism, a personal habit, a belief, a physical characteristic, ability, clothes, or family, if you can find

the thing about which a child is being teased, you will know the area in which he is most in need of help.

12. It is important for each of the very shy children to have some time with you alone but it is also important for them not to feel that they are being singled out for help. While making an earnest effort to give some special attention to the intensely withdrawn youngsters, be sure that similar attention is also given to the normal ones.

Ask one of the shy children at a time to help you for a while after school, to come early in the morning for a little extra tutoring, or to go with you on an errand in the afternoon. Take these times to learn all you can about the withdrawn child, give him time to talk, and listen for evidences of the things that are causing his troubles. Find out about any fears, hostilities, feelings of inaedquacy, pressures, or conflicts that may be making life unbearable for him. Let him know that you are a true friend who is willing to listen when he wants to talk and that you will accept and understand his feelings without blame or criticism. Besides giving him an outlet for his feelings, you may be able to think of some way to help. For example, if you believe that the child's timidity is intensified by the fact that his parents ridicule his opinions, crush his initiative, and discourage his aggressive tendencies by severe punishment and scolding, you may approach the problem from the standpoint of getting the mother and father to guard against thoughtless remarks, to respect the child's views, and to express approval when he shows some aggressiveness.

FOLLOW-UP

Children cannot be changed from withdrawing to outgoing individuals by a little spasmodic attention. Only by making them feel increasingly secure and competent can you gradually cause their timidity to disappear. It is necessary, therefore, to repeat and repeat any treatments which you find effective.

BIBLIOGRAPHY

BULLIS, H. EDMUND, and EMILY E. O'MALLEY: Human Relations in the Classroom, The Delaware State Society for Mental Hygiene, Wilmington, Del., 1947, Course I, pp. 110–118.

RATHS, LOUIS E.: An Application to Education of the Needs Theory, Louis E. Raths, Box 26, Bronxville, N.Y., 1949. Pamphlet.

TITUS, PAULINE WOODRUFF: How to Conquer Shyness, Funk & Wagnalls Company, New York, 1948.

CHAPTER 13

Helping the Daydreamer

Aims of This Lesson:

To discover the underlying reasons for the excessive daydreaming of certain children.

To help the daydreamers find satisfying activities to replace their dreams.

Every teacher has at some time experienced the hopeless feeling of being unable to teach a child who sits and gazes into space when he should be working.

A certain amount of dreaming is expected of all children and is good for them. It is the inalienable right of childhood to indulge in make-believe, to enjoy imaginary playmates, and to soar in dreams above the realm of everyday living. Dreams are essential to achievement. Only by first dreaming of an ambition or an ideal and then working to make it come true can a definite goal be reached in life.

The harmful aspect of dreaming is seen when a person is satisfied with finding what he wants in his own imagination and does nothing to bring it into reality. When a child's daydreaming reaches such proportions that it no longer fosters accomplishment, but interferes with learning, it is time for the school to become actively concerned.

Because daydreaming is not so annoying as many other types of classroom behavior, teachers frequently overlook it or fail to recognize its seriousness. It is very likely, however, that the child who is quietly daydreaming is much more in need of the teacher's attention than is the one who is disobedient, impudent, or disorderly in class. Children who are sensitive, fearful, rejected, or misunderstood often find it more pleasant to withdraw into a satisfactory world of imagination than to endure harsh, cruel reality. Unless something is done to help them, they soon develop the habit of excessive daydreaming. Some of them eventually reach the point where they so completely bury themselves in fantasy that they are helpless in the face of actual situations. In extreme cases, illusions and hallucinations, which started as dreams, later result in manic-depressive and schizophrenic illnesses.

An observing teacher can easily recognize a pupil who is likely to become a chronic daydreamer. She usually sees in him a preoccupied, timid, unhappy-looking child who is very quiet and well behaved. He causes no trouble except that, although he may be intelligent enough, he does not seem to grasp the material that is presented. Even when he is apparently listening, he is startled if called upon to recite. After he has actively participated for a brief time, his attention is lost as he again retreats into his own thoughts. He engages in very little physical activity but may be seen on the playground standing back and watching while others play. When not in school he may read to excess and see a great many motion pictures. He identifies himself with characters in books, comic strips, and movies.

A child who daydreams excessively has underlying difficulties which need attention. His dreams usually hold the key to the thing he is wishing for. Perhaps he is longing for more love from his parents, more recognition from the teacher, better marks in school, more friends, or greater physical strength. If the teacher can find out what a child is dreaming about, she will have the clue to some of his emotional, social, or physical needs. For this reason, it is not wise to make a direct effort to stop the dreaming until there has been an opportunity to study the case.

The teacher who is on the alert for the reasons back of a child's daydreaming will watch for things which seem to affect him emotionally. She will notice the type of stories he most often tells, the points at which he places the emphasis, and any definite trends in his thinking. For example, a child may be feeling economic pressure at home if he measures everything in terms of costs and if he constantly refers to money, salaries, cost of living, expenses, and luxuries. The usual tone of a child's writings, the subjects he chooses, and the endings he gives his stories often give an insight into his longings, his tensions, his conflicts with his family, and his dreams. Boys and girls who read too much may be superior students but they are often socially maladjusted. By observing the type of reading they do, it is sometimes possible to discover the lack in their lives which they are trying to fill in this way.

There are a number of reasons why children resort to daydreaming. In some cases it is because they are being pushed to reach higher standards than they are capable of. Occasionally teachers set goals that are beyond the level of ability of their pupils. More often parents have such high ideals for their offspring that they hold up unrealizable ambitions for them. When children of average ability are expected to lead the class, to bring home nothing but high marks on their report cards, or to compete with more gifted brothers and sisters, they are forced into obvious failure. Teachers and parents should face the issue squarely and modify the requirements for such children. If they do not, the children become confused and frustrated. They begin to build up a web of lies, to cheat, to deceive the teacher, or to imitate others who are accomplishing. These children may react by becoming stubborn and defiant toward those who nag them. Or they may discover the trick of allowing their thoughts to wander off into dreams that are much more satisfying than real life.

Children who are socially rejected often become shy, timid daydreamers. They may be disliked by the other children because of personal peculiarities or racial or economic differences. They may feel inferior, unappreciated by their teachers, unwanted by their parents, or jealous of other children in the family. As a result, they either find some means of getting attention or they attempt to make up for their inadequacies by dreaming of things that they would like to do or have. Feeling ill-treated, they sometimes indulge in dreams of revenge or imagine the remorse it will cause their parents to suffer when they die or run away from home.

Tom, an eighth-grade boy of low-average ability, moved into a new neighborhood when his mother married a lawyer of moderate means. In his zeal to be a good parent, the stepfather frequently called at the school to check on his son's progress. Upon finding that Tom's marks were not up to standard, he became quite strict, took away the boy's accustomed allowance, and required that he spend his evenings in his room doing his homework. Having no opportunity to mingle with other boys outside of school, and being of a quiet and retiring nature, Tom made no friends in his new environment.

Feeling that he was misunderstood at home, unsuccessful at school, and rejected socially, this boy learned to retreat into his own imagination where things could be more as he wanted them to be. He reported to his teacher that his parents were building an expensive new home in the most exclusive residential district of town. He asked the principal to obtain catalogues of fashionable boarding schools, saying that his stepfather wanted to send him away to a school where he would get the best possible preparation for college. Although he read very poorly and had a great deal of trouble with English, he attracted attention by inquiring about the possibility of starting the study of two foreign languages in the ninth grade. Soon groups of boys were seen standing around Tom at lunch period while he told them of an exciting encounter he had had with the police the night before or of a narrow escape he had experienced while speeding in his father's car in the early hours of the morning.

When Tom's teacher visited in his home she learned that there was no foundation for the stories of a new home, a preparatory school, or thrilling adventures in the evening. His mother said that the boy seldom left the house but went silently to his room right after dinner. She had been worried because she had discovered that when he was supposedly doing his homework, he was actually pouring over a ledger in which he constantly entered figures showing large incomes and expenditures. In his imagination he was receiving and spending money for all the things he wanted and could not buy.

Fortunately, Tom had an understanding teacher. She helped the mother and the stepfather see that the boy's academic ability was limited and that he could not attain the high standards they had set for him. She managed to have Tom appointed to a position on the school Service Council, which would give him a certain amount of prestige and an opportunity for more out-of-class contacts with the boys and girls. She helped him to secure a part-time job so that he could earn money of his own. When pressure was relieved at home, when life at school was more tolerable, and when social adjustments were made, the retreats into fantasy were no longer necessary.

Children who are physically handicapped shrink from the thought of being unlike others. Those who are excessively fat, thin, tall, short, freckled, cross-eyed, or otherwise different are often teased unmercifully by their fellows. If they have unusual intelligence or special talents, they may be able to compensate by excelling in some way. If not, these children are likely either to become antagonistic and revengeful or to find consolation in daydreams. For example, a boy who is small of stature may so desire to be muscular and athletic that he develops the habit of withdrawing into an imaginary world where he can be as big and brawny as he pleases. Instead of competing in games with other boys, he may surround himself with pictures of supermen and stories concerning physical prowess. A homely girl who sits endlessly sketching pretty faces, dresses, and hats may be living in a dream world where she is a beauty queen. Children who have physical disfigurements or peculiarities can be helped a great deal by teachers who give them opportunities for real accomplishment and praise them when they succeed.

Billy was the youngest resident at a home for incurables. In order to get to school it was necessary for him to board a bus by bracing himself on two crutches and making clumsy backward leaps as he dragged his almost lifeless legs up step by step. Once at school, he reached his room on the second floor by the same slow, painful method. He arrived before the other children so that he might avoid the rush on the stairs when the bell rang. He liked the extra time this afforded for talking to the teacher. He told her about spending the week ends on his uncle's farm, riding a wild pony, rounding up the cattle, and driving a tractor. Even though these activities were altogether impossible for Billy, he described them in minute detail and with a great deal of feeling.

The other children scarcely noticed this boy. While they were on the playground he sat at his desk and read detective stories and newspaper accounts of crimes and court cases. He even expressed an interest in some day becoming a fingerprint expert. Using this as a lead, the teacher brought Billy some illustrated material on fingerprint reading and made it possible for him to meet and interview persons engaged in this type of work. Billy then started making scrapbooks which he showed with pride to the other children. He really became a person of importance in the eyes of the pupils when one of the police officers who had shown an interest in him came to school on several occasions to take him on sight-seeing tours. The dreams and fantastic stories stopped. Billy still had his handicap, but he could face life with more courage since he had found some real interests to occupy his time.

After a teacher has found out what causes a child to resort to daydreaming and what he is really dreaming about and wishing for, she can usually find some way of helping him. Each daydreamer is unhappy and dissatisfied with reality and must be treated as an individual problem. Nagging, scolding, punishing, or humiliating him will do no good. In fact, such techniques will serve only to drive him deeper into his world apart. If possible, the teacher should devise some plan for helping the child to find in reality the thing he has been vainly seeking in fantasy.

Do not openly start a drive against daydreaming by telling the children that it is bad. Some children have known nothing in real life but defeat and failure. They find their only happiness, their only release from intolerable situations, and their only achievements in their dreams. If you stop them from dreaming without furnishing them something better to do, you may cause them to develop a worse type of behavior as a substitute.

When a child daydreams only at certain times during the day, it may be because he is having difficulty with geography or fractions at that hour. A little extra help in the subject he finds hard or distasteful may be enough to set him right. An understanding teacher will see that no child fails repeatedly. If he never excels in anything, she should *make* a situation in which he *can* excel and praise him for his success. Although many successes are needed, even one will work wonders. When a child has enjoyed the feeling of victory over something that he wanted to conquer, he will turn from daydreaming.

Daydreaming in class may be lessened by keeping the children so busy that they will not have time to dream and by making their activities so enjoyable that dreams are no longer fascinating. Many pupils find their minds wandering when they are required to sit and read a great number of pages without a definite objective. It is much easier to hold the attention when reading is assigned either purely for pleasure or for the purpose of preparing a summary, making a report, looking for specific information, or making an outline. Boys and girls like activity and purpose in their work.

A child whose greatest need is for opportunities to show leadership may be helped by being made chairman of a small group to investigate some question and make a report to the class. He may be asked to collect money, sell tickets, take part in a play, or manipulate puppets. Timid children who need social contacts may be appointed to serve on housekeeping, bulletin-board, and other committees. It is sometimes a good plan to group two shy children together to do a piece of work so that one or the other will be forced to take the lead.

Sometimes it is possible to discover the source of the daydreamer's difficulty by visiting in the home or by inviting the mother to come to school for a conference. It is often found that the child also daydreams at home and the parents are glad to have an opportunity to discuss the mutual problem. At this time the teacher may be able to make some specific suggestions about such things as inviting other children to the house, allowing more time for play and recreation, altering the methods of punishment used, showing more affection for the child, or changing the attitude of a domineering member of the family.

If daydreaming is the result of a broken home or some other situation that cannot be changed, perhaps the teacher can help the child to accept his lot and make the most of it. There are desirable and satisfying ways of compensating for conditions that are beyond our control. Children must be taught that success in life depends on facing their problems and working out solutions rather than on shrinking from them.

Very often it is helpful for the teacher to arrange for some time in private with the daydreamer. The interview should be a pleasant, informal occasion in which the child is allowed to do most of the talking while the teacher simply encourages him and reflects his feelings. By talking to a sympathetic listener the child may release his own tensions and may give the teacher just the clue she needs to begin treatment.

Many of the simpler cases of daydreaming can be helped by an alert and understanding teacher. When, however, the teacher senses that the problem is too complex to be handled in the classroom, she will do a great service by referring it to the school psychologist or a child-guidance clinic.

Naturally, it is a mistake to try to attach some psychological meaning to all daydreaming. Before taking any definite steps, the teacher should be sure that it is a chronic case and not one caused by a momentary attraction or a temporary escape from an uninteresting classroom situation. One boy had sat during an entire period gazing out the window while his classmates were writing an article assigned by the English teacher. At the close of the period when the others were turning in their papers, the boy stopped at the teacher's desk and said enthusiastically, "Miss Smith, guess what! The robins that have been building a nest right outside our window finally finished it today!" With a note of disdain in her voice the teacher snapped, "I'm not interested. I am a teacher of English, not of natuaral science." When classroom situations are bungled in this way, it is no wonder that some children feel the need of hiding in a land of daydreams.

ACTIVITIES SUGGESTED

It is hoped that these activities will help you discover the secret desires and the underlying difficulties of the daydreamers in the class. In selecting the ones to be used, thought should be given to the needs and the personalities of the individuals concerned. You may be able to devise more appropriate activities for your group than the ones suggested here. At any rate, the lesson should be so planned that each of the daydreamers will actively participate. It is obvious that the pupils themselves should not be told the reasons for some of the activities.

1. Tell stories about Columbus, Edison, and others who dreamed dreams and made them come true. Talk to the children about how dreams can be good and valuable but how sometimes we spend too much time imagining and dreaming. Although it is good for the soul to enjoy reveries concerning the beauties of nature and the wonders of the universe and to indulge in dreams of the great things we are going to do some day, it is still necessary that we spend much of our time on the prosaic tasks of daily life. Many children need to be constantly reminded of the distinction between fact and fancy.

2. Ask each child to try to express a real wish of his own either by painting, drawing, carving, dramatizing, modeling clay, writing a paragraph, composing a poem, giving a monologue, or doing a pantomime. The child's choice of a subject may reveal something of his interests. Be sure to allow him to interpret his pictures and models. What he says about them may serve as an approach in discussing his problems.

3. Let several children act out their favorite dreams and allow the other children to guess what they are.

4. Ask the children to close their eyes and pretend to dream for a minute. Encourage them to tell what they dreamed. Discuss the significance of some of their make-believe and the things they can do to make some of their dreams come true.

5. Make a "wishing tree" by placing a small tree on a stand in front of the room. Each child may cut out a colored leaf, write one, two, or three wishes on it, and tie it to the tree.

The same idea may be carried out by means of a "wishing chair" on which the children sit one by one while expressing a wish to the teacher. Or written wishes may be dropped into a box in the form of a "wishing well."

If the children are allowed to prepare these devices a day or so before they are to be used, they will have time to think of the things they really wish for and will not make frivolous wishes that occur to them at the moment.

After the wishes have been made, the teacher may discuss some of them (without disclosing the identity of the wishers). The class or the teacher may suggest ways of making the wishes come true.

6. Talk to the children about how people often dream of things they would like to have or to do and how they sometimes imagine themselves

as having wonderful adventures and being in exquisite surroundings. Sometimes these imaginings make very interesting stories. Ask for volunteers to tell some of the things that occur to them in their own daydreams. Pay close attention to these stories, observing significant emphases and trying to understand what is back of them. For example, if a girl tells how she visualizes interiors of homes, attractive color schemes, and plans for decorating rooms, is it perhaps because she has artistic talent and ambition to become an interior decorator or is it because her own home is so drab and colorless?

7. In the upper grades the pupils may be asked to write a paragraph on "My Biggest Problem," "My Greatest Worry," "My Greatest Desire," or "What I Think About Before Going to Sleep." In the lower grades the children may dictate stories about their wishes, worries, or thoughts while the teacher takes notes.

8. Gather the children about you in an informal circle for a friendly discussion. Ask, "What did you dream last night?" or "What do you frequently dream about?" Do not attempt to interpret their dreams for them, but ask what they think may have caused them. Reassure them by explaining that dreams are a universal experience.

Without special training you cannot be expected to analyze a child's dreams. However, since dreams are actually distorted memories of experiences that are important enough to be repeated in sleep, they may give you a clue to the things that are troubling a child. Dreams do not just happen; they have a connection with deep emotional conflicts. In younger children, unpleasant dreams often reveal fears. In older ones, they are sometimes connected with personal problems. By considering the dreams and the events that may have stimulated them, you are likely to get a hint that will help you discover some unsolved problems in the children's lives.

9. Young children may be asked to describe imaginary companions that they have had. (It has been said that bright children are more likely to have fictitious playmates than are dull ones.) Such a companion often fills a need for a lonely child. By understanding the type of imaginary companion he has, it is possible to recognize some of his needs. If a child conjures up an adult as a companion, it may mean that he longs for more attention from his parents. The characteristics, privileges, or possessions of the imaginary companion may indicate the ones which the child himself lacks. Many times children give a great deal of attention to their imaginary playmates in an

effort to escape from the duties of daily life. They sometimes endow them with magic powers which they hold over other children.

10. Sometimes a child's worries, tensions, and longings may be discovered through his imaginary stories.

A little boy (or girl) had wandered away from the rest of the group at a picnic. He suddenly realized that he had gone farther than he had intended and he was now lost in the woods. Being very tired, he dropped down at the foot of a tree to rest and soon fell asleep.

Ask each child in the class to complete this story in his own way. Most of the happy, well-adjusted children will give it a happy ending, while the fearful, maladjusted ones will be more likely to give it a grim conclusion. Some of the children may reveal some of their own dreams by telling what the character in the story dreamed.

11. Without giving any instructions or suggestions, make it possible for each child to tell a story about a picture, play with a family of paper dolls, or use miniature toys or puppets. While off his guard, the child may reveal inner anxieties, fears, and wishes. If dolls or paper dolls are used, they should form a family group exactly like the child's own. The words and actions which are ascribed to these characters may make it possible for you to discover family conflicts and feelings.

12. Ask the school psychologist to administer and interpret Rorschach Tests [1] for those who are confirmed daydreamers. This test consists of a set of cards, each of which contains an ink blot. By telling what each ink blot looks like to him, the child gives a clue to his personality and the trend of his imagination.

FOLLOW-UP

As the days go by keep a watch on the daydreamer to see whether or not he is making any improvement. Whenever he begins to slip back into his dreams, give him something absorbing to do, create in him a more lively interest in things around him, help him to make friends, and see that he wins some kind of satisfying success.

[1] *Rorschach Method of Personality Diagnosis,* by Bruno Kloper and Helen H. Davidson, World Book Company, Yonkers, N.Y., 1942.

BIBLIOGRAPHY

BULLIS, H. EDMUND, and EMILY E. O'MALLEY: *Human Relations in the Classroom,* The Delaware State Society for Mental Hygiene, Wilmington, Del., 1947, Course I, pp. 171–175.

SORENSON, HERBERT, and MARGUERITE MALM: *Psychology for Living,* McGraw-Hill Book Company, Inc., New York, 1948, pp. 196–200.

SYMONDS, PERCIVAL M.: *The Dynamics of Human Adjustment,* D. Appleton-Century Company, Inc., New York, 1946, pp. 507–511.

CHAPTER 14

Overcoming Fears

Aims of This Lesson:
To uncover feelings of fear and try to find their causes.
To plan suitable and gradual procedures for helping individuals to bring their fears to the surface, to recognize and understand them, and finally to overcome them.

Fear is a very powerful emotion which lies at the foundation of much mental ill-health. It is said that a large proportion of the phobias, neuroses, and depressions of adults have their beginnings in the fears of early life. For this reason it is imperative that we try to discover and allay childhood fears as soon as possible.

Almost all children suffer from feelings of fear at some time or other. Some are afraid of animals, darkness, thunder, lightning, illness, pain, inoculations, dentists, doctors, and policemen. Others are afraid of death, ghosts, and the unknown. Some are plagued by superstitious beliefs of all kinds. Many children are afraid of reciting, of taking part in group activities, of appearing before an audience, of meeting new situations, and of doing anything alone. One study showed that a large number of upper grade pupils said they were afraid of teachers, of taking tests, of failing, of doing wrong, of being punished, and of making their parents unhappy. Some children seem to fear almost everything.

The direct cause of fears can sometimes be easily detected. A child may be afraid of dogs because he has been bitten by one or he may be afraid of crossing the street because he has been the victim of a traffic accident. If the cause that a child gives for his anxiety is the real cause, it is a relatively easy matter to dispel the fear. But diagnosis is not always simple. Sometimes a

169

child who appears to be afraid of animals or the dark or storms may not really be afraid of these tangible things but may be expressing some inner fear that is much deeper. He may fear that his parents do not love him or that his mother may leave him. When a child is nervous, tense, and fearful of a great many things without obvious cause, the teacher should look into his general background for possible reasons. His sense of uneasiness and his unexplained dreads may be due to poor health, an unhappy home life, or a lack of friends. Before a teacher can do much toward changing their feelings, she must learn the real reasons for any fears or anxieties which the children possess and must deal with these rather than with the fears that are expressed. If disguised fears are not corrected, they continue to become more deep-seated and more thoroughly disguised.

Many childhood fears are traceable to thoughtless actions or statements of older persons. There is a close correlation between the fears of parents and those of children. A child is often afraid of insects and reptiles because his mother is afraid of them. A youngster may have a fear of school and teachers because of unpleasant things which older children have told him. Even when he has had no frightening firsthand experiences, he may be mortally afraid of many things as the result of teasing.

The most difficult fears to deal with are those intangible doubts and worries which grownups unintentionally transmit to children. Boys and girls become disturbed when they sense anxiety in the voices of their parents as they discuss strikes, layoffs, unemployment, high cost of living, communism, atomic warfare, and threatening world conditions. Sometimes they understand just enough of what is being said to start the imagination working. Children lose confidence in their main source of protection and security when they discover that adults are afraid.

Unfortunately, both parents and teachers are sometimes guilty of using corrective measures which build up fears in children. Some parents deliberately scare their children into obedience with threats of bogeymen, goblins, policemen, and firemen. They create fears by severe discipline, sometimes using the stern methods which their own parents used on them when they were growing up. Some teachers control their groups by constant scolding and intimidation. If they cannot keep the pupils interested, they keep them scared. Children may be momentarily frightened into desirable behavior, but they cannot be developed into happy, outgoing personalities in this way. Intelligent and sympathetic adults avoid using fear as a means of motivation.

Even when no apparent origin for the fears can be found, a child may be terrified at the sight of an angleworm, afraid to go into an unlighted room, or horrified at the approach of a storm. If there seems to be no other basis for such anxieties, they may be caused by a guilty conscience. The child may be suffering from guilt feelings about something he has done or has wished to do and in his subconscious mind he is fearing the punishment he feels that he deserves. A guilty conscience is usually due to the child's inability to live up to adult expectations. Parents and teachers should be careful not to set standards that are too high for the youngster at his particular age level.

Adults cause a great deal of fear among children by their constant warnings against germs, dirt, accidents, and disease. By overprotecting and overindulging their children, they also cause them to be afraid to try to do anything for themselves. Such boys and girls are as truly frightened when they leave the protection of the home as are the unloved and neglected ones.

Most children enter school with very definite fears already established. All the worries, anxieties, feelings of inadequacy, and hostilities toward members of the family which have been built up in early childhood are reflected in their school adjustment. It cannot be said, however, that all fears are the result of experiences outside of school. Many of them have their beginnings in the classroom and on the playground. Teachers and pupils unwittingly plant feelings of anxiety and dread which are difficult to erase. As a result, many youngsters are afraid of not being promoted, of not being liked by other boys and girls, of being different from others, of not having the right clothes, of being laughed at, and of being considered sissy or cowardly. Others are afraid of bullies, of certain instructors, of specific subjects, and of school in general.

Teachers often fail to realize that some form of fear is at the root of many of their classroom behavior problems. Fidgeting, squirming, nail biting, stuttering, scraping the feet on the floor, twisting the clothing, picking at the face, dishonesty, and irritability are all symptoms of insecurity, anxiety, and fearfulness.

Children who appear to be stubborn or unintelligent, who blush and are unable to talk when called upon, who seldom show independence in their work, and who are afraid to answer a question unless they are absolutely sure of the answer are usually victims of fears. Because of their underlying feelings of inadequacy, these children become nervous, excited, and frightened at the mention of tests or examinations. Instead of responding to the challenge and doing a normal amount of preparation, they go all to pieces and sometimes become physically ill.

Truancy is usually the result of fear. A child whose work is not up to standard feels self-conscious because he never succeeds. He begins to avoid companions who increase his sense of inferiority and situations which emphasize his lack of achievement. Gradually he becomes so afraid of failure that he may prefer to withdraw from social contacts and even to sit alone at home rather than to face certain defeat at school.

Some children who are aggressive and defiant in their behavior are simply trying to cover up their anxieties. They may have been hurt so much that they are constantly attempting to ward off further mistreatment. Having always felt unloved and rejected, they have not learned to cooperate. Consequently, they appear disrespectful and disobedient. Because they are neglected or jealous, they may even feign fearfulness in order to get more attention. Too often such children are so annoying and unattractive to the teacher and the other pupils that they do not receive the sympathy, understanding, and friendliness which they desperately need.

Another fearful youngster is the classroom show-off. Often this child has been teased because of his timidity until he begins to clown in self-defense. He prefers to make himself ridiculous and have his associates laugh at him rather than endure their teasing and fighting. The wise teacher regards this child's antics as a pitiful plea for mercy.

The daredevil proclaims by his foolhardy actions that he is afraid. He is generally a child who has been called "sissy," "baby," or "fraidy cat," either because of his babyish expression or dress, his smallness, or his place as youngest in the family or the class. He is so afraid of being thought weak or immature that he will risk any danger rather than be scorned or called uncomplimentary names.

A child who is unusually good, quiet, and studious or one who is timid and self-conscious may be withdrawing into a shell because of fears for which he has not been able to work out a satisfactory solution. Teachers and parents should remember that shyness is a form of fear which increases under pressure but decreases with affection, kindness, and understanding.

Sam was labeled a "crybaby" by the other sixth-grade boys. He was nervous, pale, listless, sleepy, and given to daydreaming in class. His fingernails were bitten to the quick and he cried readily. One morning he came to school with tears very near the surface. When the teacher spoke to him, he burst out weeping with, "I've been saucy to my mother again and she doesn't love me." As soon as possible the teacher made an opportunity for the child to sit down with her in private and quietly talk things out.

The conversation soon revealed that Sam was filled with fears. He was afraid of bugs, of storms, of being alone, of imaginary dangers associated with the dark, and of many other things. These fears had been aroused by a series of occurrences during his early childhood. He had often been locked in dark closets for punishment and once he had been fastened in an empty truck and left there by older boys. At one time his home had been destroyed in a flood. At another time a burglar had broken in through a window in the boy's own room. Night after night, when Sam was supposedly asleep, his father and uncle sat in the next room talking over horrors which they had experienced during the war.

A visit to the home of this child disclosed that his mother was a highly nervous person who also was afraid of the dark, of storms, and of being alone. Sam seemed to be very fond of his mother and tried to help her by running errands, washing dishes, and taking care of his little brother. But if he did anything to displease or upset her, she would turn on him, shouting, "I hate you! I hate you!" This little boy was lying awake every night pondering and worrying over all these things and then going to sleep only to have unhappy dreams about them. Is it any wonder that he was not progressing in his schoolwork?

Some childish fears are entirely outgrown in the course of time; some disappear and reappear; some shift to new objects; and others are replaced by various expressions of anxiety or tension. While new fears may not resemble the old, the original root may still be motivating their existence. As soon as it is learned that a child has fears, specific treatment should be undertaken lest the fears persist in some form throughout life.

A child's fears are very real to him. To tell him that they are foolish and groundless is a waste of time. A fearful youngster can no more help being afraid than he can help being sick or afflicted. Certainly he cannot be reasoned or shamed into being brave. It is sheer folly to say to a child, "You are acting like a baby. Ten years old and afraid to go to the dentist!" Calm reassurance and an example of fearlessness on the part of parents and teachers are more effective than a great deal of talking.

Children should not be taught that it is cowardly to be afraid. For their own protection, it is intelligent to fear things that are actually dangerous. To take away all fear would be to remove one of the child's greatest safeguards.

The best cure for a fear is to admit it, bring it out into the open, and talk about it, even joke about it. Fear will continue to haunt the person who does not face it and come to grips with it. Children are usually eager to overcome their fears and, if given an opportunity, will talk about them quite readily. It is useless to try to discover the source of a fear simply by asking, "Why are you afraid?" The child probably doesn't know the answer. By casual conversation, however, it is possible to get a clue. When a child reaches the point where he will talk freely about the thing that is troubling him, he will usually be able to recognize the cause for himself and the fear will be likely to disappear.

A little boy was afraid to enter any bathroom and refused to take a bath unless the door was left wide open. If the door became closed while he was in the bathroom, he screamed with genuine fright. At a loss to understand this unusual fear, the parents encouraged the boy to talk about bathrooms in general and about those in various homes he had visited in particular. When the bathroom in his cousin's home was mentioned, the little boy seemed suddenly to remember something. With a horrified look in his eyes, he told how he had been present when his little cousin had accidentally locked herself in the bathroom and had been hysterical until her father had scaled the wall, climbed in through a window, and unbolted the door from the inside. It was an easy matter for the parents then to explain how this incident was the cause of the fear, how the little cousin was unnecessarily panicky, and how their own bathroom door could not be locked in the same way. Miraculously, the fear disappeared.

If fear persists in spite of all efforts to dispel it, and if the actual object of the fear is not in itself a sufficient cause, it is necessary to discover the things which are associated in the child's mind with this object. By continuing to talk about everything related to his fear, the real cause can eventually be uncovered.

A little girl was always terrified at the sight of cobwebs. The teacher took pains to explain the existence of webs, to point out spiders in the process of making them, and to let the girl see other children handle them unafraid. This was of no avail. The fear did not subside until the child had related all the experiences with cobwebs that she could recall. This brought to light the story of domestic trouble in her home. Several years before while her father was at work each evening a suitor called on her mother. This man teased the little girl by putting cobwebs in her hair and telling her frightening stories about them. One evening when the father returned early from work, the mother in a fit of rage left the home with her paramour. In the course of the separation and divorce which followed there were a great many heated arguments over the custody of the child. The cobwebs were merely a symbol of this little girl's fear that neither of her parents loved or wanted her and that she would be homeless. When she realized this, the spider webs were completely forgotten.

Some of the most common fears of childhood are so general in nature that they can be treated through group discussions, explanations, and demonstrations. A great deal can be done by means of class discussions to eradicate superstitious beliefs and vague apprehensions caused by terrifying stories, radio programs, and motion pictures. Since practically all fears of children are learned, they must be overcome by relearning. Many times children who have developed fears can be helped by having a pleasant experience with the thing or the situation which they have come to fear.

Although some of the fears of school children can be handled through group lessons, most of them are of such a character that they call for individual attention. For example, if a child shrinks from reciting before his classmates, he should not be forced to stand in front of the class and talk. Rather, he should be called on when he volunteers. He should be allowed to work in a small group at first. Sometimes it is a good plan to place several timid children together. If a child is found to be shy or fearful, teachers should not be sarcastic with him and should not allow other children to tease or ridicule him. One of the best cures for fear is self-assurance and self-esteem. Some way should be found to help shy, timid, frightened children build up confidence in themselves. Boys and girls often forget their fears as they become intensely interested in a skill or hobby.

When a child's fear seems to be caused by a general feeling of insecurity, something may be wrong at home. It may be that the child simply needs some extra love and attention. He should be encouraged to express himself through play, creative activities, and conversation until he gives a clue to the cause of the trouble. A visit in the home or a conference with the mother may give both teacher and parent an insight into the problem.

School people frequently have to deal with the fear of school itself. A well-behaved, conscientious child from a good home may literally become ill at the thought of school. His constant absence due to nausea, diarrhea, headaches, abdominal pains, and weeping spells may become a serious problem to both parents and teachers. The illness often occurs following some change in family life such as illness of the mother, illness of the child himself, marriage of an older brother or sister, or moving to a new home. Because the symptoms disappear on holidays, this is not a disease which can be cured with medicine. The child may claim to dread school because he is afraid of a nagging teacher, a bully, a difficult subject, or even a physical-education class. Actually this so-called "fear of school" is a fear of being away from home. It nearly always occurs in a child who is overdependent upon his mother and is afraid to leave her. Strangely, this seeming reliance on the mother may sometimes be the child's struggle to free himself from domineering parents. Although the fact that he is attempting to draw away from a too close attachment to his mother is good, the method he uses is bad.

There are several errors which are commonly made in handling a case of fear of school. Too often teachers, truant officers, and parents aggravate the problem by harsh and unsympathetic methods of forcing the child into school. Many times a principal or teacher tries to treat the symptoms rather than the cause by undertaking to reason the child out of his fears, by removing him from the class of the teacher or the children whom he professes to fear, or in other ways making school life especially pleasant and easy for him. Sometimes the child is given physical treatment in the form of rest, medicine, a vacation in the country, or a semester or more out of school for the sake of his nerves. If the latter method proves to be effective, it is because the child decides to assert himself by going to school rather than by staying at home.

The most important factor in the cure of a fear of school is a change in the mother's attitude. She may unconsciously like having the child at home and may feel antagonistic toward the school. She must be made to realize and accept the fact that the child's difficulty is probably a matter of family relationships and that she needs to relax her hold on him or to refrain from dominating him. It is extremely important to get the child back to school every day even if he stays for only a short time and does not report to his class. If possible, the youngster who says that he is afraid of school should have the opportunity to save face by being made to feel that it is his own decision to return. It may help if he is allowed to air his grievances and to suggest minor changes in his program.

Children cannot do their best work when they are worried and afraid. In so far as possible, therefore, the school should attempt to alleviate fears which already exist in the minds of its children and should make a sincere effort not to create new ones. Classroom teachers can do a great deal toward freeing children of tensions and anxieties. When, however, a fear becomes so intense that it interferes with sleep, play, and happiness, it is advisable to seek professional help from the school psychologist, the child-guidance clinic, or a psychiatrist.

ACTIVITIES SUGGESTED

It is understood that these activities must be suited to the level of the pupils. Some of them can be used only in the upper grades; some, only in the lower grades. Care should be taken not to arouse any new fears by allowing some child to dwell on horrifying experiences which may frighten the other pupils.

1. Without letting the class realize that you are trying to find out about their own fears, ask that each child write on a slip of paper some of the things which he has noticed that people are afraid of. Discuss these fears. If they concern water, storms, darkness, or animals, explain how unnecessary it is to be afraid. Give scientific facts. Let the children talk until they have exhausted their thoughts on the subject.

Try to get the pupils to discover and recognize the sources of their fears. For example, if a boy is afraid of water, is it because he has been pushed into deep water unexpectedly? If he is afraid of policemen, is it because his parents have threatened him with jail? If he is afraid of the dark or of small spaces, is it because he has been locked in closets as a means of punishment?

2. As another method of discovering fears, have the pupils write answers to questions similar to the following, explaining that identities will not be revealed in discussing answers:

a. Do you often worry about your lessons and schoolwork?

b. Do you dread getting your report card?

c. Do you mind talking in front of our class about things that interest you?

d. Have you ever been afraid of a teacher?

e. Are you afraid to go to the principal's office?

f. Are you afraid of anybody in this room?

g. Have you ever been afraid of any older person? Who?

h. Do you lie awake long after going to bed at night?

i. Do you often have bad dreams?

j. Do you often think about things that are dangerous, such as falling, etc.?

k. Are you afraid of storms?

l. Are you afraid of going into the attic, basement, or a dark room at your home?

m. Are you afraid of being alone or of going places alone?

n. Are you afraid of dogs or other domestic animals?

o. Do older boys and girls ever try to frighten you?

p. Do you ever try to frighten girls and boys who are smaller than you?

q. Are you afraid of any particular person? Who?

r. Are you afraid of any particular thing? What?

The following chart shows a sampling of the answers given to these questions by one class. A study of this chart showed that the greatest number of fears was expressed by the class bully, that the poorest and the most conscientious students feared schoolwork and grades, and that the fears of some of the children explained their behavior.

FEARS

NAME	1. Schoolwork	2. Report cards	3. Oral reports	4. Teacher	5. Principal	6. Pupil	7. Older person	8. Sleeplessness	9. Bad dreams	10. Dangers	11. Storms	12. Darkness	13. Solitude	14. Animals	15. Bullies	16. Scaring others	17. Any person	18. Any thing	TOTAL
1. Jimmy	X		X		X		X	X	X	X	X				X	X	X	X	12
2. Marshall	X	X			X	X		X	X	X				X				X	9
3. Charlotte						X			X	X	X	X		X		X	X		8
4. Lois	X								X	X	X	X	X					X	7
5. Norma									X	X	X				X		X	X	6
6. Sandra	X							X	X	X		X							5
7. Henry				X						X						X		X	4
8. Ronnie		X						X	X										3
9. Ray								X	X										2
10. Robert										X									1
11. Lynne																			0
TOTAL	4	2	1	1	2	2	1	5	8	8	4	3	1	2	2	3	3	5	

3. During a language lesson have each child write a true story about some frightening experience he has had or about the things he frequently thinks about while lying awake at night. Use this as a basis for discovering fears and for giving pupils an opportunity to bring their fears out into the open. Explain that fears tend to decrease when they are expressed.

Encourage the younger ones to work out the cause of their fears in dramatic play, through clay modeling, drawing, or stories that they tell. If a child has had an operation, witnessed a wreck, or been frightened in the darkness, he will get rid of his terror more quickly by playing it out. The small child who is afraid of storms, animals, or doctors may find relief in repeatedly making drawings of these things. For further suggestions, see Rosemary Lippitt's *Psychodrama in the Home,* published by Beacon House, Inc., New York, 1947.

4. If you teach very young children, you may want to send notes to the parents asking if the children are experiencing any fears at home and explaining that you plan to try to help them overcome their fears.

5. Gather the children around you in a close, informal group and talk to them about their fears. Ask various ones to think of something they are afraid of and to try to recall the particular occasion when they first felt this fear. Pay careful attention to all details and record them in anecdotal records after the class.

6. Tell some timely stories of bravery and of persons who overcame the same fears that the children in your class have. The pupils will be especially interested in knowing how the teacher managed to get rid of some fear of her own.

7. Tell the children that they should not be ashamed of fear. Being afraid sometimes helps them to escape from danger. For their own protection, boys and girls should have a reasonable fear of crossing the street in heavy traffic, of swimming in water that is unsafe, of being careless with fire, and of using weapons and fireworks. This is quite different from being afraid of things that do not actually exist or that are not really harmful. Discuss the foolhardy actions of some children who do not want to appear afraid and who will do anything they are dared to do.

8. Talk about how fear sometimes causes people to act unwisely without thinking. A child who is entering school for the first time is often so afraid of going into a strange situation that he cries and clings to his mother. A boy who has broken a windowpane at school may be so afraid of punishment that he runs away without reporting it to a teacher. A hit-and-run driver may be too frightened to stop and help the person whom he has injured. A fire in a theater may create such a panic that everyone rushes wildly out and jams the exits.

Lead the children in a discussion of the importance of keeping calm in an emergency. Also talk about the value of facing one's fears and taking the consequence of one's deeds without running away. Fear continues to follow the person who will not come to grips with it.

9. Ask the class to make a list of common superstitions such as the ones regarding breaking a mirror, walking under a ladder, and carrying a rabbit's foot. Assign certain pupils to carry on experiments to prove or disprove each of these superstitions. For example, they may check accident statistics for Friday, the thirteenth, and compare them with statistics for other days.

(Actually, fewer accidents occur on Friday, the thirteenth.) One child may carry a good-luck charm and another carry none. At the end of a week they may compare notes on their good or ill fortunes. When all reports have been made, ask the class to decide by vote whether they believe or do not believe in each of the superstitions listed.

10. Many childhood fears are aroused or intensified by ghost and mystery stories on the screen, on the radio, and in comic books. Help the children to understand that the things which seem so terrifying are purely imaginary. Explain how motion pictures are made, how illusions are created, and how hideous faces are made up for the screen. Show how some of the noises are made for sound pictures and radio. Allow the pupils to plan and create some sound effects which seem real when heard in connection with exciting drama.

11. Play techniques may be used in the lower grades for helping children cope with their fears. By analyzing their pretendings and dramatizations, the teacher may discover clues to the worries and anxieties of young children. For example, when playing house a child may demonstrate fear of a parent by enacting the part of a tyrannical father or nagging mother.

12. An infant is afraid of only two things: loud noises and falling. All other fears are acquired. Let some of the children tell how babies in their homes have become afraid of dogs, cats, or rabbits, either by being barked at, scratched, or bitten; how they have become afraid of storms or darkness by being left alone when it was thundering and lightning; or how they have acquired some other fear which has remained with them.

13. A little boy was once terrified by being locked in a garage by older boys. It took him many years to outgrow this and other fears. When he had a little brother of his own, he did everything possible to keep older boys from teasing and frightening him.

Talk with the children about ways of preventing younger brothers and sisters from becoming afraid (by refraining from teasing them and making fun of their fears, by explaining things to them instead of laughing at their uneasiness, and by taking care never to act as if they are afraid of things that are not really dangerous.)

Suggest that the boys and girls plan some games, stories, or activities which they may use at home to help allay fear among younger members of the family. Example: Hide a doll, a Teddy bear, or some other object in a dark room, and allow the small child to find it; or throw a ball into a dark room and have the child go in and get it. In this way he will learn to have fun in the dark instead of being afraid.

14. Children should be taught the power of prayer. Those who have faith in a sustaining power have a permanent guarantee against fear.

15. The following films are suggested for use with this lesson:

Overcoming Fear (for junior and senior high school), 16 mm., sound, 13½ min., Coronet Films, Chicago, 1950. This unusual film shows how specific fears can be overcome. It opens with the story of a boy who knows how to swim but still fears the water. Reasons for many common fears are explained and ways of getting rid of them are suggested.

Science and Superstition (for intermediate, junior, and senior high school), 16 mm., sound, 11 min., Coronet Films, Chicago, 1947. The students in this picture prove that superstitions about the groundhog, the rabbit's foot, and other such things are inaccurate. They base their conclusions on research and experimental evidence.

FOLLOW-UP

From time to time, make some casual observation of the children who have professed to have definite fears. Toward the end of the term, again use questions similar to those suggested in Activity 2 and compare the results.

BIBLIOGRAPHY

BEVERLY, BERT I.: *A Psychology of Growth,* Whittlesey House, McGraw-Hill Book Company, Inc., New York, 1947, Chap. 7.

JERSILD, ARTHUR T.: *Child Psychology,* Prentice-Hall, Inc., New York, 1947, pp. 260–287.

OVERSTREET, BONARO W.: *Understanding Fear in Ourselves and Others,* Harper & Brothers, New York, 1951.

PATRI, ANGELO: *How to Help Your Child Grow Up,* Rand McNally & Company, Chicago, 1948, Chap. 4.

RATHS, LOUIS E.: *An Application to Education of the Needs Theory,* Louis E. Raths, Box 26, Bronxville, N.Y., 1949. Pamphlet.

CHAPTER 15

Considering the Causes of
Absence and Tardiness

Aims of This Lesson:

To recognize chronic unexplained absence as an evidence of difficulty in the home, in the school, or in the emotional make-up of the child himself.

To seek a complete understanding of the problems which lie at the root of individual cases of absenteeism.

To create a classroom atmosphere that makes children want to be among those present.

To develop in pupils habits of regularity and punctuality.

Absenteeism is a major problem in most schools. In those states which allot public funds for education on the basis of average daily attendance, the absence of a pupil means a financial loss to the school. But whether or not there is a tangible loss, nonattendance always impedes the progress of the entire group as well as of the individual who is absent.

Being keenly aware of the value of regular attendance, teachers devise numerous and varied plans to promote it. They try contests and awards, threats and punishments. Sometimes they put too much stress on the importance of perfect attendance as a goal. The record on the roll book, the plaque on the door, or the prize which the class wins is not the significant thing. When teachers make it their main business to strive for the happiness and the physical and mental health of pupils, good attendance is a natural result.

Because of loyalty to the group, pressure from their classmates, or a desire to please the teacher, some children go to school when they are physically unable to be there. The attendance record will be better in the long run if youngsters are encouraged to stay at home when they have colds or when they have not completely recovered from an illness. It should be remembered, too, that travel and other out-of-school activities are sometimes more valuable than an equal amount of time spent in school. It is possible for a whole class to benefit from the interesting experience of one child. For example, an entire group may participate in helping a child collect information for an anticipated trip, in receiving cards and descriptive folders from him en route, and in hearing a report and seeing souvenirs after his return.

Aside from the cases of absence that are legitimate and justifiable, there is a far greater number that are unexplained and unnecessary. One of the many responsibilities of the school is to investigate the causes of chronic absenteeism and to find ways of eliminating or correcting them. When repeated absences are explained on the basis of headaches, upset stomach, or inclement weather, the excuses may be authentic or they may be a sham to cover up the real reason. By keeping an accurate record and using some simple code for the causes of absence, it is possible to make a study of absenteeism. In this way it may be observed that Tom's absence always occurs on Tuesdays and Thursdays, the days on which gym classes are scheduled— and Tom is very conscious of the fact that he cannot compete with the other boys in physical activities. It may be seen that Ellen is invariably absent on Mondays. Further investigation may show that, in spite of the other excuses offered, she is kept at home on that day to help her mother with the laundry. John's absence six times during the past two months because of a sore throat indicates that his tonsils need attention. A carefully kept record of attendance has many implications for the alert teacher.

Communicable diseases, skin conditions, digestive disturbances, injuries, and other physical disorders always cause a certain amount of nonattendance. Aside from these medical causes, absences are largely due to home conditions, attitudes toward school, and emotional upsets.

Undesirable home conditions may be the actual reason for absence or they may be used as an excuse for nonattendance that is really due to a more deep-seated cause. It is not unusual for children in some schools to stay at home because of a lack of food, clothes, shoes, or transportation. Most cases of poverty are met with sympathy from the teacher and are referred without delay to welfare agencies or other sources of help.

Some parents create an indifference toward education by unnecessarily keeping pupils at home to take care of the younger children, to do the housework, to run errands, to help in the father's place of business, to go on shopping tours, or to take week-end trips. Others unwittingly foster a dislike for school by telling the children how they themselves hated school, annoyed the teachers, and stayed away at every opportunity when they were growing up. Conferences with parents often help them to realize the importance of regular school attendance and to understand the effect of their own actions and opinions on the attitudes of the children. A few tactful suggestions concerning improvements in home management may enable an overworked mother to get along without keeping a child out of school to help. If circumstances in the home cannot be altered, however, at least the teacher can accept the child's absence with understanding and without blaming, criticizing, or embarrassing him.

It is sometimes difficult for teachers to realize that the cause of absence may be in the school itself. Children find many excuses to stay away from the teacher who is grouchy, faultfinding, and lacking in imagination and the ability to make work seem like fun. Sometimes they stay out of school merely because they feel that the teacher is unfair to them or does not like them. It is quite common for a child who has been sharply reprimanded to remain at home the following day because of embarrassment, wounded feelings, or a desire to spite the teacher. When it is necessary to scold a child, it is equally necessary to find some way of reestablishing his self-esteem as soon as possible.

There are few real attendance problems in the class of the teacher who has a cheerful, pleasant disposition, who sincerely likes children, and who plans interesting and challenging activities for them. In fact, the children in such surroundings are often so eager to know what absorbing experience is next in store for them that they will go to school even when they are not physically able to be there.

The child who is ashamed of being the largest or the oldest in the class, the one who is discouraged because of failure, or the one who finds the curriculum unchallenging may use absence as a means of escape from a situation that has become too difficult or too distasteful for him. The solution may be found by placing this child in a different group, by helping him to experience success and accomplishment, by coaching him until he has more self-confidence, or by giving him some responsibility that will make him feel needed in the group. The teacher who keeps her eyes open to opportunities can usually find some simple way to win a child, at least until the underlying cause of his absence has been discovered.

One teacher had been unable to interest a boy who was frequently absent from school for trivial reasons. His only accomplishment seemed to be chewing bubble gum. On one of his infrequent days at school he happened to notice the similarity of the illustrations in the history lesson to the wrappers on his bubble gum. He observed that the pieces of gum were wrapped in pictures of various historical events. He became interested in the stories connected with the pictures, started a scrapbook for himself, and came early to school each day to show the teacher his newly acquired wrappers. Not only did the child gain some knowledge of social studies, but his feeling of friendliness toward the teacher gave her the opportunity she needed to study his other needs and interests.

Members of an adventurous gang frequently stay away because they find school so much less stimulating than their out-of-school activities. Such children can sometimes be won through the gang leader. An absorbing project in which the leader has a specially responsible part and in which the members of his gang are included may be the answer. Through other boys in the class it is often possible to interest these youngsters in joining the boy scouts, a YMCA club, or other similar group.

Although any child may sometimes be tempted to cut school on the spur of the moment when there is some special atrtaction, habitual absence is usually the result of some deep-seated trouble that needs attention. If the direct cause cannot be traced to poverty, retardation, or dislike of the teacher, it is almost sure to be found in an emotional disturbance of the child himself. The same underlying conflicts which cause children to steal, fight, bully, destroy property, have temper tantrums, run away from home, and become antagonistic toward authority may also cause them to play truant. Truancy, like daydreaming, fearfulness, and nervous habits, should be regarded by the teacher as a child's signal that something is wrong.

A great many habitual truants are children who feel a lack of real love and affection in their homes or who are uncertain about the feelings of their parents for each other. Such children usually have so many frustrating situations in their lives that they fight back at the world in general in whatever way they can. They may have been nagged and punished over trifles until they have come to feel defiant toward all authority. Since both school and home represent authority to them, they express their resentment toward dictatorial or tyrannical parents by refusing to accept the routine of school life.

When a youngster has had an unhappy relationship with one of his parents, he may dislike teachers of the same sex. For example, a forceful man teacher may be to the child a counterpart of his overstrict father. A woman teacher may be unconsciously associated with a neurotic mother, an unpleasant stepmother, or a bossy grandmother. Although the child himself is usually unable to understand or to explain his feeling, he has a vague sense of anxiety. His urge to escape from an uncomfortable situation may compel him to stay away from both home and school.

A child may have a long history of absence before it is discovered that his explanations of being ill, having to help at home, or keeping a dental appointment cannot always be taken at face value. Even when he is frank enough to say that he does not like the school or the teacher, the real reason for his feeling of insecurity and unhappiness may not be learned until a thorough investigation is made. There are always determining factors in the background or the environment of the truant. If the teacher is unable to discover them by her own efforts, she should seek help from some other source within the school or from an outside agency.

Elsie was a respectful, obedient child who never caused any trouble at school. However, poor attendance apparently kept her from being interested in her work. She dreamed away her time but never allowed the teacher to get any clue to her problem. After a day out of school she always brought a note from her stepmother stating that she had been kept at home to take care of the younger children, that she had been sent on an important errand, or that the family had been out of town for the week end. A home visit by the teacher revealed that Elsie's father was away a great deal of the time because of his work, that there were four younger half brothers and sisters, and that the stepmother was a complaining person who probably was in ill-health, as Elsie had said. So the absence excuses were accepted until one morning when Elsie came to the door of the principal's office and asked for a private interview. She was weeping bitterly but between sobs she explained that her stepmother had threatened to cut off her hair when she returned from school that afternoon. The girl's one distinguishing feature was her beautiful, red, curly hair and she was especially proud of it because it was exactly like her own mother's. Although nothing could hurt so much as the possibility of losing her gorgeous tresses, she showed the welts made on her back when her stepmother had beaten her because she had not properly scoured the kitchen sink that morning.

The child then poured out a long story of abuse and mistreatment. She told how she was always called very early in the morning to prepare breakfast for the family, to dress the younger children, and then to wash the dishes and clean the kitchen before she was allowed to go to school. The afternoons brought still heavier duties until there was no time that she could call her own. When the work was not done to the entire satisfaction of the stepmother, a beating was sure to follow. If the child attempted to talk with her father about the situation, he invariably sided with his wife and believed her version of the story. He openly favored the younger children and made Elsie subservient to them. She had been afraid to report the real trouble to the school, but she had often secretly planned to run away. It was on these occasions that she had been truant, although fear of being caught and taken back to her stepmother had caused her to return home at the end of the day. She had carefully forged her own excuse notes. After the truth of these stories had been ascertained, Elsie was referred to the juvenile court for protection and was subsequently placed in a foster home. The stepmother was sentenced to the workhouse on a charge of cruelty.

One of the most frequent causes of nonattendance in young children is school phobia. Although the child may claim to be afraid of the teacher or of certain children, his trouble is more likely to be a fear of leaving home or of being separated from his mother. He may actually become so ill from headaches, nausea, dizziness, or abdominal pains that he is unable either to go to school in the morning or to remain there throughout the day. The situation is often brought about unconsciously by a possessive or overprotective mother who is glad to have the child at home and who makes his apparent illness so pleasant for him that he wants more than ever to stay away from school. One of the greatest single factors in a case of aversion to school may be a feeling of jealousy toward a younger child who remains at home, a desire for more of the mother's care and attention, or a vague fear that some harm may come to the family during the child's absence. It is generally agreed that the best treatment is continuous unbroken contact with the school. Attendance should be regular even if the child does no more than report to the principal's office each day or if he remains for only a part of the day at first. A problem of school phobia requires that the teacher be patient and sympathetic and that the parents be made aware of the significance of the child's fears and of their own attitudes and feelings (see pages 147–148 and 175–176).

Danny, an intelligent fourth-grader, constantly complained of colds, coughs, sore throat, and any other ailments that would furnish reasonable excuses for staying at home. After a call from the visiting teacher this child would appear at school in the morning but before noon he would cry and beg to leave because of illness. After the school had made possible a tonsillectomy, had given him nourishing food, and had finally threatened him with referral to juvenile court, Danny attended with fair regularity for a while. However, he frequently resorted to illness as a means of getting to go home before dismissal time.

A visit in Danny's home would make one wonder why he should want so much to be there. He lived with his mother and grandmother in a single room of a dark, dirty, cheerless rooming house. His bed was a heap of ragged blankets on the floor. His father had deserted the family when the child was quite young. His mother, to whom the little fellow was strongly attached, had left town to get a job and had been unable to see him except on occasional week ends. During this time Danny had been shifted back and forth from grandmother to aunt. Now, however, his mother had lost her job and had come home to stay temporarily. It was not a dislike of school, but a fear that his mother might leave again, that made Danny feel compelled to stay at home. When the mother remarried and established a permanent home, the child realized that he had a secure base to which he could return each day and the problem of nonattendance at school disappeared.

Every case of absence should be a major concern of the teacher. Even though an occasional day out of school may seem harmless enough, it is easy for nonattendance to become chronic. Habitual truancy does not usually appear overnight but instead it develops gradually from an almost unnoticed beginning. Then, although truancy does not necessarily result in delinquency, there is the possibility that the child who evades the school law may later go a step further and become involved in more serious violations. For this reason, teachers should try to recognize and study early signs of trouble which, if ignored, are likely to have serious aftereffects. Emotional disturbances that are not dealt with as they appear but are allowed to continue into adolescence may develop into firmly fixed behavior patterns that are extremely difficult to change. The earlier treatment of potential truancy is started, the less time it will take and the more effective it will be.

It is natural for the teacher to react to habitual truancy by wanting to punish the child and to force him to conform to the regulations. But this method only aggravates the problem and makes the youngster dislike school even more. If the truant knows he is going to be punished when he gets back to school, he will postpone his return for another day or so. Since he usually is already an unhappy, insecure child who is trying to find a way of escape from his difficulties, harsh treatment will cause him to feel still more misunderstood and rejected.

Aggressive children who are behavior problems in the classroom are the ones who are most likely to be punished for their absenteeism. The teacher usually has less patience with them than with the fearful, timid children who withdraw from social contacts by staying out of school but manage to give acceptable excuses for their absence. Psychologists believe that the child who is unconsciously trying to solve his problem in any way at all, even though it is through truancy, has a better chance of achieving mental health than the one who attends school and complies with other rules and regulations but at the same time has all his troubled emotions stored up within himself. Both the aggressive and the withdrawing cases need understanding and sympathetic treatment.

The only lasting cure for truancy can be effected by finding what the child is trying to run away from and then helping him to get a different outlook on life. If the teacher discovers that she herself is the cause of the trouble, she should accept the child's feeling without resentment or irritation and be glad that she has an opportunity to change the situation. If she learns that the child is lonely, unhappy, or neglected at home, she should try to give him at school, in a small measure at least, some of the satisfactions which he does not find elsewhere.

A pupil who has been absent should be made to realize that he has been missed but he should never be allowed to feel that the teacher holds a grudge because of his truancy. Upon his return to school it may help to give him some job or responsibility which, without seeming to reward him, will at least let him know that there are no unkind feelings toward him. One good procedure is to get him interested in some long-term project that will whet his desire to be present every day.

Tardiness is due to the same basic causes as irregular attendance and should be treated in much the same way. It may be the result of indifferent parents, poor organization in the home, or too many responsibilities imposed upon the child. A youngster who must prepare his own breakfast and get started to school on his own initiative because his mother sleeps late deserves a great deal of consideration from the teacher. The motherless child who must take care of younger children in the family and do much of the housework before leaving home also needs understanding and encouragement. But the child who is tardy because he is allowing himself to become dilatory needs to have some corrective measures applied. To be sure, it is first necessary to find out whether the underlying cause of the tardiness is physical weakness, a lack of incentive, the example of parents, or some mental trait such as a habit of indecision or a lack of self-confidence which slows down the child's actions.

The teacher should be conscious of the late-comers and help them in every possible way to acquire the habit of tackling all jobs without delay. She can often induce young procrastinators to get to school on time by scheduling their favorite activities at the first period of the day, by allowing them to do something which they especially enjoy before school each morning, or by planning interesting opening exercises. The value of promptness can be emphasized on numerous occasions throughout the day. It must be remembered, however, that if too great a penalty is attached to tardiness, some children who have difficulty in getting to school on time will stay out all day rather than risk being late.

It is extremely important that the foundation for habits of responsibility and punctuality be laid in early childhood. If the task has not been done by parents, it naturally falls to the lot of teachers of the lower grades. If teachers fail, the job is likely to remain undone.

ACTIVITIES SUGGESTED

Because some of the activities of this lesson are aimed primarily at the habitually absent children, it will be well to use them on a day when attendance is good or to plan some special attraction which will induce all children to be present. Select only the activities which are likely to have a value or an appeal for your particular group.

If there are no truants in your class, plan the lesson by keeping in mind the children whose behavior patterns are such that they might at some future time resort to truancy as a means of combating their difficulties. Also keep in mind the tendencies of those children who are potential tardiness cases.

1. In order to keep pupils interested in being present every day, you may employ some of the devices used in advertising. A large question mark, a part of a picture, and a word which will engage the attention may be placed on the blackboard to herald a forthcoming event. If Mondays and Fridays are the days when attendance is usually poorest, it is a good idea to plan some especially attractive features for these days. Children who are tantalized by the words, "Guess what we are going to do on Friday," written across the blackboard are likely to be present to satisfy their curiosity.

2. Look to the causes of absence in your own class for possibilities for preventive teaching. For example, if a child has recently been absent because of a communicable disease, talk to the group about the cause, prevention, duration, and treatment of the particular disease and about their responsibility for stopping the spread of contagion. An absence due to an injury may lead naturally to a discussion of accident hazards about the home

CONSIDERING THE CAUSES OF ABSENCE AND TARDINESS 191

and school, safety rules that should be observed, and first-aid information that all children should have. A committee may be appointed to observe and report hazards about the school building and grounds which need to be corrected.

3. Find ways of incorporating in the regular classwork some ideas concerning good attendance and punctuality. Ask the secretary of the class to keep for a period of two or three weeks a strict accounting of the types of medical absences of pupils in the class. The number of cases of colds, digestive disturbances, toothache, headache, injuries, and other causes can be used as data for arithmetic problems.

As part of the language lessons plan to have oral and written reports concerning the most frequent causes of absence among the group and suggestions for eliminating these causes. Let the art lessons center around the theme of regular attendance.

4. Allow the younger children to dramatize situations which have caused recent absence in their class, assigning to different ones the role of doctor, dentist, nurse, and the mother who admonishes the sick child to use his handkerchief to stop the spread of germs, who urges the other children to avoid toothache by good dental care, or who reminds her boys and girls to eat a good breakfast so that they will feel strong and alert during the day. Numerous possibilities will suggest themselves.

5. If you do not have accurate information about the causes of all absence and tardiness, you may gain an insight into the interests of the youngsters by frequently asking them to tell you stories about the things they do outside of school. Although the children who are often absent are the objects of your concern, do not let them feel that they are being singled out for this activity.

6. Encourage the pupils to talk freely about the times when they have been absent without a real reason, letting them realize that nothing they say will be held against them. Introduce the discussion by asking some child who talks readily to tell about a time when he was tempted to stay away from school, what caused him to feel as he did, and what he did about it. As others are gradually drawn into the conversation some of them will probably confess how they have actually played truant. Be careful not to moralize or to say anything which will prevent the pupils from releasing any antagonisms or hostilities that they may feel.

7. Set up situations which are actually typical of your group and allow the children to act them out. Choose as characters those who are frequently absent or tardy and urge them to act as they would in real life. Have different children to take the leading parts as the dramatizations are enacted over and over. Then ask the class to vote on the persons who they think have given the most honest portrayals. The acting should be strictly improvised and the children in the audience should be permitted to comment freely. The purpose is to get the pupils to take an honest view of their own habits of rationalization, compensation, and other means of handling their emotional conflicts. Suggested situations:

a. Two boys are on their way to school. One recalls that there is to be a test in mathematics today. The other mentions that it is too fine a spring day to be penned up in a schoolroom. Just then they pass a building under construction. The noise and din of the concrete mixers, shovels, and cranes, and the activities of the carpenters, stone masons, and bricklayers are very attractive to boys who are not especially eager to get to school anyway. Pretend to be these two boys and demonstrate what you would really do and say.

b. A boy is on his way to school when his foot slips on the wet pavement and he falls into a puddle of muddy water. His clothes get so wet that he is forced to return home to change. When he reaches home he finds that his favorite cousins from out of town have just arrived to spend the day. After changing his clothes, he glances at the clock and discovers that it is already past time for school to open. Pretend that you are the boy and show what you would say and do.

c. Because they went to a movie last night, two girls have failed to finish their notebooks which are due today. This morning one of the girls stops at the home of the other so that they can walk to school together. She finds her friend listening to an interesting radio program. Her mother has already left for a day of shopping in town and will not be home until late in the afternoon. Pretend that two of you are these girls and dramatize exactly what you would do.

Further suggestions for such dramatizations can be found in *Psychodrama in the Schools,* by Nahum E. Shoobs, published by Beacon House, Inc., New York, 1944 (monograph).

8. Hold a discussion concerning the ill effects of absence both on the individual and on the group. See that this leads to a consideration of the diffi-

culty of catching up with the class after an absence of several days, the effect of absence on grades, and the loss of interest as a result of being out of school.

9. Appoint some responsible child to interview a member of the Board of Education or to obtain a yearbook or other source of information concerning the cost of education in your city. Let the children know how much your school system spends each year for teachers' salaries, school equipment and supplies, maintenance of buildings, janitorial service, clerical work, heat, light, and other items. Find out the annual and the daily per capita cost for the education of elementary school children in your city. Help the pupils to see how each child is planned for when numbers are taken into consideration in employing the required number of teachers, furnishing the rooms, and ordering the supplies. The money is spent for them whether or not they are in school to receive the benefit of it. Pupils should no more want to miss a day of school than they would want to miss a ball game or a movie to which they had been given free tickets. Without moralizing or preaching, emphasize the point that those who forfeit their right to the education provided for them are real losers.

10. The child who is out of school because of long or frequent illnesses is likely to feel left out of things or even to dread facing the responsibility of school again. Such a child appreciates being remembered by notes from his classmates as well as by collections of stories they have written, drawings they have made, and samples of any special holiday decorations they have used. When a sick child is convalescing and is able to do handwork, he may be kept in touch by being asked to make a scrapbook or a poster for a special project at school. If his mother signifies that he is well enough for homework, certain children may be responsible for writing his assignments and seeing that they are delivered to him. This training in thoughtfulness for others is good for the well child and it may mean a great deal to the mental health of the ill one.

11. Among the chronic absentees, the ones who are hesitant to talk before the group are probably most in need of your friendship and understanding. Try to find occasions to engage these shy children in bits of private conversation before and after school and at lunch period. Gradually you may be able to find out why they try to avoid school. It will do no good to ask them point-blank questions because they are not aware of the real reasons for their actions. But by giving them an opportunity to talk to you alone, by being a

sympathetic listener, and by attempting to understand their feelings, you may be able to help them.

12. Discuss the matter of tardiness. Ask the children to mention some of the reasons for their own tardiness and make a blackboard list of the most common excuses given. The list will probably look something like this:

"I could not find my books."
"I had to do my homework before leaving the house."
"I had to wait for my friend who was not ready."
"Our clock was slow."
"We overslept this morning."
"I forgot my notebook and had to return for it."

Talk with the group about the advisability of having their belongings ready the night before, of allowing an extra fifteen minutes as a margin of time to take care of unexpected delays, and other precautions that may be taken to avoid tardiness.

13. Talk to the children about the meaning of the word "procrastination." Help them to see how the person who dawdles, wastes time, and has a tendency to postpone tasks is usually the one who is consistently late getting to school. Urge the children who are having this difficulty to form the habit of tackling all jobs immediately without putting them off until after dinner, until tomorrow, or until next week.

Organize a campaign for promptness. Make the pupils so conscious of the importance of attacking all work briskly that the last one to get started on a job will feel like the loser in a race. The only way to establish habits of promptness is by practice. Have the children notice the things about which they are especially dilatory, such as coming into the room after play period, getting out materials for work, handing in homework papers, and putting away supplies at the end of a period. Let them decide upon some system of rewards or penalties for those who are especially prompt or unduly slow in these matters.

14. Tell the class some true stories of procrastinators you have known and how they were cured.

15. Take a poll to determine what your particular group considers to be the most enjoyable lesson or classroom activity. Try to place this feature at the beginning of the day as an incentive for getting to school on time in the morning.

FOLLOW-UP

As the year goes on consider each case of frequent, unexplained absence as possible truancy. In these cases you are very likely to find leads to problems of maladjustment which go far deeper than the immediate cause of the absence.

BIBLIOGRAPHY

Children Absent from School, Citizens' Committee on Children of New York City, Inc., New York, 1949.

DOUGHERTY, JAMES HENRY, FRANK HERMON GORMAN, and CLAUDE ANDERSON PHILLIPS, *Elementary School Organization and Management,* The Macmillan Company, New York, 1950, pp. 55–59.

SHOOBS, NAHUM E.: *Psychodrama in the Schools,* Beacon House, Inc., New York, 1944. Monograph.

WALLIN, J. E. WALLACE: *Personality Maladjustments and Mental Hygiene,* McGraw-Hill Book Company, Inc., New York, 1949, pp. 330–337.

CHAPTER 16

Developing Responsibility

Aims of This Lesson:

To create an atmosphere and set an example which will encourage responsible behavior.

To instill in each child a sense of his obligation to look after himself, to be responsive to the needs of others, and to exercise initiative in meeting new situations.

To foster cooperative relationships between all members of the group, both leaders and followers.

One of the chief concerns of teachers is the development of responsibility among pupils. It sometimes seems that all too frequently children must be prodded to do their homework, to bring their materials to school, and to supply the help they have promised for class projects. In spite of daily reminders, boys and girls forget to bring their musical instruments, to practice their lessons, to return library books, and to keep dental appointments. They forget their promises or fail to keep their word to classmates and teachers.

Among the many reasons for this laxity in children is the example set by the adults in their lives. Youngsters who grow up in homes where parents do not hesitate to shirk church, club, and community responsibilities are not likely to take their own obligations seriously. When mothers and fathers are indifferent about taking care of their possessions, keeping their appointments, or looking after the welfare of others, it is small wonder that the children are disorderly, thoughtless, and irresponsible. It is extremely difficult for slipshod adults to sell younger persons on the virtues of reliability.

Many children who come from homes where there are servants or from small apartments where there is little work to be done are not expected to

196

assume any responsibility whatever about the house. They expect to have their clothes gotten out and put away, their rooms cleaned, and their lunch money, books, and other supplies handed to them as they leave for school. Some youngsters never do things on their own initiative because they have oversolicitous parents who pamper them and cater to their every wish. Their mothers may actually encourage dawdling, idleness, and immaturity because of their own psychological need to have someone dependent on them. Then there are the parents who are so busy or so impatient that they never take the time or the trouble to train their children to accept any specific responsibilities. They find it easier to do all the work themselves than to watch the awkward attempts of those who are just learning. Parents who, for any of these reasons, continue to encourage children to depend on them for everything may expect the youngsters to grow into adults who will shrink from accepting responsibilities, making decisions, or tackling new jobs for themselves.

Some parents go to the other extreme and put so much stress on the importance of assuming responsibility that they make the whole idea seem tiresome to youngsters. By arbitrarily assigning tasks, demanding that they be done in a specific way, and expecting perfect performance, they defeat their own purpose. The incentive to be a responsible member of home and society cannot be instilled just by talking to a child and constantly reminding him of his obligations or by setting up rules and regulations and rigidly enforcing them. Neither can the importance of dependability be impressed upon a child by constantly saying to him, "You must learn to be more responsible." Such an approach is likely to make him antagonistic and indifferent. Instead of taking the initiative in doing more tasks about the house, he will probably spend his time trying to avoid them.

Parents who believe that good training consists in forcing children to do numerous tasks which they dislike may succeed in getting them to work well under supervision but at the same time they may fail to develop in them the more desirable capacity to take the lead in meeting new situations. An elementary school child may not be able to see the necessity for doing routine housework or looking after younger children. At his stage of development the most important thing in the world is to learn to get along with his contemporaries. When he functions well on a school committee, organizes a club, or plans and prepares refreshments for a group of his friends, he is actually becoming a much more responsible individual than when he simply remembers to hang up his clothes and to dry the dishes. Adults who scold and nag about details that are important to their own peace of mind sometimes neglect to look at the over-all picture.

One morning, in his enthusiasm over collecting and wrapping the cardboard boxes and the empty spools which he wanted to contribute to the school workshop, a little kindergarten boy forgot to clear the table after breakfast. On his return from school that afternoon he brought enough tickets to enable the family to attend a concert. He had heard his parents lamenting the fact that no more tickets were available to the public. So, of his own accord, he had contacted the band instructor and arranged to procure the tickets through the music department. His mother had no fear that this child was not developing a sense of responsibility merely because he failed to do his regular job at home.

No one will deny that each member of the family should do his part to keep the household running smoothly. In fact, training in this respect should begin at a very early age. Step by step the little child can learn to take care of his own wants so that he will not need to be dependent upon others. He should feed and dress himself, put his toys away, and gradually reach the point where he can help with simple household tasks such as emptying ash trays and putting away the used daily papers. Later he can learn to make his bed, hang up his clothes, set the table, do some simple cooking, wash dishes, mop, sweep, make minor household repairs, run errands, and do numerous other helpful jobs. But even though learning to manage his own affairs and to share in some of the work of the home are important phases in a child's development, they should not be overemphasized to the extent that unpleasantness is associated with them.

Because the job of training children to assume responsibility cannot be done by the home alone, it is only natural that it should be shared by the school. The group activities and the relationships with friends at school provide excellent opportunities for practice in sharing responsibility, in cooperating, and in meeting varied situations. Training for responsibility is such an important part of a child's education that it should not be done in a general or spasmodic way. It should be considered a major objective which is kept in mind and made a part of all activities both inside and outside the classroom.

A sense of responsibility can be started in the kindergarten by letting each child know that he is expected to remove and put on his own wraps, to be liable for the condition of his own work materials, to replace the equipment and supplies that have been used, to leave the room clean and orderly, and to assume responsibility not only for his own property but for that of the other children and of the school. It is in this first year of school life that overdependent youngsters can discover the satisfaction of doing things for themselves, overprotected ones can have opportunities to practice resourcefulness, and those who have had very little opportunity to associate with others of their own age can learn to cooperate and share responsibilities.

The kind of responsibility that a child can be expected to carry will depend upon his age, his physical strength, his intelligence, and his maturity. Some children fail to measure up to their commitments because they are entrusted with duties that are not in keeping with their capacities. A four-year-old girl was asked to take a neighbor's baby for a walk while the mother went shopping. When the mother returned she was horrified to find that the little girl had left the baby in its carriage a block from home while she wandered off to play. Children should not have to experience failure and discouragement simply because adults ask too much of them. Neither should they be denied the opportunity to assume as much responsibility as they are capable of handling. From such sources as Gesell and Ilg's *The Child from Five to Ten* [1] it is possible to get an idea of what the majority of children of various age levels can be expected to do.

A study of the background and the environment of pupils will also help the teacher determine the degree of responsibility they can shoulder. Too much is sometimes expected of children who have not been taught at home to assume responsibility or who have circumstances in their lives which prevent them from doing exactly what is required of them. A seventh-grade girl was one of thirteen children who lived with their parents in four small rooms. Although this child was capable and cooperative at school, she seldom brought in the assigned homework. During a quiet talk after school she explained to the teacher that her home was in a state of constant confusion, that it was late at night before all the children were finally asleep, and that any books or papers that she took home were sure to be torn and marked by the younger ones. While discussing the situation with the teacher, it occurred to the girl that she might be able to study for a while each evening at the home of a neighbor. But even if there had been no such obvious solution, the teacher would not in the future have chided her for neglect of duty but would probably have found a way for her to make up the work at school. It is often necessary to make allowances for children who are

[1] Arnold Gesell and Frances L. Ilg, *The Child from Five to Ten,* Harper & Brothers, New York, 1946.

seemingly irresponsible. Even a small improvement in their habits may constitute a major victory.

Children do not develop self-reliance and dependability by having certain duties assigned to them, by being told exactly how to perform them, and by being coaxed, reminded, and prodded until they have completed the tasks. By forcing youngsters to accept specific responsibilities and by punishing them or curtailing their privileges when they fail, adults succeed only in building up rebellion and resentment. The habit of responsibility cannot be coerced. It grows of its own accord when children find it pleasant to be able to look after their own affairs and to feel that other persons are depending upon them. Teachers and parents help most when they set an example of cooperativeness and helpfulness and when they create an atmosphere that is conducive to responsible behavior. They do a great deal toward making dependability a satisfying trait when they provide opportunities for young people to practice resourcefulness and initiative, when they encourage spontaneous and independent action, when they recognize and praise a job well done, and when they withhold unnecessary criticism of minor details.

In every classroom there are numerous interesting and challenging jobs which fall within the range of ability of the pupils and which really need to be done. It is good for certain children to feel that it is their own particular responsibility to erase the blackboard, distribute supplies, answer the door, check on the light or the room temperature, arrange the nature collections, take care of the lost and found articles, sell pencils or other supplies, account for class money, or look after special equipment. But a sense of responsibility cannot be devloped simply by having a child clean the erasers or keep the books arranged in neat rows. Along with the actual performance of the duty must be the feeling that this is an important and necessary task and not merely a piece of busywork designed to keep one occupied.

It is natural for children to work more willingly at jobs which they themselves have chosen than at tasks which have been arbitrarily delegated to them by adults. Self-reliance is much more evident in classrooms where pupils discuss the things that need to be done and volunteer to be responsible for duties that are somewhat in keeping with their interests and abilities. For example, the job of accounting for ticket money or taking lunch orders will cause less strain and tension for the child who is accurate in mathematics than for one who is unsure of his calculations. Likewise, taking care of the fish, the animals, or the plants will be much more satisfying to the child who is a real nature lover.

When a youngster has once offered to do a particular task which is consistent with his ability, he should be encouraged to finish it even though his enthusiasm lags. He should not be allowed to think that someone else will complete the job for him. The teacher can more effectively keep him working if she offers him some occasional assistance than if she constantly reminds him of his obligation at the risk of seeming to nag. When a child really tries, it is unwise to let him experience constant failure. But when he willfully slights a duty, he needs to realize the effect of his neglect both on himself and on the group.

In addition to being responsible for the performance of certain tasks at home and at school, young persons need to be keenly aware of their duties to themselves and to their associates. It is definitely their responsibility to acquire the knowledge and skills expected of boys and girls of their age, to manage their finances, to budget their time, to take care of their belongings, to make wise decisions, and to follow through to completion whatever they start. They have an obligation to others to do what they say they will do, to be conscious of the safety of other people, to do anything that needs to be done to keep the organization of school or home running smoothly, and to give their support and cooperation to the group either as leaders or as followers.

Children need a great deal of practice in solving their own problems, in meeting new situations, and in functioning as part of a group. They can get a wide variety of valuable experiences in a classroom where they are free to express opinions, to formulate plans, and to carry out original ideas. It takes time and patience to help children develop initiative and self-reliance. Like parents, teachers find it much easier to take complete charge than to stand by and watch children bungle and make mistakes. But they lose their greatest opportunities when they exclude children from the planning and allow them to participate only in the less interesting details. Class trips furnish much richer experiences for pupils who have a part in the planning, who realize that their suggestions are accepted and used, and who feel responsible for asking intelligent questions and accumulating important information. Classroom decorations may not be so tastefully arranged, picnic menus may not be so complete, and letters to the mothers may not be so well worded as if the teacher had managed them alone but the youngsters who have been in charge have had another opportunity to grow in responsibility. Teachers give the greatest boosts to habits of dependability when they praise all efforts to exercise initiative, when they withhold harsh criticism and discouraging remarks, and when they learn to be satisfied with less than perfection in minor details.

Children become responsible only as they feel that they are trusted. There are still schoolrooms in which pupils are required to get permission for every move they make. It is evident that the teacher does not consider them capable of managing even the smallest matters because they are not allowed on their own initiative to sharpen a pencil, get an extra piece of paper, consult the dictionary, or look at the globe. Materials should be kept within easy reach so that all youngsters can at least be depended upon to take care of their own needs.

Many children have learned to be entirely responsible for their conduct only while they are being watched. When the teacher is out of the room, bedlam reigns. Pupils who are quiet and orderly under such circumstances are labeled as sissies and cowards by the others. Every teacher should work toward the time when children will behave acceptably because they are trusted and depended upon to use good judgment and to be mature in their actions. It should be possible to leave the room at any time knowing that all members of the class will respect the leadership of a chosen child or that they will carry on without anyone in charge. It is a very poor technique to appoint one pupil to stand guard and report any of his classmates who whisper or move out of their places in the teacher's absence. Some children who are thus placed in authority regard the assignment as evidence of superiority and use their position to exploit the others. Some of them give false accounts rather than tattle on their friends.

Children who learn to be trustworthy and resourceful in the classroom will know how to be useful members of the home and the community. They will be able to anticipate things that need to be done, to volunteer for jobs that they can do well and, having once accepted an assignment, to see it through to completion. A sense of responsibility cannot be taught like a lesson in spelling or mathematics. But it can gradually be developed by teachers and parents who have faith in children, who do not expect too much or too little of them, and who provide adequate opportunities for them to prove their dependability.

ACTIVITIES SUGGESTED

Although most teachers are daily striving to develop a sense of responsibility, a planned lesson on the subject may make both teacher and pupils more conscious of the extent to which further emphasis is needed. Select only those activities which seem best suited to your particular group.

Try to find out what is keeping some children from cooperating with the group and from assuming individual responsibility. If it is a difficulty which cannot be corrected, at least you will be more sympathetic with the child and will better understand and accept his seeming lack of maturity.

1. As a means of finding out what responsibilities the children have at home, ask them to make lists of the duties which they perform regularly as their contribution to the family welfare. These should not be things that they are supposed to do, but the ones that they actually do. Compile the lists and discuss them with the group, commenting on the duties which are most common, the ones that are unusual, and the reasons for the differences in responsibilities of families of different sizes living in different types of homes with varying needs.

2. Have the group make a blackboard list of the home duties which they think can reasonably be expected to be done by persons of their own age, by those a year younger, and by those a year older. Make the point that children can generally be expected to assume more responsibility each year. At the close of the discussion ask the pupils to mention some jobs which need to be done in their own homes and which they feel that they could do. These should include tasks which need to be done only occasionally as well as regular routine duties. Then talk about various emergencies which sometimes arise in any home and about specific ways in which boys and girls of their age can take the initiative.

3. Children sometimes have their reasons for feeling rebellious about the duties which are delegated to them at home. Give them an opportunity to tell what they think about the jobs they are expected to do, the fairness of the distribution of work among the various members of the family, the penalties that are attached to neglect of duty, and the cooperation they receive. It will do them good to express their grievances and to hear how others feel about their mutual problems. Do not criticize or moralize but let the children know that you understand their feelings. Later it may be possible to talk with some of the parents and to help straighten out misunderstandings. One child who was given a chance to talk on this subject told how she was expected to buy the groceries each afternoon before her mother came home from work. But the mother frequently failed to see that there was sufficient money in the specified place in the kitchen. After thinking about the situation with her classmates, the child decided to take the responsibility of going over the grocery list with her mother the evening before, estimating the cost, and checking to see that the money was on hand.

4. In order to acquaint the parents with your purpose and to enlist their help, you may want to send home a letter similar to the one below:

Dear Parents:

During the next few weeks at school we shall be concentrating on the matter of accepting responsibility. Because we believe that the project will be much more effective with your cooperation, we are hoping that at the same time you also will emphasize the importance of assuming responsibility at home.

If you have not already done so, perhaps you and your child can decide on some suitable task for which (s)he may be entirely responsible. It will be in line with our program if you will encourage initiative and resourcefulness in the discharge of this duty. For example, if the child is to be responsible for cleaning his room, won't you allow him to arrange the furnishings and the decorations according to his own taste? If he is to help with the cooking, won't you let him also help with the planning of the menus?

Some information from you will help us in our approach to the problem at school. Will you please answer the following questions and return them to us:

1. What regular duties does your child perform at home?
2. How does he execute these duties? (Please check.)
   _____ Always willingly, cheerfully, without being reminded.
   _____ Fairly well most of the time.
   _____ Frequently forgets or slights job.
   _____ Usually grumbles, neglects part of work or shirks altogether.
3. Does your child of his own accord assume any responsibility for doing tasks not regularly assigned to him?
4. Does he have any opportunities at home to manage situations that call for resourcefulness?
5. What regularly scheduled out-of-school lessons, appointments, or part-time jobs does he have?
6. How does he meet these obligations? (Please check.)
   _____ Very conscientiously.
   _____ Fairly well.
   _____ Rather laxly.
   _____ Very poorly.

Thank you very much for your cooperation.

Sincerely,

5. Ask that the group discuss and list duties for which they feel pupils of their own age level could be responsible at school. Allow them to decide who could probably do each of the tasks well and to volunteer to be responsible for some jobs that have not previously been done by the children.

6. From your own experience you may be able to tell some interesting and inspiring stories of former pupils who learned to accept responsibilities and to manage new situations well.

7. Urge those children who have difficulty remembering to do things for which they are responsible to make a schedule of their definite duties for each day of the week. A special little notebook or a particular section in a regular notebook should be set aside for this purpose. As each task on the list is finished, it should be checked off.

8. In order to establish the habit of making and carrying out plans, take a few minutes each morning to help the pupils make a list of all the things they hope to accomplish during the day. These should include the regular routine and any special things to be remembered, such as writing notes to a sick classmate. The list should be kept at a special place on the blackboard so that the items can be checked off one by one as they are finished.

9. Talk with the children about the responsibilities connected with owning pets. Ask each child who owns a pet to tell in detail about its care. Find out if the owners actually assume the responsibility or if they leave the job to their mothers.

10. Discuss the folly of promising to do more than one has time and ability to do well. Help the boys and girls to realize that it is better to refuse to take on a new responsibility if they are not sure that they can carry on with it. The same child may want to belong to the scouts, sing in the choir, take music lessons, keep a pet, deliver newspapers, make a stamp collection, and play football with a neighborhood team. Each new activity brings added responsibilities and less time to spend on other things. One should think carefully about what one wants to give up in order to take on a new interest.

11. As a means of getting children to think about the way they react to responsibility, ask each one to fill out a questionnaire similar to the following, using "yes," "sometimes," and "no" as answers:

RESPONSIBILITY

At school:

—— Do you bring to class the materials you are expected to have?

—— Do you listen to instructions as they are given?

—— Do you behave as well when the teacher is out of the room as when she is watching you?

—— When some other pupil is in charge of an activity, do you do your part to make it a success?

—— Do you remember to do particular jobs for which the class is depending on you?

—— Do you take the lead when you see something that needs to be done in your room?

At home:

—— Do you do your special jobs at home without running away before they are finished?

—— Do you keep your clothes and other possessions in order?

—— Do you do your part to help when other members of the family are entertaining guests?

—— Do you make an effort to get to meals on time?

—— Do you keep your promises to your parents and to other members of your family?

—— When your parents are away from home, are you able to take care of most situations that arise?

12. An overnight camping trip, a picnic, or a party is a good means of giving practical experience in assuming responsibility. Certain children can be called upon to collect the money, plan the menus, look after the necessary supplies, prepare and serve the food, wash the dishes, plan the entertainment, and pack the equipment for going home. They will be able to see the result if even one person fails in his obligation.

13. Class discussions or dramatizations adapted to the grade level and the interests of the particular group may be built around such simple stories as the following:

a. Henry's friend who lives in the same block had been out of school for a week because of illness. He had asked Henry to get his assignments and bring his books to him on Friday afternoon so that he could study during the week end. Henry forgot all about this until he came in view of his friend's home that afternoon. It was a mile back to school. What do you think Henry should have done? What would you have done?

b. George had agreed to feed their dog while the neighbors were on vacation. One morning he started with his family on an all-day outing. They were halfway to the river and it was almost time for the excursion boat to sail when George suddenly remembered that he had not given the dog his food and water. What do you think George should have done? What would you have done?

c. Anna and her sister Eva share the responsibility of setting the table, preparing the vegetables, and helping to serve the evening meal. One afternoon when their mother was going to shop until late, Eva came home ill from school. Just when it was time for Anna to start doing her work, some of her friends came and asked her to go skating with them. This was a tempting invitation because skating was her favorite sport and she had a new pair of skates. What do you think Anna should have done? What would you have done?

d. Bobby had borrowed money from Tommy for his lunch with the understanding that he would repay him the following day. The next morning Tommy did not bring any money to school because he was depending on Bobby's repayment. Just as the tardy bell rang Bobby remembered the teacher's announcement that pupils who had not brought money for their newspaper subscriptions that day would be unable to subscribe at all. Bobby did not have enough money to take care of both obligations. What do you think he should have done? What would you have done?

e. Janet's mother and father were away from home. A car stopped in front of the house and some strangers got out and came to the door. They introduced themselves as old friends of the family whom Janet had often heard about but had never met. It was a cold day and they were very weary after a long journey. What do you think Janet should have done? Tell exactly what you would have done.

14. This is the logical time to talk with children of all grade levels about their report cards and their responsibility to do the best schoolwork of which they are capable. Encourage each child to tell how his parents react to his grades. If the children feel free to express themselves, you will probably find that some parents are indifferent to the reports, some never feel that a child's

best effort is quite good enough, some put entirely too much pressure on the child to make high grades at any cost, and some offer such attractive bribes that the child loses sight of the value of what he is learning. Parents often exact promises from a child that he will make better marks next time. If the difficulty which caused the low marks in the first place is not removed, the child can probably do no better and he will feel that he has failed to keep his bargain. For such a child, report cards are a constant source of fear, anxiety, and unhappiness. Conferences with the parents may result in a better understanding of the problem by both parents and teacher.

15. A child's progress in the matter of assuming responsibility may be recorded by means of some such device as the *Winnetka Scale for Rating School Behavior and Attitudes,* by Dorothy Van Alstyne and the Winnetka Public School Faculty, Winnetka Educational Press, Winnetka, Ill., 1937. This scale permits the teacher to rate behavior of children from nursery school through sixth grade in terms of classroom situations. It provides for two ratings a year over a three-year period and for a graph of each child's level of cooperation, social consciousness, emotional security, leadership, and responsibility at the end of each grade.

16. Even children in the intermediate grades are not too young to begin to carry on their meetings according to simplified parliamentary procedure. If you allow them to organize the class, see to it that the officers have a chance to function and are not simply figureheads. Explain the relationship of committee chairmen and committee members and have some committees appointed with definite duties to perform.

Help the children to understand that sometimes they will be leaders and sometimes they will be followers and that it is important that they learn to be equally dependable in either role. Talk with them about the obligations of class officers and about the responsibility of voting for those persons who show initiative and are willing to work rather than for the ones who are good looking or good talkers. It should be understood that when the teacher is out of the room for any reason, it will be the duty of the president or the vice-president to assume the leadership of the class.

17. Some excellent motion pictures are available for use with this lesson. The following are suggested:

Am I Trustworthy? (for primary and intermediate grades), 16 mm., sound, 10 min., Coronet Films, Chicago, 1950. This film shows that students who practice trustworthiness in the little things of everyday life, such as returning borrowed articles, keeping promises, and doing assigned tasks well, can also be trusted with more important matters.

Beginning Responsibility: Taking Care of Things (for preschool and primary grades), 16 mm., sound, 10 min., Coronet Films, Chicago, 1951. This film explains how and why children should care for their possessions at home and at school. It shows the importance of having definite places to keep things, of putting articles back where they belong, of cleaning up after play time, and storing and handling things properly to prevent accidents or damage.

Developing Responsibility (for primary, intermediate, and junior high school), 16 mm., sound, 10 min., Coronet Films, Chicago, 1948. This story of a boy and a dog teaches that although responsibilities often entail hard work, difficult decisions, and missing out on some fun, the rewards more than compensate.

How to Cooperate (for intermediate grades and junior high school), 16 mm., sound, 10 min., Coronet Films, Chicago, 1950. From this film students learn what cooperation is, the value to be derived from it, and some of the situations in which cooperation is most necessary.

Parliamentary Procedures in Action (for intermediate, junior, and senior high school), 16 mm., sound, 13½ min., Coronet Films, Chicago, 1941. This film shows a high school club whose members employ the proper procedures for seconding motions, amending motions, calling for a division of the house, rising to a point of order, tabling a motion, and all the other commonly used parliamentary forms.

Ways to Good Habits (for primary, intermediate, and junior high school), 16 mm., sound, 10 min., Coronet Films, Chicago, 1950. Through real, clearly understandable situations this film demonstrates how to substitute good habits for bad ones and motivates students to build good habits of their own.

The following filmstrips from the Child Cooperation and Self-discipline Series, Simmel-Meservey, Inc., Beverly Hills, Calif., 1949, are also suggested:

Jimmy Wouldn't Listen (for primary grades). Jimmy would not put things in their places and, as a result, the picture which he had drawn and which should have been on display fell to the floor and was walked on.

The New Book (for primary grades). A new book speaks to the children about their habits in caring for books.

Schoolground Discoverer (for primary and intermediate grades). Animated pictures of a school building, trash cans, etc., emphasize the importance of keeping the schoolgrounds clean.

BIBLIOGRAPHY

BAILARD, VIRGINIA, and HARRY C. McKOWN: *So You Were Elected!* McGraw-Hill Book Company, Inc., New York, 1946.

BENEDICT, AGNES E., and ADELE FRANKLIN: *The Happy Home,* Appleton-Century-Crofts, Inc., New York, 1949, Chap. 6.

BULLIS, H. EDMUND, and EMILY E. O'MALLEY: *Human Relations in the Classroom,* The Delaware State Society for Mental Hygiene, Wilmington, Del., 1947, Course 1, pp. 127–130.

OTTO, HENRY J.: *Principles of Elementary Education,* Rinehart & Company, Inc., New York, 1949, Chap. 8.

Spiritual Values in the Elementary School, Twenty-sixth Yearbook, Department of Elementary School Principals, National Education Association, Washington, D.C., 1947, Chap. II.

CHAPTER 17

Encouraging Fair Play

Aims of This Lesson:

To create a spirit of fair play that will carry over into every aspect of daily living.

To give special attention to those children who fail to respond to the accepted standards of good sportsmanship.

To encourage an attitude of tolerance for beliefs and practices that are different from one's own.

A great deal is said and done to promote good sportsmanship on the playground. In games and athletic contests of all kinds children are taught to abide by the rules, to treat their opponents with courtesy, to be good team workers, to win without boasting, and to lose without grumbling. Even the youngest children are constantly reminded to share and to take turns in their play. Probably because there are a greater number of obvious opportunities for a give-and-take relationship in the physical-education program than in the classroom, youngsters sometimes come to regard fair play as belonging exclusively in the realm of sports.

Sharing a ball and taking turns in line are not the beginning and the end of fair play. It is equally important that children learn to practice fairness in every area of their daily living. They need to observe rules of good sportsmanship in all their dealings with parents, teachers, and friends at home, in the neighborhood, and in the classroom.

Children who have grown up in sheltered homes where there have been few contacts with others of their own age must first learn the difficult lesson of becoming socially adjusted when they enter school. They gradually come to realize that belonging to a group involves more than cooperative play. It

211

means complying with regulations, respecting the rights of others, and even doing some things that one does not like to do. The standards of fair play demand that boys and girls refrain from taking unjust advantages of each other, destroying the work of others, using more than their share of materials, interrupting those who are reciting, preventing classmates from studying by enticing them to play, and monopolizing the teacher's time and attention by making constant unnecessary pleas for help. It is just as necessary that children learn to share ideas and interesting information as that they share playground equipment. The pupil who contributes to a school project by bringing an appropriate picture, a pertinent clipping, or other related material for the entire group to use is sharing in the finest way.

As children grow older they should realize that it is a part of fair play to listen thoughtfully to other persons, to weigh their opinions, and to respect their viewpoints even if they cannot agree. Good sportsmanship demands that they accept and abide by the consensus of the group when it is for the good of all. It also demands that they neither shirk their share of a group responsibility nor try to become the self-appointed directors of every class project. Youngsters who observe the rules of fair play are willing to acknowledge that they are at least partially at fault without trying to shift the blame to others when things go wrong. They are quick to recognize ability in their classmates and to praise them for their achievements.

Simply by living and working with other children under the guidance of an intelligent teacher most boys and girls grasp the idea that fair play is essential. Sometimes, however, a child does not accept the standards of the group but continues to want whatever others have, to strive for all the teacher's attention, to refuse any help from his classmates, or to prefer always to work alone. Such a child is usually expressing some emotional lack in his life. Perhaps he needs more opportunities to feel important, more reassurance and affection, more chances to vent his aggressive feelings, or less pressure and tension from some source. As in all cases of maladjustment, the teacher should talk with the child and with his parents and observe him closely in order to discover the cause of his feelings. If it is impossible to find the underlying reason for his poor sportsmanship or to improve the quality of his relationships, professional help should be called in.

A child who seems to feel that he must excel at any cost in some particular field may be unconsciously driven by his jealousy of a brother or sister who always surpasses him in some way. One who consistently cheats in order to get high grades and to win at games may have been made to feel that it is a disgrace to be the loser in any form of competition. Parents and teachers sometimes set unattainable goals for children and then try to force them to reach these goals. In an effort to conform, the children may lie, cheat, or become emotionally upset.

A pupil who gets low marks in school may feel compelled to defend himself by shifting the blame to the teacher, the grading system, or some other person, condition, or circumstance. He will learn to shoulder his own responsibility more quickly if adults will accept his shortcomings without scolding and nagging, will praise him for any real effort or accomplishment, and will encourage him to try again.

Although it is good for children to acquire the habit of success, it is also necessary for them to be fortified against the time when they will inevitably meet failure. Some adults endeavor to shield young children from all disappointments and hardships. They make it possible for them to win every game they play and to get whatever they want without effort. False successes only make a child lose interest and take away his incentive to improve his game and to increase his skill. Occasional failures help him to develop persistence and to learn how to accept defeat without becoming hopelessly discouraged.

It is not good for a child either to win or to lose consistently. The one who always does outstanding scholastic work must be handled in such a way that he will not become an intellectual snob who is disliked by his associates. On the other hand, the unfortunate child who is seldom able to gain any sort of recognition must be prevented from acquiring a painful sense of inferiority or an intense distaste for school, for either is apt to manifest itself in daydreaming, cheating, truancy, or some other form of maladjustment. For the sake of good mental health, each child must feel that none of his classmates can excel in everything and that he can do at least some things as well as or better than they.

A visitor to a kindergarten room saw a five-year-old boy seated at the piano playing the accompaniment for a song which the others were singing. A little boy near the door whispered, "Doesn't Danny play well? He made up the music, but the rest of us made up the words to the song." After the visitor had complimented the children on the lovely song, the group suggested that Danny play more of his original compositions and that he read from the morning newspaper. This gifted child had learned to read well before entering school and the other children were very proud of his accomplishment. He was quick to say, however, that he could not skip, dance, draw, or throw balls nearly so well as the other boys and girls. The teacher of this group had taught them to recognize the talents of the superior child in their midst but she had also taught him to realize his limitations and to appreciate the abilities of his classmates. With less intelligent handling, this only child of a well-do-do family might have developed a smugness which would have made him a social outcast.

Children would more readily learn to be fair and square in all aspects of their daily living if adults would set them a better example. Too often the things that parents and teachers say are inconsistent with what they do. It is useless for them to preach the doctrine of fair play if they themselves cheat at games, take unfair advantages in business dealings, spread unkind rumors, beg off on committee appointments, and fail to do their share of the work in church, club, and community projects.

Boys and girls quickly adopt their parents' prejudices and intolerant feelings. Among the very young there are no problems of bigotry and hatred. They rate each other on their merits as individuals and not as members of a race, a nation, or a group. They would continue to be fair-minded if they did not learn from adults to feel hostile toward new ideas, strange religious sects, foreigners, or people who live in different sections of town. Since children usually have no real foundations for their prejudices, they can be easily influenced by a teacher who is sympathetic and considerate in her attitude toward all people.

Naturally, the approach used in the teaching of tolerance will depend to some extent upon the pattern of segregation in the local school system, the types of minority groups in the community, and the general attitude toward these groups. But there must be more than an occasional social studies lesson on our neighbors in other lands or a discussion of the cultural contributions of different nationalities. The principles of fair play require that teachers and pupils recognize the brotherhood of all persons, including those on their own streets and in their own school.

Teachers can most effectively free their pupils from prejudice by giving them accurate information. If there appears to be an intolerant attitude toward a particular race or religion, a special effort should be made to let the children meet a member of the race or the religious sect and learn about his beliefs and customs firsthand. Pupils should be encouraged to get the opinions of parents, neighbors, and friends, and to exchange ideas with their classmates. They should read and make observations until they are able to clarify their thinking and to feel quite sure that they are expressing their own ideas and not the thoughts that have been put into their minds by others.

In order to teach children to practice fair play in all the aspects of daily living, it is necessary to give them a working knowledge of the Golden Rule. They will not be likely to take an unfair advantage of another person if they have learned to understand his viewpoint, to be sensitive to his feelings, and to accord him the same treatment that they would like for themselves.

ACTIVITIES SUGGESTED

The needs of your class will determine the particular phase of fair play which should receive the major emphasis. Use only those activities which will be likely to create the desired feelings and attitudes. Be sure to make any changes which will render the suggested activities more appropriate.

1. Every child likes to be known as a good sport. Help the group to formulate their own code of sportsmanship. This code will probably include the thoughts that a good sport always keeps the rules, plays for the fun of the game and the success of the team rather than for his own glory, treats his opponents with courtesy, congratulates the winner or thanks the loser for giving him a good game, and abides by the decisions of the referees.

2. Discuss with the class some of the ways in which boys and girls may be good sports in other ways than at play. Ask them to tell how they think a good sport would react in each of the following situations:

   a. The teacher is unexpectedly called to the telephone and no one is left in charge of the class.
   b. A new substitute teacher has charge of your class for a day.
   c. A girl hopes to be chosen for the leading part in a play, but her friend is chosen instead.
   d. A boy who draws very well had hoped to be placed on the committee to make posters for an exhibit but instead he is given the job of greeting guests as they arrive.
   e. A pupil misbehaves in class and the teacher, thinking that the offender is a different child, reprimands the wrong one.
   f. A timid pupil who reads very poorly makes some rather ridiculous errors when reading a paragraph before the class.
   g. An unpopular girl who is always very bossy and disagreeable with her classmates is asked to lead a group discussion.
   h. Some of the younger children are giving an assembly program. The production is very juvenile and the speakers cannot be heard in the rear of the auditorium.

i. A committee has worked hard planning a class party but somehow the games they have arranged do not seem to interest the group.

j. A boy wants a new bicycle and his sister wants a new party dress. The parents cannot afford to buy both of these items at the same time.

k. While at a concert two school children keep thinking of things they would like to whisper to each other.

3. Ask the children to mention some striking examples of good and of poor sportsmanship which they have observed at home, at school, on the street, and on the playground. Let them feel free to include the actions of parents, teachers, and neighbors in these stories.

4. Tell the children some true stories of good and of poor sportsmanship which you have witnessed in the course of your own teaching.

5. Point out opportunities for fair play in the classroom until the younger children are conscious of the fairness of being responsible for the condition of their own materials and work space, of putting away their crayons, papers, tools, and blocks, of washing their paste sticks and paintbrushes, of picking up scraps from the floor, of sweeping up the sand, and of replacing disarranged furniture. Help them to feel that it is a matter of good sportsmanship to help the others after they have completed their own work, but that it is unfair to dawdle purposely in order to have someone else do all the work. Make a special point of praising the children for any evidences of fair play.

6. In some kindergarten and primary classes it is the custom for children to share their birthday parties by bringing to school cake, ice cream, candy, and favors for all the members of the class. Parents of children who are not having birthdays sometimes bring cookies, balloons, or other small gifts for each member of the group. The children who are unable to make such gestures need to realize that there are many valuable contributions which they can offer. Help all the pupils to think of some of the delightful things which they may share with their classmates. Examples:

A book from home or the public library
A story learned out of school
An imaginary story
Interesting experiences
Information about mechanical things
Information about nature

Magazine pictures

Newspaper clippings

Fish, turtle, bunny, flowers, rocks, unusual leaves, or other items
  brought from home

7. Games of sharing may be built around some of the toys or items of
equipment which are especially popular. A large rocking horse, the most
coveted object in one kindergarten room, was a constant source of wran-
gling until the teacher suggested that one child "ride around the block" while
the others waited their turns at the "stable." The horse was no longer
thought of as something to squabble over but as the center of an exciting
game.

8. Children of the primary and intermediate grades will enjoy reading
Munro Leaf's *Fair Play*, published by Frederick A. Stokes Company, New
York, 1939. It explains how our government is founded on respect for the
rights of individual citizens and how laws are intended to protect all of
us. It presents the idea that a part of a child's training for citizenship comes
from learning such practices of fair play as taking turns on playground
equipment, standing in line at a ticket office, obeying the rules in games,
walking on the right side of the sidewalk, and asking a friend's permission
before using his baseball bat.

9. Find out whether pupils in your class hold any feelings of enmity
toward individuals or groups who may differ from them in beliefs or
customs. Encourage an open and frank discussion of the feelings. By considering the characteristics which Catholics, Protestants, Christians, Jews,
Negroes, Caucasians, or any other majority or minority groups have in
common with other peoples, it will be found that they are all more similar
than different.

If a child says that he does not like foreigners, try to get him to give a
real reason for his feeling. Ask him if his parents have the same dislike. If
he says that he does not like a certain teacher who has not yet taught him,
ask if it is because some other child has influenced him. By skillfully leading the discussion, you can get children to see for themselves how often they
have formed definite opinions without knowing the facts. Discuss various
common prejudices, explaining that they are simply unreasonable objections
to something about which a person is not well enough informed to pass
judgment.

10. Ask children of the upper grades to mention some prejudices of their parents and suggest that they find out from their mothers and fathers the real reasons for their objections, if any, to certain political parties, religious sects, capitalists, their bosses, or other persons or organizations. In order to get frank answers and to avoid embarrassment, the prejudices and possible reasons may be written anonymously and discussed later.

11. Grasp every opportunity to help children learn more about people of other races, nationalities, and creeds than their own. Invite a foreigner to speak to the group and to show articles of interest from his country. Take representatives of the class to see a program or an exhibit or to visit a school or a church of a people who are different from themselves. If possible, plan to let a committee from your class witness the naturalization of a group of foreigners. Be sure that any such activities are undertaken in a spirit of friendship and not merely as a matter of curiosity.

12. Ask each child to watch for evidences of intolerance in the actions of persons on the street, in stores, in busses, parks, trains, restaurants, hotels, and other public places, and to report them to the class. Simply by talking about them the children will become conscious of the injustice of some commonly accepted practices.

13. Allow the pupils to use their own ideas in planning plays, pageants, stories, poems, posters, drawings, or slogans which will express their feelings about fair play, tolerance, and brotherhood.

14. If there are members of a misunderstood or ill-treated minority group in your class, you may be able to point out things in their inheritance of which they should be proud and to call attention to some of the things which their people do especially well. In quiet talks with these children find out how they are treated by their classmates and plan ways of making them more acceptable to the boys and girls who are potential friends.

15. The following films are suggested for use with this lesson:

> *Let's Play Fair* (for primary, intermediate, junior high school), 16 mm., sound, 10 min., Coronet Films, Chicago, 1949. Two brothers discover that sharing, taking turns, obeying rules, respecting the property of others, and being considerate of the feelings of others are some of the basic elements of fair play.
>
> *Good Sportsmanship* (for intermediate and junior high school), 16 mm., sound, 10 min., Coronet Films, Chicago, 1950. Through lively

story situations, this film clearly demonstrates the importance of sportsmanship in all phases of daily living.

Let's Share with Others (for primary grades), 16 mm., sound, 10 min., Coronet Films, Chicago, 1950. Various examples are shown in this film to demonstrate to children the new values and pleasures that come with sharing.

The Greenie (for elementary, junior and senior high school), 16 mm., sound, 11 min., Teaching Film Custodians, Inc., New York, 1942. As a group of boys get to know and understand a Polish refugee lad, they overcome their initial prejudice and ridicule, and accord him a place in their circle. (The films of Teaching Film Custodians, Inc., are intended for educational use only and are provided on a long-term lease basis.)

The House I Live In (for elementary, junior and senior high school), 16 mm., sound, 11 min., Young America Films, Inc., New York, 1947. This film stars Frank Sinatra in a plea for racial and religious tolerance as he talks to a group of boys who thoughtlessly have started to persecute a boy of another religious group.

The following filmstrips are also suggested:

Share the Sandpile, Share the Ball, Working Together (for primary grades), Child Cooperation and Self-discipline Series, Simmel-Meservey, Inc., Beverly Hills, Calif., 1949.

These filmstrips, made in black and white outline, emphasize the importance of taking turns, sharing, and playing together. The third one illustrates cooperation by showing the contributions various children make in building a playhouse.

Little Cottontail Series (for primary grades), colored, Stillfilm, Inc., Hollywood, Calif., 1950 (first series), 1951 (second series).

The first series is made up of eight filmstrips entitled Kindness, Consideration, Sharing, Honesty, Thoughtfulness, Fair Play, Thankfulness, and Acceptance. It is the story of a little lost cottontail who, although he was different, was befriended by a family of jack rabbits. After a succession of experiences in learning to share and to cooperate, the little cottontail was finally accepted as a real member of the family.

The second series is composed of filmstrips on Helpfulness, Promptness, Willingness, Preparedness, Encouragement, Protectiveness, Cleanliness, and

220 · ELEMENTARY SCHOOL GUIDANCE

Neighborliness. These stories illustrate the right adjustments to be made to school and community play groups.

BIBLIOGRAPHY

BEAUMONT, HENRY, and FREEMAN GLENN MACOMBER: *Psychological Factors in Education*, McGraw-Hill Book Company, Inc., New York, 1949, Chaps. V, XI.

BULLIS, H. EDMUND: *Human Relations in the Classroom*, The Delaware State Society for Mental Hygiene, Wilmington, Del., 1948, Course II, pp. 107–112.

———— and EMILY E. O'MALLEY: *Human Relations in the Classroom*, The Delaware State Society for Mental Hygiene, Wilmington, Del., 1947, Course I, pp. 135–139.

GESELL, ARNOLD, and FRANCES L. ILG: *The Child from Five to Ten*, Harper & Brothers, New York, 1946, Chaps. 16, 19.

KILPATRICK, WILLIAM HEARD, and WILLIAM VAN TIL: *Intercultural Attitudes in the Making*, Harper & Brothers, New York, 1947.

NEUGARTEN, BERNICE L., and PAUL J. MISNER: *Getting Along in School*, Science Research Associates, Inc., Chicago, 1951. Pamphlet.

CHAPTER 18

Cultivating Good Manners

Aims of This Lesson:

To show that courtesy is simply another way of expressing friendliness and thoughtfulness.

To set a continuous example of mannerliness by being as polite to the boys and girls as to adults.

To explain and provide practice in the use of some of the social customs of our time.

It is generally agreed that the best time to start teaching a child good manners is when he is a toddler. Many preschool children, however, get very little home training in social conduct. Those who have learned all the niceties that young children can be expected to practice often drop them when they start to school and get the impression from the remarks of the gang that acts of courtesy label them as sissies. Whether or not the task of teaching good manners has been well started at home, a large part of the job still remains to be done by the school.

A child naturally behaves as he has learned to behave by observing others. No amount of drilling him in the accepted rules of etiquette is as effective as the eaxmples which he sees in his everyday living. Like a mirror, he reflects the courtesy and consideration or the boorishness and thoughtlessness of the adults around him. It is small wonder that children push and shove in line when they have seen their elders do the same thing. They are sometimes disrespectful to older persons because they have heard unkind remarks at home about grandparents and other aged relatives. Many children are altogether unskilled in the matter of making introductions because their parents never bother to introduce them to their friends. They frequently ask

221

too many personal and improper questions as a result of hearing their inquisitive mothers subject others to persistent questioning.

Boys and girls are confused by double standards. They do not understand a code that requires them to put on company manners only on certain occasions and allows them to be as rude and uncouth as they please at other times. They wonder at the inconsistency of parents and teachers who do not practice the manners they preach. They rebel at the idea that grownups are so much more considerate of other adults than they are of children. A mother may gush over a bouquet brought to her by a neighbor but scold and show extreme annoyance if her own child brings into the house a handful of short-stemmed flowers plucked from the garden. Parents are sometimes rude to the neighborhood children who come to play but they expect their youngsters to be models of politeness when older persons come to call. The father who stops on the street and chats for half an hour with an acquaintance while his child stands waiting may be very impatient if the boy wants to pause and talk for a minute with a young friend of his own. Mothers who issue commands with a brusque "Come here" or "Bring me that" often require that all requests to them be made in a polite, solicitous manner.

Teachers are sometimes guilty of the same type of discourtesy. They interrupt when a child is speaking; they cut him short in the middle of a story; they walk away and leave him still talking; or they brush him off by telling him to run along because they are busy. They read over a child's shoulder and use the pencils and erasers on his desk without asking his leave although they never allow children to take such liberties with their own possessions. They humiliate youngsters by publicly calling attention to their unpleasant mannerisms. They wound their pride by scolding them for spilling paint or turning over a vase of flowers. Instead of correcting children in public, it is much more considerate to wait and speak to them at a later time about ways of avoiding a repetition of the offense. Teachers and pupils would profit by having the same understanding as the members of one family who agreed among themselves that, no matter what the circumstances might be, they would never embarrass each other in the presence of company.

It does not make sense to children when they are drilled on the importance of consideration for others and are, in turn, treated as if they had no feelings whatsoever. Youngsters are even more sensitive than adults. Although they may not say anything when they are hurt, their resentment is sure to show in their actions at some later time. In the long run, children give back the same treatment which they receive. They respond much more favorably to a person who respects their feelings and who treats them with the same courtesy that would be accorded an adult in a similar situation.

Because they have so often seen politeness put on and taken off like a garment, many children have come to consider it a sham. They are not interested in learning a set of conventions just for the sake of acquiring a veneer that will please their elders. One small boy expressed a common feeling of many of his contemporaries when he said, "Who made all these rules anyway? And what right did they have to decide what is proper for me to do?"

Some of the details of courtesy will be learned and practiced more willingly if they are presented as ways of showing friendliness, thoughtfulness, and consideration for the feelings of others rather than as arbitrary requirements of the adult world. Although boys and girls may feel that much of our code of proper behavior is unnecessary, they can understand that good manners often help to make and hold friendships and to smooth out difficult situations. They are quick to see the element of fair play in waiting their turn when others are ahead of them, in giving a seat to an older person, in being prompt for meals, and in being careful not to interrupt when another person is talking. They can understand that good table manners are desirable because it is more pleasant to eat with persons who are careful about their manners than with those who drink noisily, bolt their food, or chew with their mouths open.

Many a child comes to realize the value of courtesy when he sees a lack of good manners cause hurt feelings and loss of friends. He knows that it is natural for a person to resent having his feet stepped on, his lunch tray knocked out of his hands, or his ink spilled if it is done intentionally. To be sure, there is no way of knowing that a mishap is accidental unless the offender takes the trouble to stop and say that he is sorry. The magic words "Excuse me," "I am sorry," "Thank you," and "Please" relieve many awkward situations and make everyday living much more pleasant.

All children should be taught some of the basic rules of behavior which will make life easier and happier for them. But since common usage often causes accepted practices to become outmoded within a few years, it is not necessary to burden youngsters with a great many confusing details of etiquette. It is far better to create in them an attitude of thoughtfulness and consideration for the rights and feelings of others.

Parents and teachers sometimes become discouraged. After all their efforts to teach boys and girls civilized customs, they see them gobble their food, whoop through the halls, slam doors, and yell to each other in the most discourteous manner. These are likely to be only symptoms of one of the stages through which young people pass in the process of growing up. To them, noise and commotion are necessary to having fun. But this does not mean that all training has been in vain. If good manners have been a part of a child's way of living, he will not lose them even though he lays them aside for a while. When he reaches adolescence and begins to want to be attractive to the opposite sex, he will be glad that he knows some of the rules. Nothing gives a young person more self-confidence than a working knowledge of social conventions.

Manners must be taught. But the teaching must be done in such a way that children will experience the joy of being able to please others and the satisfaction of knowing how to act in any social situation. No amount of lecturing, nagging, scolding, shaming, or punishing will ever make them genuinely courteous.

ACTIVITIES SUGGESTED

Most teachers are constantly reminding and drilling their pupils on the little niceties of social behavior. Nevertheless, it is sometimes advisable to plan a series of lessons in which special emphasis is given to the matter of good manners. Such lessons are usually more effective if they are a part of a school-wide campaign for courtesy.

The approach used and the particular methods employed will naturally depend upon the needs of the group. The amount of time spent on the various phases of courtesy will be determined by the age level and the home backgrounds of the pupils. By talking with the children about their ideas of good and bad manners and by observing the group carefully, you can readily decide which behavior problems most need to be stressed. It is a good plan to keep a notebook and make entries as you notice types of conduct which might be helped through group work.

The suggestions given below are intended merely as a guide. In so far as possible, encourage the children to propose activities and to work out details for the lessons.

1. Try to arouse interest by creating an attractive setting for these lessons. Have the pupils make posters or bulletin-board displays using magazine pictures illustrating good manners at home, at school, on the street, in stores, on busses, and in church. Write on the blackboard each day some brief,

catchy quotations or reminders to be friendly and thoughtful. See that several good children's books on manners are available to the pupils.

2. Introduce this project by talking with the children about the importance of good manners from the standpoint of making themselves more likable, of being more comfortable in the company of other persons who know the rules, and of making other people feel happy and at ease. Help them to formulate some simple, usable rules for their own behavior.

3. Provide a box in which children are encouraged to deposit notes concerning any school behavior problems which they think need attention. Anonymous questions regarding proper manners for certain occasions may also be asked. The box should be opened periodically so that the questions can be read and discussed by the group.

4. Have the children make parallel lists of proper and improper conduct in the school corridors, the assembly, the lunchroom, and the school office. From the combined ideas of the group, a list of accepted school manners may be made up, attractively lettered, and placed in a conspicuous place in the room as a constant reminder.

5. Cartoons may be drawn in pairs and entitled, "Do This—Not This," using stick figures to show the desirable and the undesirable behavior in everyday situations. In this way youngsters may express their opinions of classmates who put chewing gum in the drinking fountains, drop papers on the lunchroom floor, bump into people in the halls, annoy others on the school bus, and whistle, shout, or run in the halls.

6. At the close of each day a few minutes may be set aside when the children are asked to mention any outstanding examples of courtesy which they have observed during the day. They should be told to take particular notice of thoughtful actions in the lunchroom, in the halls, and on the playground.

7. Gather the group around in a circle and hold an informal discussion concerning the examples of good and bad manners which they have noticed on the street, in busses, in stores, in church, and in places of amusement. Stress the unfairness of such practices as whispering at a concert and preventing others from enjoying the music, throwing candy and chewing-gum papers on the floor in public buildings, and distracting the driver by unnecessary boisterousness on a bus.

8. Younger children may mention all the different occasions when they should say "Please," "Thank you," "Pardon me," "I am sorry," and "May I?" In groups of two or three let them act out simple situations in which these terms are used.

9. Timid children who do not like to face an audience may participate in shadow plays in which they make silhouettes by standing behind a sheet with a light back of them. In this way they may demonstrate correct procedure in various social situations. A reader may explain the acts as they are presented, or the children in the audience may be asked to guess the phase of good manners that is being portrayed, as they would do in a game of charades.

10. Boys and girls who like to create may make a television program on some phase of good manners and show it to the class. They are sure to think of ingenious ways of turning a box into a television set and of making the pictures on long strips of paper that can be unrolled behind an opening in the box. Other children may take the speaking parts and make the sound effects.

11. As this lesson is developed a great many possibilities for dramatizations may occur to both teacher and pupils. Although tact should be exercised in every case, it is well to let the aggressive, attention-getting children, as well as the crude and ill-mannered ones, have numerous opportunities to take active parts. This will allow them to gain legitimate attention and also to observe the attitude of the group toward rudeness.

12. Tell the class a story of real courtesy which does not have to do with any superficial rules of etiquette but with feelings of genuine kindness for another person.

Some of the pupils may be able to tell of personal experiences when they were made happy or comfortable by the kind or thoughtful deed of some other child.

13. Discuss some of the details of good table manners. Emphasize the importance of being prompt for meals, of keeping elbows off the table, of waiting to start eating until the older people at the table have begun, of eating quietly and slowly, and of talking only of pleasant things while at the table. Find out if all the children are familiar with the rules concerning the use of napkins and silver, the passing of dishes, and the proper way to manage soup, bread, butter, and other foods.

Give a demonstration of the correct way to be seated at the table, to use the knife and fork, to eat various common foods, and to leave the table. Then permit the children to practice in groups of two or more at the front of the room while the others observe and offer comments as each demonstration is completed.

14. Give some instruction in simple table settings for family meals. Each day for a period of time an attractive arrangement may be made by a different group of children and left on a small table where all may have a chance to see it.

15. Plan a skit showing a family meal in which some of the children display perfect table etiquette and some of them, faulty manners. This is always more effective when real food is served. It should be supervised and practiced in advance so that points which will be especially helpful to members of the particular group may be stressed. While the skit is being presented, the children in the audience may try to detect all the examples of good and bad table manners. Allow ample time for discussion at the conclusion of the activity.

16. Because of the many occasions when it is necessary for them to introduce their young friends to each other, their teacher to their parents, and the parents of their friends to their own parents, children should be taught some simple, easy rules for making introductions. They will feel more at ease if they are sure about when to make introductions, how to acknowledge them, when to stand, and when to shake hands. This complicated matter can be simplified by reminding children to mention first the older, the more important, or the more respected person and to use the easy form of "Mrs. Long, this is Jack Short." It may help to give a few definite rules for remembering which name to call first in making introductions. Example:

First	Last
Adult	Child
Woman	Man
Girl	Boy
Older woman	Younger woman
Older man	Younger man
Married woman	Unmarried woman

Let the pupils plan and dramatize various situations in which it is necessary for young people to make introductions. Ease and self-confidence will come only through practice.

228 ELEMENTARY SCHOOL GUIDANCE

17. Explain how important it is for all boys and girls to know how to use the telephone correctly. Emphasize such points as speaking pleasantly and distinctly, answering by giving one's name or telephone number, and having a pad and pencil convenient for taking notes. Let the pupils carry on some imaginary telephone conversations, allowing different ones to take the parts of the person making the call, the switchboard operator, and the person answering the call. Examples:

 a. Call your mother and ask if you may stay after school and practice a play.
 b. Order a taxicab to come to your home, giving your name and address and the time when the cab will be needed.
 c. Call the grocery store and give an order.
 d. Call a classmate and ask him to explain to the teacher that you are ill and would like to have your homework assignments.

18. Using as a basis the information which you have presented in these lessons, give an objective test on manners. The children themselves may like to suggest questions for the test. Examples (to be answered "True" or "False"):

———— Boys should always stand when being introduced.

———— Forks are placed at the right side of the dinner plate.

———— A whole slice of bread should always be buttered at one time.

———— Boys and girls are expected to open doors for mothers, teachers, and other ladies.

19. Frank Luther's recording, *Manners Can Be Fun,* Decca Records, Inc., New York, can be used to make this lesson on good manners more meaningful for younger children. This record is based on Munro Leaf's clever little book, *Manners Can Be Fun,* published by Frederick A. Stokes Company, Philadelphia, 1936.

20. The use of motion pictures and filmstrips will encourage discussion and impress upon the children some of the fundamentals which you wish to teach. The following are suggested:

Everyday Courtesy (for intermediate grades and junior high school), 16 mm., sound, 10 min., Coronet Films, Chicago, 1948. This film shows a school exhibit of the pupils' work on courtesy. It deals with written invitations, acceptances, regrets, proper introductions, telephone manners, and the use of polite phrases in everyday situations.

Good Table Manners (for intermediate grades and junior high school), 16 mm., sound, 10 min., Coronet Films, Chicago, 1951. This film stresses the point that good table manners depend primarily upon attitude. It shows a fourteen-year-old boy brought face-to-face with himself as a young man of twenty-one entering an adult world in which he is constantly concerned with making a good impression.

Parties Are Fun (for primary and intermediate grades), 16 mm., sound, 10 min., Coronet Films, Chicago, 1950. This film gives an understanding of the work involved in planning and preparing for a party and offers guidance in accepted standards for party behavior among students of the lower grades.

The following filmstrips are also recommended:

Conduct and Behavior Series (for intermediate grades), colored, 27 frames in each filmstrip, Curriculum Films, New York, 1950. This series includes these titles:

1. *In School* shows a normal class in which the children are neat, quiet, and orderly when the teacher is out of the room, when there is a visitor, during morning milk time, and while passing through the halls.
2. *On the Playground* shows how children observe the rules of safety, share the playground equipment, and play fair.
3. *On the Street* depicts the consideration of a boy for his small sister, his mother, a blind man, and a woman with many packages.
4. *At Home* pictures two children helping their mother keep the home clean and neat, taking care of their own clothes and toys, showing consideration for the baby, and being careful not to disturb their father when he is busy.
5. *Visiting Friends* introduces the rudiments of polite behavior for both guests and hosts.
6. *Travelling* illustrates politeness and consideration on train and bus trips.
7. *Shopping* demonstrates courtesy and consideration when shopping in a clothing store, fruit store, and candy store.
8. *In Public Buildings* shows thougthfulness and respect for property in the library, the museum, and the theater.
9. *The Picnic* portrays a typical family picnic where all three children help with the preparation, cooking, and cleaning up, observe the proper safety precautions, and show due consideration for others.

10. *Responsibility* pictures the two children of the series taking care of their own appearance and possessions, both in school and at home. It shows that they think of others and enjoy the privileges that accompany their grown-up responsibilities.

FOLLOW-UP

Whenever a children's party, a school function, or a visiting day for parents presents the need for a knowledge of correct social conduct, grasp the opportunity to rehearse the children for the occasion. Give them a chance to ask any questions that occur to them and afterward review the good manners displayed.

BIBLIOGRAPHY

ALLEN, BETTY, and MITCHELL PIRIE BRIGGS: *Behave Yourself!* J. B. Lippincott Company, Philadelphia, 1945.

BETZ, BETTY: *Your Manners Are Showing,* Grosset & Dunlap, Inc., New York, 1946.

LEAF, MUNRO: *How to Behave and Why,* J. B. Lippincott Company, Philadelphia, 1946.

McKOWN, HARRY C.: *Home Room Guidance,* McGraw-Hill Book Company, Inc., New York, 1946, pp. 407–423.

PATRI, ANGELO: *How to Help Your Child Grow Up,* Rand McNally & Company, Chicago, 1948, Chaps. 18, 21, 23, 24.

Your Ticket to Popularity: Good Manners, Girl Scouts of the U.S.A., New York, and Boy Scouts of America, New York, 1950. Pamphlet.

CHAPTER 19

Improving Family Relationships

Aims of This Lesson:

To help children understand that there are reasons for the things parents do and that every upheaval in family living does not mean a threat to their security.

To create in each child a feeling of respect and admiration for the traditions and customs peculiar to his own family.

To help boys and girls formulate some sort of satisfying philosophy which will enable them to face both major tragedies and small annoyances in their daily living.

To start children thinking in terms of the kinds of homes they would like to establish for themselves some day.

Teachers are prone to blame much of a child's behavior on his home background but to shy away from doing anything about it. They often feel that family life is a private matter which is entirely out of their jurisdiction and that they should observe a hands-off attitude concerning it. But since a child's ability to learn is greatly affected by the emotional state in which he leaves home each morning, it is not only the teacher's right but her duty to do what she can to help him to understand, overcome, or live above any surroundings which tend to hinder him.

Children continue all their lives to follow the pattern of behavior, good or bad, which they have learned in their homes. Their relations with teachers and classmates are colored by their attitudes toward parents, brothers, sisters, and other relatives. If their early experiences have been such that they have learned to like and trust people, they will be self-confident and outgoing in their contacts with others outside the home. If they have been reared in an environment which has provided a wide variety of experiences and responsibilities and the freedom to express themselves, they are more likely to be cooperative, considerate, resourceful, and self-reliant.

On the other hand, children from broken, unhappy, or otherwise unsatisfactory homes are almost certain to show the effects in undesirable relationships outside the home. If they have to fight to make a place for themselves in their own families, they are likely to be on the defensive with other persons also. If they have parents who are overcritical, dictatorial, and demanding of too great accomplishment, they are likely to feel unloved and insecure. If they are victims of overprotective mothers, they usually react by becoming either bossy and dominating or timid and withdrawing. When parents are quarrelsome, nervous, and subject to frequent outbursts of anger, it is no wonder that children learn to act the same way.

Since behavior problems so often have their roots in home problems, it would seem that the point of attack should be through the parents. But simply to diagnose a case and to place the blame on the home is not enough. It does no more good to censure and berate parents than it does to scold and punish children. There should be some systematic plan for acquainting parents with the goals of modern education, impressing upon them the importance of good relations with their children, and showing them the effect of a child's mental health on his progress in school. Some of the larger school systems have full-time consultants whose job it is to bring parents into the schools and to interpret the educational program to them. In some schools appropriate reading material is placed on racks or tables in the halls and provision is made for groups of parents to see pertinent motion pictures on emotional problems of family life. A great deal is often accomplished through lectures, panel discussions, and study groups. The most direct plan and the one which is most often effective, however, is the private interview between parent and teacher.

Even parents who are well versed in the approved methods of handling children sometimes need to be reminded of factors that make for solidarity in the family. For example, mothers and fathers sometimes lose sight of the fact that children are usually more reasonable, cooperative, and unselfish when they are treated as responsible people and allowed to share some of the problems adults have to face. Youngsters like to be consulted about the way the home is to be decorated, the food that is to be served when their guests are present, the jobs for which they are to be responsible, and the way a family holiday is to be spent. In many homes all issues are settled democratically by means of the family council.

It is difficult for some parents to realize that their children are steadily growing up and that, as a result, they need gradually to have less supervision and more opportunities to assume responsibility. Mothers and fathers who are unwilling to release their hold bit by bit force children to become defiant, belligerent, and disobedient in their unconscious effort to pull away from absolute parental control. By allowing boys and girls to have their own way in trivial matters such as following the current fads in clothing and copying the latest slang expressions, adults can expect to have greater influence when they take a firm stand on more vital issues.

Teachers can help parents to realize the importance of spending time with their children, doing interesting things with them, and helping them to feel that they have a real place in the family while they are still very young. It is only in this way that they can hope to have children continue to like and trust them, to ask their advice, and to seek their company when they reach adolescence and young adulthood. One of the best ways to ensure good parent-child relationships is by planning picnics, hunting and fishing trips, long walks, and other recreational activities and hobbies that the entire family can enjoy together. Children who have a variety of interesting things to do will not have to seek entertainment away from home or depend solely on radio, television, and motion pictures for enjoyment.

Tactful, sympathetic teachers can do much toward interpreting the emotional needs of children to their parents. Often, however, the homes that are most in need of help from the school cannot be reached by the usual means. It is difficult for mothers to come for programs or interviews when they are employed, when they feel that they are not so well dressed as the other mothers or the teachers, when there is no means of transportation, when there is illness in the family, or when there is no one with whom to leave the younger children.

Whether or not it is possible to make direct contacts with parents, much can be done to improve home relations by working with the pupils themselves. Children who feel inferior, inadequate, unloved, or neglected are in need of real help. Good homes give youngsters the satisfaction of feeling needed, important, and respected, but all homes are not good homes. In many cases the parents do not realize that an emotional need exists or they are unable to do anything about it. Unless teachers recognize the problem and undertake, in so far as possible, to solve it, it may remain unsolved.

For many children home life is full of trials. Situations which seem trivial to the outsider may be very serious to the child who is involved. A youngster whose mother has scolded him severely just before he started to school may daydream throughout the day, annoy the other children, forget to hand in his spelling paper, miss every problem in arithmetic, and pick a fight on the playground. In the back of his mind there may be the vague, gnawing thought that he is misunderstood or that his mother does not love him. More often than adults realize, children take them literally when they make such statements as, "If you disobey me again, I am going to pack my things and leave home," "When you act like that, I hate you," or "If you do not keep your promise, I shall know that you don't love me." They worry and brood over such remarks until they actually are uncertain of their place in the family's affections. Most parents love their children dearly and would be surprised to know that boys and girls ever entertain a thought to the contrary. But when a child feels that he is not wanted at home, the hurt is just as real as if it were true. A kind, sympathetic teacher who enjoys the confidence of children can sense that something is wrong and can do much to reassure such a child.

Problems that loom very large may not seem nearly so tragic when they are discussed with others. Children get a great deal of relief by being able to release pent-up emotions in private informal talks with the teacher or in open discussions with their classmates. There is a certain satisfaction in knowing that others of their own age have similar worries. By skillfully leading the discussion and doing very little of the talking herself, it is possible for the teacher to help children discover the reasons for many of their home problems.

It is not unusual for boys and girls to feel misunderstood, ill-treated, and discriminated against because they must come in off the street at an earlier hour than others in the neighborhood, because they are required to have a set time for doing their homework, because they have to go to bed sooner than they like, or because they must practice their music, run errands, or do certain chores about the home. Other common complaints among children are that their allowances are too small, that they do not enjoy as many privileges as the older children, that they do not get as much attention as the younger ones, or that they are not allowed as many clothes, toys, or movies as their friends. When such feelings are present, children often sulk, rebel, or hide their resentment. They need to experience the satisfaction that comes from talking matters over calmly with their parents, explaining their own points of view, and listening with open minds to the adult point of view. Teachers can give children of all ages the needed practice in expressing their opinions and presenting their claims intelligently. They can teach them the advantage of approaching any adult as responsible, thinking individuals, not as whining, complaining juveniles. Teachers can help children, too, to understand that most restrictions are intended to protect rather than to hurt them and that slights by parents are more often imagined than real.

Youngsters need to be reminded how their parents cared for them when they were infants, nursed them through childhood diseases, rendered first aid when they were injured, dressed them, fed them, took them to school, and were conscious of all their needs during the years when they were very young. As they grow older and are able to do more things for themselves, it is sometimes difficult for parents to realize that they are no longer help- less babies. The best way for boys and girls to earn the right to more privileges is to prove that they are reliable and dependable. Parents are usually willing to give children greater freedom when they show that they are ready for it.

It is natural for young people to want to identify themselves with their own generation by dressing, speaking, and acting exactly like others of their age. This causes constant friction in many homes where parents make a desperate struggle to hold the children to standards of their own. Children should learn to accept the fact that different families have different customs and beliefs. As members of the household, they should abide by the regula- tions and practices of the family and respect the wishes of their parents in routine matters. At the same time, however, they should be learning to think for themselves so that when they are older they will be prepared to make their own decisions. The racial, religious, economic, and social prej- udices, the false standards of value, and the fears, resentments, and antago- nisms that parents feel need not be adopted *in toto* by their children. Many of the ideals that have been instilled in youngsters since they were infants are "right" or "wrong" only in a relative sense, depending upon the incli- nations of their elders. Teachers have numerous opportunities to help boys and girls weigh the ideas and opinions of many people and to form their own conclusions without feeling any disloyalty toward their parents.

Children frequently wonder why parents behave as they do. It does no harm to explain to them that there may be psychological reasons. When father kicks the cat, shouts at the baby, or slams the door and walks out of the house, it may be that he has had a very bad day at work and that he is really getting out his bad feelings against the boss or one of his fellow workers. When mother is unusually cross and does not give the children the little attentions to which they are accustomed, it may be that she is tired, sick, or worried. Mothers and fathers are only human and sometimes they act very much as children would act under the same circumstances. They were brought up by parents who lived a good many years ago and who may have been very strict in their discipline. It is natural for them to use the same methods of child rearing that were used on them when they were young. But although they are sometimes disagreeable when things go wrong, this is no indication that they do not love their children. By studying the situation, boys and girls can usually learn to understand their parents' moods and can make it a habit to do the things that please them and to refrain from doing things that irritate them.

Children sometimes need to be reminded that home life can run more smoothly for them if they are conscious of the rights of other members of the family. Many conflicts would be avoided if each one would protect the home furnishings and the personal belongings of the others, respect their privacy, and do a fair share of the work. Monopoly of the radio, the telephone, and the bathroom, rivalry and competition between brothers and sisters, failure to be on time for meals, and other common causes of friction in the home can be relieved immeasurably by taking an objective look at them, analyzing the causes of the trouble, and trying to work out a solution that is satisfactory to all concerned.

Although family problems that are common to many children can be discussed and analyzed by the group, there are always a few difficulties that need special handling. The interested teacher can find numerous ways of giving some personal attention to children who have been reared in orphanages or foster homes, to those whose parents have recently been separated or divorced, or to those who may be feeling antagonistic toward newly acquired stepparents. She can make fewer demands of children who are becoming adjusted to a new way of living because an older relative has moved into the home, a brother or sister has married and brought a new member to live with the family, or a parent has suffered a permanent disability. When youngsters are upset by these and numerous other family problems, they often resort to daydreaming and brooding and their schoolwork suffers. They need to unburden themselves to someone outside the home. An understanding teacher is usually the one to whom they turn.

When a classmate, a teacher, or a member of a child's family is taken by death, many children are unprepared for the shock. They need teachers who will talk to them about the experience rather than try to avoid any mention of it. While young children should not be troubled with involved explanations concerning death, they need calm reassurance. Failure to answer their questions only makes them more anxious and fearful.

One young child had been told by a well-meaning old lady that death was like a long sleep, that the lifeless body was placed in a beautiful box covered with flowers, and then there was a funeral and burial. She added that people had been known to be buried alive. Unaware that this conversation had taken place, the parents of the child later became puzzled over her restlessness and inability to sleep and her teacher showed concern at her drowsiness and lack of concentration in class. Sometime later it was learned that the little girl had been forcing herself to lie awake nights in the fear that if she went to sleep she might be thought dead. Although they may not disclose the fact, many introverted, withdrawing children are troubled by thoughts of death and the hereafter.

Children are less afraid of death when they realize that it does not come to most persons until they are old and tired and their bodies are worn out and incapacitated. There are relatively few deaths among young persons who observe health and safety rules. Most boys and girls will accept the fact that all nature is in the care and under the laws of the God of the universe, that the loved one who has died is safe, and that the hurt which is felt over the parting will grow less as time goes on. When there is tragedy in a child's life, whether it be a major disappointment of some kind, the death of a pet, or the loss of a devoted member of the family, it will be easier to bear if a sympathetic teacher shares his sorrow and allows him to discuss it with her. Teachers' and parents' own beliefs and attitudes and the way in which they answer questions are extremely important. A philosophy that satisfies the adults in whom he has confidence will usually satisfy the child.

Many children are miserable because they are ashamed of their homes, their families, or their neighborhoods. They would rather appear unsociable and be left out of good times than to bear the humiliation of inviting their friends into their own homes. It is not unusual for a child to try to hide the fact that his parents are foreigners, his father is a drunkard, his little sister is mentally deficient, his aged grandmother is cranky and unreasonable, there is no bathroom in his home, or his living quarters are shabby and unattractive. For the sake of good mental health it is essential that children learn to accept their lot without shame or apology and without trying to live a lie. Adults can help them to realize that many of the material things that seem so important to them are really superficial and not half so necessary in a home as a warm, friendly, hospitable atmosphere. Although a child may be powerless to change some undesirable features of his home, he can do much to offset them by developing a pleasing personality that makes others seek him out in spite of his surroundings.

No school child is too young to start thinking about the time when he will have a home and children of his own. If his present environment is not satisfactory, at least he can look forward to making the desired improvements when he is head of his own house. Remembering that it is only through the children of today that there can be better parents of the next generation, teachers should grasp every opportunity to imbue young persons with some of the fundamental ideals of homemaking. Casual observations about the characteristics of a good mate, the personality traits that make for harmony among members of a family, and the physical aspects of a satisfactory home may carry a great deal of weight.

One eighth-grade girl was the product of an unhappy, broken home. She had been shifted from mother to father and then to grandparents and aunts. In the homes of each of her parents she had seen the younger stepchildren nagged, scolded, and pushed around. An interested teacher took this girl to live in her own home for a while in order that she might see another way of life. In wide-eyed amazement she remarked, "I never knew that a little child could be disciplined in any way except by a spanking or a slap on the face. Nobody ever spoke kindly or explained things to us as you do to your children. When I have a family of my own, I am going to give my children all the love that I wanted and failed to get when I was growing up."

Every child needs to be able to feel a special pride in his home. Some homes have very little in their favor. If, however, the teacher can help a child to ferret out some feature of which he can be proud, she will give him a great boost in morale. Children can be impressed with the significance of family customs by being asked to tell in school about their ancestry, family traditions, unique ways of celebrating birthdays, Christmas, and other special days, recreations that members of the family enjoy together, special dishes that the mother prepares, and unusual practices of the older people in the family. If a child's immediate family seems to have nothing to commend it, perhaps there is a relative, an ancestor, or a bit of history that makes him glad he belongs to a particular clan. It is important for children to realize that the greatness of members of their families may consist in the good deeds which they do in a quiet, unassuming way. The most substantial, wholesome, and worth-while families are not always the ones that are most widely known.

ACTIVITIES SUGGESTED

The information about the home background of your pupils which was obtained at the beginning of the year (Chapter 1, Activities 1, 2, 8, 11, 12) will give you an insight into the needs of your class in connection with this lesson. If the activities suggested here do not meet the requirements of your group, substitute more appropriate ones.

1. Ask each child to describe the happiest home he knows, whether it is his own or the home of a friend or acquaintance. Get him to try to analyze this home and to tell what it is that makes it outstanding. Ask what the members of this family do together for fun, what they do to make children who come to the house feel welcome, and how the various members treat each other.

2. Encourage the children to talk about the good times which they have with their own families. Ask them to enumerate some of the things that come to mind when they think about home. In answer to this question, some young people mentioned "popping corn in the evening," "singing together while Mother plays the piano," "working with Dad in our basement workshop," and "eating Sunday night supper in the living room."

3. Suggest that a poll be taken to discover the most frequent causes of parents' complaints concerning children. It will probably be found that mothers and fathers dislike the fact that children dawdle, leave their rooms in a messy, jumbled condition, scatter articles about the house and fail to put them back in their proper places, fail to take care of books, gloves, caps, and other personal belongings, and grumble about doing their share of the family chores. Combine these into one list and ask the children to plan definite ways in which they can eliminate the causes of the complaints. After a period of several weeks take the poll again and mark off the complaints that are no longer heard at home.

4. The older children may have panel discussions on such subjects as, "What tasks should school children of our age be expected to do around the house?" and "What privileges should boys and girls of our age be allowed to enjoy without the supervision of parents?" It may add to the interest and the effectiveness of these discussions if several parents are invited to participate in them along with the children.

5. Children of any grade level can discuss or dramatize various acts of courtesy and consideration which should be practiced in the home

Toward parents
Toward younger brother and sisters
Toward older brothers and sisters
Toward grandparents or other elderly persons
Toward employees in the home
Toward guests

6. As a means of helping them get rid of some of their resentments, lead a friendly, informal conversation in which all pupils are encouraged to express any grievances they may feel toward their homes or families. Endeavor to remain neutral during the discussion, being careful neither to support the children in their complaints nor to oppose them by siding with the parents. Teachers are prone to defend the views of parents partly because they feel that it is necessary and partly because adult opinions seem so much more reasonable to them. As a result, children generally come to think of teachers as adults who are in league with parents.

Group discussions may be centered around such subjects as the following:

a. The reasons for older persons sometimes having to live with relatives, the problems which this often creates, the reasons why old people see things differently than children do, and some of the things children can do to make for more pleasant relationships with grandparents, aunts, and uncles.

b. The many services which parents are constantly rendering their children, the unexpected surprises they plan, and the unselfishness they show in denying themselves in order to give to their children.

c. The reasons which parents probably have when they impose duties or restrictions that children feel are unfair.

d. The types of disciplinary measures used in the homes of individuals in the class, how the children respond to correction, and what they think about punishment.

e. The advantages or privileges accorded to older or younger brothers or sisters of members of the class, the duties required of each member of the family, and the fairness which probably exists in the distribution of these responsibilities.

f. The things about the children's homes and families of which they are especially proud, the customs they would like to copy when they have homes of their own, and any undesirable features they would like to change.

7. Try to create in all children a definite interest in their home surroundings. Talk with them about their rooms. Ask each child to tell with whom he shares his sleeping quarters, how his room is furnished, and the changes he would like to make if he could. Emphasize the importance of neatness in making a room attractive. Discuss the use of color, pictures, plants, and decorations for adding beauty. Let each child plan and make something for his own room. This may be a rack for hanging his clothes, a painted bottle or jar to serve as a flower vase, a box for holding some of his "treasures," a decorated wastebasket, or a simple magazine rack. If he does not have a room of his own, he may plan something that will make the living room more attractive or the kitchen more convenient for his mother. Those children who have lawns may extend this activity to an interest in pulling weeds, cutting grass, planting flowers, or beautifying the surroundings in some other way.

8. Talk with the group about how children sometimes feel like running away from home. If any of the pupils volunteer that they have experienced such feelings, ask them why they felt as they did, what they did about it, and the result. Explain how children who feel slighted or mistreated by their families sometimes think that, by running away, they can punish their parents or make them sorry. Tell a story to illustrate the folly of trying to solve a home problem by running away from it.

9. Have the older children write answers to questions similar to the ones suggested below but adapted to their age and grade level. When allowed to express their views on discipline, children often reveal the methods used in their own homes. If a pupil consistently mentions cruel, harsh punishment in these activities, it may be advisable to have a talk with his parents about their methods of discipline.

The younger children may dramatize the situations and discuss them.

a. Nancy (aged ten years) had spent a great deal of time preparing a scrapbook for a school exhibit. After it was completed and ready to be taken to school on the following morning, her little brother Arthur (aged five years) decided to add his personal touch by marking on each page with colored crayons. What should be done with Arthur?

b. Ella (aged six years) wears the outgrown clothes of her sister Marcia (aged nine), she gets a smaller allowance, and is granted fewer privileges than her older sister. One day when their mother had promised that Ella might go skating with Marcia and some of her friends, the group slipped away and left Ella behind. What should be done about Marcia?

c. Henry (aged twelve years) is an only child and his parents have tried to make life very pleasant for him. But he has become so accustomed to being indulged that now he never wants to help with any of the work about the house. When he is asked to mow the grass or clean the basement on Saturday morning, he raves and complains that he never has time to do the important things that he has planned. What should be done about Henry?

10. Take advantage of the examples of democratic family living in children's literature to help you apply the principles of good home relationships in the everyday lives of the pupils. Instead of using real family problems for discussion, the same purpose may be served without risk of embarrassment by referring to storybook situations. There are excellent materials on every grade level that can be used as bases for stimulating discussions, creative writing, drawing, and dramatic activities.

11. Motion pictures may be used very effectively with this lesson. The following are suggested:

Appreciating Our Parents (for primary and intermediate grades), 16 mm., sound, 10 min., Coronet Films, Chicago, 1950. This film helps to promote a more genuine appreciation of parents and the sacrifices they make, to establish attitudes of respect and affection for mothers and fathers, and to give boys and girls an insight into their own role in the parent-child relationship.

Dad's Wish (for elementary grades), 1 reel, 7 min., Family Life Series, Teaching Film Custodians, Inc., New York, 1951. This film deals with a family situation in which the mother explains to her little girl why they cannot have everything they want in life, and the father makes it clear to his daughter that he is happy with what he has. The film is intended for educational use only and is provided on a long-term lease basis.

Earning and Giving (for elementary grades), 1 reel, 7 min., Family Life Series, Teaching Film Custodians, Inc., New York, 1951. This picture shows a little girl performing family chores, saving her pay, and planning and purchasing Christmas gifts for her parents. Provided on a long-term lease basis, this film is to be used for educational purposes only.

Family Life (for junior and senior high school), 16 mm., sound, 10 min., Coronet Films, Chicago, 1948. This picture outlines a program for achieving happiness in the family through good management of schedules, responsibilities, privileges, and finances.

Family Team Work (for elementary, junior and senior high school), 16 mm., sound, 18 min., Frith Films, Hollywood, Calif., 1947. This portrays a family in which there is affection, understanding, and cooperation, and in which parents and children share both home and outside activities.

Homer and the Kid Brother (for elementary and secondary school), 1 reel, 9 min., Family Life Series, Teaching Film Custodians, Inc., New York, 1951. This picture dramatizes excellent brother relationships. Homer patiently answers all his little brother's questions and gives him a sense of companionship and security. The film is provided on a long-term lease basis and is intended for educational use only.

Patty Garman, Little Helper (for elementary grades), 16 mm., sound, 11 min., Frith Films, Hollywood, Calif., 1946. This portrays a self-reliant and helpful little girl in her relationships with her family on the farm.

Sharing Work at Home (for junior and senior high school), 16 mm., sound, 10 min., Coronet Films, Chicago, 1949. This film shows the importance of cooperation in the home and offers some good suggestions for improved family living.

Your Family (for primary and intermediate grades), 16 mm., sound, 10 min., Coronet Films, Chicago, 1948. This is a delightful story of a happy family in which there is mutual understanding and acceptance of responsibility.

12. The subject of family relationships may be presented to parents by means of plays and informal discussions given before study groups or PTA meetings. The following program ideas are suggested for this purpose:

The Will B. Mature Family, The National Association for Mental Health, New York. This dramatic sketch shows how mental-health principles may be applied to everyday family living. It consists of five episodes representing common harassing problems in the life of a typical family (Mr. and Mrs. Mature and three children, aged thirteen, six, and two and one-half years). Each episode may be read aloud or dramatized. Then the audience may be divided into groups to discuss the problems left unsolved. Afterward the audience may reassemble to hear reports from a panel formed of one member from each group. A psychiatrist, if available, may point out the mental-hygiene principles involved.

Temperate Zone, The National Association for Mental Health, New York, 1949. Three plays for parents about the climate of the home, *Scattered Showers, Fresh Variable Winds,* and *High Pressure Area,* deal with preschool youngsters, ten-year-olds, and teen-agers respectively, and show the difference between discipline that merely exacts obedience and that which helps the child achieve self-discipline. The three half-hour dramatic sketches are planned to be used at each of three successive parent meetings and followed by a discussion period. A Discussion Guide, by Lawrence K. Frank, is provided with the plays.

13. Carefully selected motion pictures are a good means of impressing parents with the importance of meeting children's emotional needs early in life before they cause irreparable damage. The following films are suggested for use with groups of parents or teachers:

Children's Emotions, 16 mm., sound, 20 min., McGraw-Hill Book Company, Inc., New York, 1950. This film for parents of young children is correlated with Elizabeth B. Hurlock's book, *Child Growth and Development,* McGraw-Hill Book Company, Inc., New York, 1949. It shows through living examples how adult influences, both bad and good, affect children's emotions.

Feeling of Hostility, 16 mm., sound, 27 min., National Film Board of Canada, Ottawa, 1948. (Distributors, 620 Fifth Avenue, New York City.) This is the case history of Clare, an outwardly successful woman who is lonely and unhappy because of the many disappointments which she experienced during her childhood.

Feeling of Rejection, 16 mm., sound, 23 min., National Film Board of Canada, Ottawa, 1947. (Distributors, 620 Fifth Avenue, New York City.) This is a visual case history of a neurotic young woman whose trouble began when parents who did not understand her needs sheltered her too much and molded her into a model child.

Helping the Child Accept the Do's, 16 mm., sound, 11 min., Personality Development Series, Encyclopaedia Britannica Films, Inc., Wilmette, Ill., 1948. This picture portrays the young child learning to live in a world of convention and proper behavior and explains how his personality is shaped by the way he accepts his parents' methods of training him.

Helping the Child Face the Don'ts, 16 mm., sound, 11 min., Personality Development Series, Encyclopaedia Britannica Films, Inc., Wilmette, Ill., 1948. This film shows how young children meet a world of "don'ts" and how their personalities are affected by the ways in which restrictions are imposed upon them.

Life with Junior, 16 mm., sound, 18 min., March of Time Forum Edition, New York, 1949. This picture shows a typical day in the life of a ten-year-old boy and presents some of the aspects of child training in the home, the school, and the community.

Meeting Emotional Needs in Childhood, 16 mm., sound, 33 min., New York University Film Library, New York, 1947. This film illustrates the fact that adults are products of their childhood and that children who have a satisfactory home life are better equipped for social relationships at school and elsewhere.

Over-dependency, 16 mm., sound, 32 min., National Film Board of Canada, Ottawa, 1949. (Distributors, 620 Fifth Avenue, New York City.) This is the case history of a young man whose life is crippled by behavior patterns carried over from a too dependent childhood.

Preface to a Life, 16 mm., sound, 27 min., Castle Films, New York, 1950. This film dramatizes the influences which neighbors, friends, associates, and especially parents bring to bear on the personality of a child from the very beginning of his life.

14. Records may also be used for programs on child training and family living. The following 15-minute recorded programs may be obtained from the Promotion Department, The National Association for Mental Health, New York:

The Inquiring Parent is a total of forty-four transcribed radio programs (three series) in each of which Dr. Luther Woodward and the Inquiring Parent discuss some important phase of child care and training. Everyday problems that arise in almost all family situations are presented and constructive ways of dealing with them are suggested.

Hi, Neighbor! is a series of ten plays dramatizing the mental health aspects of family living and showing how emotional problems can be solved through effective use of nonpsychiatric community resources—schools, hospitals, recreation centers, etc. The content is keyed to the pamphlet, *Mental Health Is a Family Affair,* by Dallas Pratt and Jack Neher, Public Affairs Committee, Inc., New York, 1949.

15. Prepare a table or shelf marked "For Parents" and place on it books, pamphlets, and magazines which parents are encouraged to borrow. Through an article on some phase of mental health which is especially applicable to his child's case, you may be able to afford a parent more direct help than you could give in numerous conferences. See the recommended reading list for parents at the end of Chapter 1.

The following publications of Child Study Association of America, Inc., New York 21, will help you to provide an up-to-date reading list for children and parents:

Books of the Year for Children.
Parents' Bookshelf: A Selected List of Books for Parents, revised yearly.
The Year's Books for Parents and Teachers, yearly supplement.

The following periodicals carry articles of interest to parents:

Child-Family Digest, Lieutenant Gayle Aiken III Memorial Foundation, New Orleans, La.
Child Study, Child Study Association of America, Inc., New York 21.
Childhood Education, Association for Childhood Education, Washington 6, D.C.
Mental Hygiene, National Committee for Mental Hygiene, Inc., New York 19.
National Parent-Teacher, National Congress of Parents and Teachers, Chicago.
Parents' Magazine, Parents' Institute, Inc., Chicago 39.
Progressive Education, American Fellowship, New York 10.
Today's Health, American Medical Association, Chicago.
Understanding the Child, National Committee for Mental Hygiene, New York 19.

The following pamphlets are suggested for use by parents:

a. Association for Childhood Education International, Washington 5:
For Parents Particularly, 1949.

b. Bureau of Publications, Teachers College, Columbia University, New York:

BARUCH, DOROTHY W.: *Understanding Young Children,* 1949.

HUNNICUTT, C. W.: *Answering Children's Questions,* 1949.

HYMES, JAMES L., JR.: *Being a Good Parent,* 1949.

HYMES, JAMES L., JR.: *Discipline,* 1949.

LETTON, MILDRED CELIA: *Your Child's Leisure Time,* 1949.

MAYER, JANE: *Getting Along in the Family,* 1949.

REDL, FRITZ: *Understanding Children's Behavior,* 1949.

SYMONDS, PERCIVAL M.: *The Dynamics of Parent-Child Relationships,* 1949.

c. Child Study Association of America, Inc., New York 19:

ATKIN, EDITH LESSER: *Aggressiveness in Children,* 1950.

BURGESS, HELEN STEERS: *Discipline. What Is It?* 1948.

d. The National Association for Mental Health, Inc., New York 19:

RAUTMAN, ARTHUR L.: *Adoptive Parents Need Help Too,* 1949.

SPOCK, BENJAMIN: *Avoiding Behavior Problems,* 1945.

e. New York Committee on Mental Hygiene, New York 10:

RIDENOUR, NINA, and ISABEL JOHNSON: *Some Special Problems of Children—Aged 2 to 5 Years,* 1949.

To Foster Parents: This Is Your Foster Child, 1944.

f. Public Affairs Committee, Inc., New York 16:

BARUCH, DOROTHY W.: *How to Discipline Your Children,* 1949.

DUVALL, EVELYN MILLIS: *Keeping Up with Teen-Agers,* 1947.

FRANK, JOSETTE: *Comics, Radio, Movies—and Children,* 1949.

HYMES, JAMES L., JR.: *How to Tell Your Child about Sex,* 1949.

LAMBERT, CLARA: *Understand Your Child—from 6 to 12,* 1949.

NEISSER, WALTER, and EDITH NEISSER: *Making the Grade as Dad,* 1950.

PRATT, DALLAS, and JACK NEHER, *Mental Health Is a Family Affair,* 1949.

THORMAN, GEORGE: *Broken Homes,* 1947.

———: *Toward Mental Health,* 1946.

g. Science Research Associates, Inc., Chicago 10:

ENGLISH, O. SPURGEON, and STUART M. FINCH: *Emotional Problems of Growing Up,* 1951.

JENKINS, GLADYS GARDNER, and JOY NEUMAN: *How to Live with Parents,* 1948.

MENNINGER, WILLIAM C.: *Self-Understanding—A First Step to Understanding Children,* 1951.

NEISSER, EDITH G.: *How to Live with Children,* 1950.

h. State of New York Department of Mental Hygiene, Albany, N.Y.:

YOUNG, CHIC: *Blondie,* produced by Joe Musial, 1950. (A comic book in full color, illustrating four basic mental-health principles applied to family living.)

i. United States Department of Labor, Children's Bureau, Washington, D.C.:

Your Child from Six to Twelve, 1949.

Children Are Our Teachers, by Marion L. Faegre, 1949. (Outline and suggestions for group study to be used with *Your Child from Six to Twelve.*)

BIBLIOGRAPHY

BENEDICT, AGNES E., and ADELE FRANKLIN: *The Happy Home,* Appleton-Century-Crofts, Inc., New York, 1949.

BULLIS, H. EDMUND: *Human Relations in the Classroom,* The Delaware State Society for Mental Hygiene, Wilmington, Del., 1948, Course II, pp. 95–98, 135–140.

————, and EMILY E. O'MALLEY: *Human Relations in the Classroom,* The Delaware State Society for Mental Hygiene, Wilmington, Del., 1947, Course I, pp. 94–103.

DUVALL, EVELYN M.: *Family Living,* The Macmillan Company, New York, 1950.

ELLENWOOD, JAMES LEE: *Just and Durable Parents,* Charles Scribner's Sons, New York, 1948.

FRANK, MARY, and LAWRENCE K. FRANK: *How to Help Your Child in School,* The Viking Press, Inc., New York, 1950, Chaps. V, VI.

GABBARD, HAZEL F.: *Working with Parents* (A Handbook), United States Office of Education, Washington, D.C., 1949.

OLSON, WILLARD C.: *Child Development,* D. C. Heath and Company, Boston, 1949, Chap. IX.

OTT, HENRY J.: *Principles of Elementary Education,* Rinehart & Company, Inc., New York, 1949, Chap. 3.

TABA, HILDA, and DEBORAH ELKINS: *With Focus on Human Relations,* American Council on Education, Washington, D.C., 1950, Chaps. III, IV, V.

CHAPTER 20

Creating Wholesome Pupil-Teacher Relations

Aims of This Lesson:

To help teachers see themselves as the children see them.

To cause teachers to feel concerned about the effect of their own personalities upon the mental health of the pupils.

The successful teacher of today is an emotionally adjusted individual. She is conscious of the influence of her own personality upon her pupils and adjusts her life in such a way that it will not affect them negatively. She likes children and lets them know it. Teaching them and working and planning with them is not a laborious task but a pleasure to her.

Only a few years ago teachers were primarily concerned with dispensing facts relative to the three R's. Teaching the basic skills is just as important now as it was then but it is not enough. Today superior teachers are interested in each child's total personality, not simply in his ability to acquire factual information. They feel extremely responsible for their share in his social and emotional adjustment as well as in his academic achievement.

Knowing the child must precede formal instruction. Although many teachers claim to believe this truism, they merely give lip service to it but do not put the idea into practice. They dislike the thought of taking time from the teaching of reading, arithmetic, and history and devoting it to a study of the physical, emotional, and social needs of pupils. Actually, time spent in learning about children and helping them to become better adjusted is time saved. By helping boys and girls to solve their personal problems, teachers make it possible for them to learn faster and with less effort both now and in the years to come. Emotional maladjustments that are not treated early in life tend to become more serious as persons grow older. In the final analysis, all teachers want their pupils to become successful and worth-while citizens. The only point of departure from this ultimate aim is the method used. One type of teacher strives to reach her goal by teaching subject matter only. The other works toward her objective by developing the whole child, which automatically includes a teaching of the basic skills.

It is easy enough to say that John steals, Bill is a bully, Mary has temper tantrums, or Arthur is disliked by the other boys. All these conclusions may be quite obvious. But why are these children as they are? And what can be done for them? It is unethical and unfair to probe into a child's background and find that his father is an alcoholic or that his mother has deserted the family and then use the information only as a bit of gossip to pass on to the other teachers. It is the responsibility of the teacher to become familiar with the symptoms of emotional disorders so that she can discover maladjustments while they are still in the early stages. In localities where it is impossible to obtain professional assistance from child-guidance clinics, psychiatric social workers, or school psychologists, it is doubly important that teachers understand the principles of mental hygiene. Emotionally upset children who are misjudged and unintelligently handled at home may never receive any real help except from teachers.

A great deal can be learned about individuals and many group problems can be solved through regularly scheduled guidance lessons. Children like activities based on the needs of their daily lives. Even the teacher sometimes benefits from group-guidance projects. For example, a drive for friendly relationships naturally requires that the teacher herself be friendly with both her pupils and her colleagues. A campaign for acceptable social customs necessitates the teacher's practicing good manners and treating children with respect and consideration.

But more important than well-planned group lessons is the teacher's own personality. Just as the principal creates the atmosphere in the school as a whole, the teacher determines the relationships which exist in her room. It is not unusual to hear teachers discuss among themselves the merits of their respective classes. One talks about how she enjoys her delightful group while another constantly complains about how bad the children are and how happy she will be to send them on to the next grade at the end of the term. If the truth were known, the pupils probably feel no differently about her. The same class that is such a trial to one teacher may prove to be an excellent group under a different instructor. Why is this? Is it the children or is it the way they are handled?

The teacher is the key to a good or a poor learning situation. The children simply reflect her moods and her disposition. If she displays a sense of humor and is gay and vivacious, the pupils are likely to be cheerful, helpful, and responsive. If she is cross, tense, and irritable, the children react in the same manner. A teacher who is emotionally unstable produces emotionally unstable pupils. An overaggressive, domineering one either causes children to become fearful, timid, and withdrawn or antagonizes them to the extent that they seek relief by bullying and teasing other children, by feigning illness, or by staying away from school. A teacher who nags, belittles, or shames her pupils into conformity with a great many petty rules and regulations often drives them to lie and cheat in order to meet the difficult standards. It goes without saying that a calm, self-controlled, courteous teacher always has an entirely different class situation than the restless, worried, impatient one who is a screaming bundle of nerves.

Judged by traditional standards, one woman had taught rather successfully for a long time. But she had an innate feeling of intolerance and aversion toward children. Her forced smiles did not conceal her disapproval. Although she was quite familiar with the modern philosophy, techniques, and procedures, she failed to put them into practice. On numerous occasions she told her pupils how stupid they were and how much she disliked them. It was only natural for the children to reflect her feelings and to respond in the same way that she had acted toward them. As can well be imagined, the situation in the classroom was a series of attacks and counterattacks by both teacher and children. This woman's knowledge of subject matter and her superficial understanding of child psychology were not enough to offset her hostile feelings. Her philosophy of life, her facial expressions, her prejudices, and her mannerisms and peculiarities have probably left a lasting impression on many children. No matter how efficient a teacher may be in other respects, she misses the highest aim of her profession if she does not contribute to the development of pleasant, well-balanced, dynamic personalities.

All children, especially the very young ones who are getting their first impressions of school life, deserve to have pleasant, friendly teachers who will instill in them a love of learning. A child's experiences in the early grades often set the pattern of his future adjustment to school. Many potential problems simply never develop when teachers of small children create an atmosphere of warmth, affection, and understanding. On the other hand, many children transfer their dislike for their first teachers to a dislike for education in general and drop out of school as soon as possible. It is not uncommon for older students to choose high school and even college subjects on the basis of attitudes acquired in elementary school.

It is of the utmost importance that teachers do everything possible to make schoolwork interesting, enjoyable, challenging, and profitable. The years of childhood are brief and every day is precious. School seems hardly worth while when hours and hours of time are frittered away in useless activities and unrelated busywork. Children like teachers who plan interesting projects, who vary their methods, and who allow the pupils ample freedom to help initiate and carry out plans. They especially appreciate teachers who respect their viewpoints, pay attention to what they say, think, and feel, and in other ways treat them as real persons.

Seemingly unimportant things often make for wholesome relationships between teachers and pupils. Trips, hikes, parties, and picnics entail work but they also afford a tremendous amount of satisfaction. By giving teachers and children an opportunity to know each other better and to experience a feeling of comradeship, they help to eliminate misunderstandings and to improve classroom morale. When teachers and pupils are able to have fun and to laugh together, there is less room for friction or tension.

Teachers have a real responsibility to add some color and happiness to the lives of children whose homes are drab and unattractive or filled with bickering and unrest. Although the school can never take the place of the home, it can be a fair part-time substitute. A loving, understanding teacher can do a great deal to fill the need of a motherless child who lives with grandparents or other relatives or one who lives in a foster home or an orphanage. Children who feel uncertain of the love of their parents should at least be able to feel secure in their relationship with a consistently kind and sympathetic teacher.

Children like teachers who are pretty. All teachers are not good-looking by adult standards but they can all be attractive and vivacious and wear a happy smile. Those who radiate friendliness, kindness, and cheerfulness are considered beautiful by their pupils. A new dress and a trip to the beauty shop are usually well worth the expense and the time involved.

Youngsters respond more readily to teachers who have pleasant voices and who are able to control their classes without too much wordiness. Since adults influence the behavior of children largely by talking, it is important that they occasionally take stock of the things they say. If they find themselves using an overabundance of negative expressions such as "Don't,"

"Stop," and "No, no," they should make a conscious effort to be more positive in their approach. By studying and analyzing the sentences they most often employ to show approval and disapproval, they can eliminate some of the overworked and meaningless platitudes and the endless commands with which they bombard children. Pleasant requests, encouraging comments, and sincere praise are much more effective.

Adults should be able to observe children objectively without feeling that every undesirable thing they do or say is intended as a personal affront against them. Very often when children are impudent or antagonistic, they are simply reacting to life in general and not to the teacher. They may be rebelling at pressure from parents or at some difficult circumstance imposed upon them by their environment. They may even be reflecting the instability of a former teacher. It is not the task of educators to rebuke or intimidate youngsters for expressing their feelings but to try to discover and remedy the cause of the trouble.

The old "spare the rod and spoil the child" philosophy of yesterday is fast disappearing. Because educators have found that corporal punishment only tends to aggravate discipline problems, many school administrators have forbidden its use. Teachers often feel blocked and frustrated because they are not permitted to impose their will upon children through force. As a consequence, they sometimes find release for their feelings by stamping their feet, clapping their hands, shouting, scolding, nagging, threatening, keeping children in during recess or after school, causing them to stand in the hall, or assigning extra homework as punishment. These techniques place both teacher and children under a terrific strain and, at best, bring only temporary conformity. Teachers who must resort to such practices are themselves in need of help.

By planning a system of intervisitation, a principal or supervisor can give teachers who have poor classroom situations an opportunity to observe and get new ideas from those who are more skilled in handling certain problems.

A plan of mutual rating may also be helpful to some teachers. The faculty as a whole may participate in formulating a check list of items on which they believe the personality and the mental health of teachers depend. Then each teacher may rate the other members of the staff on these items. In this way each one is rated on the basis of collective judgments rather than the opinion of a single person. An entire faculty is not usually prejudiced or unfair in its rating. Although an individual may have pull with his superior, he has to deserve the esteem of a group. In order to be effective, mutual ratings should be made frequently. The desire to rank well in the eyes of their colleagues and to improve their standing with each rating is a stimulus to teachers. Such ratings are also helpful to the principal in that they enable him to approach a teacher without bias, to tell her how she stands with teachers, parents, and pupils, and to suggest ways in which she may improve.

A kindness which is seldom performed by a colleague is to suggest to a teacher that she may be in need of psychiatric treatment. Principals often shy away from this responsibility because they are afraid of offending a sensitive person. Teachers who are interested in the mental health of their pupils do not hesitate to make a tactful suggestion to the parents when they think that a child should go to the mental clinic. They urge children to know themselves. Is it too much to expect that they also try to know themselves, to become aware of their shortcomings, and to do something to remedy them? When a teacher who is relatively healthy finds herself becoming irritable and antagonistic, when she scolds, nags, and loses her sense of humor, when she is constantly labeled as mean and unfair by a large number of pupils, and when she realizes that she is beginning to dislike children, it is time for her to check on her own mental health and to consult a specialist.

The physical well-being of a teacher has more to do with her ability to get along with her pupils than she sometimes realizes. Nervousness, fatigue, irritability, and grouchiness are often symptoms of approaching illness. It is hard to smile, act pleasant, and deal patiently with children when one is ill. A sick person becomes emotional over little things that she would normally be able to overlook or laugh off. The teacher who is ill has no place in the classroom. She owes it to herself and her pupils to seek medical advice.

In the past the job of educating the children of the nation was left entirely to the school. The distinct line which was drawn between the responsibilities of home and school is well illustrated by the old story of the teacher who sent a dirty little boy home for a bath. The child soon returned bringing a note from his mother which said, "Don't smell Johnnie. Learn him." Today, however, both parents and teachers realize the need for close cooperation between home and school. Parents are interested in what goes on within the walls of a school building. Teachers need to encourage this attitude because many of their problems are the direct result of home environment. It is only through establishing a friendly relationship with parents that they can hope to treat some cases of emotional disturbance at the root and to prevent others from developing.

Parents support the school and they have a right to know how their children are progressing. They are entitled to some of the teacher's time and to a pleasant and courteous reception when they ask for a conference. Although they are interested in their children and want to help them, their chief difficulty is usually in not knowing what to do or how to do it. Teachers who are tactful and considerate in their approach find that most parents are understanding and eager to cooperate.

Some mothers and fathers hesitate to bring a problem to the teacher's attention because they fear that she may become resentful and vent her feelings on their child. Parents sometimes avoid going to school for a conference because they are made to feel inferior. This happens when teachers put themselves on pedestals and act as if they know all the answers. Any teacher can have the respect, the cooperation, and the gratitude of parents if she is a cultured, agreeable person who likes children and is sincerely concerned about their development. She needs to approach a parent from the standpoint that the two of them have a mutual interest—the child. She also needs to do a great deal of listening, to let the parent know that she understands his problem and his viewpoint, and to refrain from making adverse criticisms or presenting a definite solution. The parent will be much more likely to follow through with a plan which he has worked out for himself as a result of being allowed to talk until he has gotten a clear insight into the nature of the trouble.

Fathers and mothers like to be proud of their children. They feel embarrassed, uncomfortable, and dissatisfied with the school if they never get anything but unfavorable reports. In some localities a note from the teacher can mean nothing but bad news about a child's behavior or work. Much better results can be obtained by the reverse procedure. One teacher has endeared herself to parents and children alike by watching for chances to make complimentary reports. She sends home an exceptionally good school paper with a comment written across the corner, writes a brief note to say what a fine oral report a child has made, or calls a mother to tell her about signs of improvement in a child's social adjustment. Receiving some kind of recognition from this teacher has come to be a matter of neighborhood pride. Parents realize that here is a person who is genuinely interested in their children and is not constantly looking for the bad in them. As a result, they accept any adverse criticism graciously and do everything possible to cooperate. This intelligent teacher is not only making her own situation more pleasant, but she is building up in the children a love for school which will affect their attitudes when they are the parents of the next generation.

A good way to convey to the parents an idea of what the teacher is doing, how she is teaching the core subjects, her major objectives for the year, and what the home can do to help is to plan a program of visitations. At the beginning of the year all parents may be invited to school to meet the teacher, to see the setting in which the child is to work, and to find out what is expected of children on that particular grade or age level. Then small groups may be scheduled to come at specified times throughout the year to observe their children at work. In this way busy teachers who find it impossible to visit in all the homes have an opportunity to know the parents and thereby to understand the children better. When parents can observe the performance of their own children in relation to the group, they have a much more reliable way of judging their achievement. Those parents who never visit the school sometimes get distorted ideas by listening to childish interpretations of classroom situations. After meeting the teacher and talking with her, they are in a much better position to understand and appreciate her viewpoint when difficulties arise.

No treatise on pupil-teacher relations would be complete without mentioning the necessity for becoming familiar with the wealth of material which has been written on the subject. Some teachers spend many hours of their leisure time reading current literature. Those who claim that they never have time to read need to reschedule their day. No one would consult a physician who never reads a medical journal nor finds out about the newest scientific discoveries in his field. How can teachers expect the public to have faith in them if they are not familiar with the latest accepted practices in education? They owe it to their pupils, to themselves, and to their profession to keep abreast of the times by attending workshops and summer sessions of college and by reading the latest books on methods of teaching, child psychology, and mental hygiene.

ACTIVITIES SUGGESTED

Throughout all the preceding lessons it has been suggested that you find out by means of questionnaires, open discussions, and private interviews how children feel about their family and friends. Since so great a portion of the child's life is spent under the direct influence of teachers, it is important to know how he feels about them also. One of the main objectives of this lesson is to give pupils an opportunity to rate their teachers without fear of being penalized for anything they say. The point will be missed, however, unless you as a teacher are able to take an objective attitude toward the project and to realize that relationships cannot be improved unless they are first recognized and understood.

Select only those activities which you feel can be used to advantage.

1. Discuss with the pupils some of the things teachers do to help keep their classrooms running smoothly. Tell them about the responsibilities of your position and why it is important for you to do certain things which may seem unfair or unnecessary to them.

2. Allow each child to keep on his desk for one day a sheet of paper having three columns ruled from top to bottom. Ask that a single mark be made in column 1, 2, or 3 whenever one of the following actions is observed:

a. Teacher nagging, scolding, saying, "Don't do that," "Don't make so much noise," or making other negative or sarcastic remarks about little things.

b. Teacher finding it necessary to reprimand an individual for disturbing the class or failing to do his work.

c. Children doing things that are disturbing to the class or annoying to the teacher but which the teacher either does not notice or allows to go uncorrected.

1 Teacher's scolding about little things	2 Teacher's correcting real misbehavior	3 Children's need for correction

Explain to the children that they are not expected to give their entire time and attention to this little study, but that they are simply to record what they happen to notice. At the close of the day allow time to discuss some of the observations so that you can help the pupils understand why it is sometimes necessary to reprove a child and why at other times it may be desirable to let his behavior go apparently overlooked.

3. Younger children may be allowed to play school, taking the parts of teacher and pupils. Older boys and girls may plan simple skits enacting school scenes or activities in which various members of the faculty participate. Urge them to make the portrayals of the teachers as accurate as possible, using their typical mannerisms and favorite expressions. By observing these dramatizations, you will become conscious of the phrases and gestures

which you use constantly in your teaching and which may become quite tiresome to children.

4. Ask the pupils to write or talk on the subject of "The Teacher Who Helped Me Most" or "The Teacher I Liked Best," mentioning all the reasons why they feel as they do about the particular teachers. To make the reports objective in nature, the present teacher should not be included. These papers or talks are sure to reveal the fact that pupils like teachers who are emotionally well adjusted, who have pleasant personalities, and who are fair in their dealings.

5. In an effort to get the children to express their feelings toward their present teacher, ask them to list the things they like and the things they do not like about her. Insist that they give this project their most serious thought and that they hand in the papers *unsigned*. The important thing is not to find out what an individual thinks about you but to get the total feeling of the group. If a child harbors any resentment toward you, it will do him good to be able to write it down and get it out of his system.

In order to make this a two-way activity, you may want to list on the blackboard the good and the bad traits of the class as you see them. For your own mental health, it is better to have a frank and open discussion of the faults and the virtues of the children than to be constantly nagging and feeling upset about them.

6. It is a good plan to set aside a little time when the children are encouraged to bring out into the open any grievances which they feel toward the school in general. They may be asked to mention any features which they think could be improved and any practices which they feel would make for better school morale. After an uninhibited expression of feelings, some classes realize that they have very little cause for complaint. If this activity causes the children to feel rebellious or antagonistic, however, there may be real reasons for the teacher to be concerned.

7. Take a poll among the children of your group to determine what they think about the playground games that are most fun, the type of lesson that is most interesting, the part of the school day that is most enjoyable, and the times when they are happiest at school. When you have found out what your particular group likes most to do, you can apply the information in making other lessons and activities more enjoyable to them.

8. For you own satisfaction, you may like to find your rating in the teaching profession by using one or more of the following scales:

a. ALMY, H. C., and HERBERT SORENSON: *Rating Scale for Teachers,* Public School Publishing Co., Bloomington, Ill., 1930. This scale provides for the rating of a teacher by an administrator on twenty traits of character and personality.

b. KELLEY, IDA B., and KEITH J. PERKINS: *How I Teach* (Analysis of Teaching Practices), Educational Test Bureau, Educational Publishers, Inc., Minneapolis, Minn., 1942. This examination is used by school administrators for finding out the attitudes of teachers and prospective teachers toward the problems of children and to check their knowledge of mental hygiene principles. It is also used by teacher training institutions for determining how much progress students have made in understanding children.

c. TSCHECHTELIN, SISTER M. AMATORA: *A Diagnostic Teacher Rating Scale* (Grades 4 to 8), Division of Educational Reference, Purdue University, Lafayette, Ind. This is a list of questions on which children anonymously rate their teachers.

d. WHITTIER, HELEN, JAMES W. H. BAKER, and Others, *A Self-Rating Scale for Teachers,* Houghton Mifflin Company, Boston, 1947. This scale provides for scores in professional qualifications, professional technique, personality traits, and social traits of the teacher. It is intended for the use of no one but the teacher herself and the questions are framed in such a way that the teacher is the only one who can give a meaningful response.

9. The motion pictures listed below are correlated with Dr. Raleigh Schorling's text, *Student Teaching,* published by McGraw-Hill Book Company, Inc., New York, in 1947. Although the films are based on problems of secondary school, they portray situations that are also found in the lower grades and should be very helpful to elementary school teachers. They are excellent for use in faculty meetings or for small groups of teachers or students who are interested in a better understanding of children.

Learning to Understand Children: A Diagnostic Approach (21 min.). This picture shows a case study of an emotionally and socially maladjusted fifteen-year-old girl and the techniques used by her teacher in diagnosing her difficulties. These include observation of the child's behavior, study of her previous records, personal interviews, home visits, and plans for remedial measures.

Learning to Understand Children: A Remedial Program (23 min.). This is a continuation of the same case, showing remedial procedures which may be used in dealing with many types of maladjustments.

Maintaining Classroom Discipline (14 min.). This film shows a class in which the work is neither instructive nor pleasant because the teacher has failed to stimulate interest and the students have sought relief from boredom in misbehavior. Then, by contrast, it shows how the same situations could have been handled by using approved techniques of class control.

Broader Concepts of Method: Developing Pupil Interest (13 min.). This film presents a comparison of the effects on student attitudes, responses, and learning when there is a formal, teacher-dominated, lesson-hearing type of recitation and when there is an informal group-discussion type of lesson in which students are permitted to share in the planning of an interesting class project.

Broader Concepts of Method: Teacher and Pupils Planning and Working Together (19 min.). This picture shows how the teacher can provide tactful guidance when students are learning to work together, to organize themselves into functional groups, to make and carry out plans for investigation, to present their findings in a final report, and to put into practice some of their recommendations.

10. In order to secure professional help for extremely maladjusted children, it may be necessary for you to know the location of the mental hygiene clinic, the personal consultation clinic, or the child-study school nearest you. This information may be obtained by writing to The National Committee for Mental Hygiene, Inc., New York. A *Directory of Psychiatric Clinics in the United States* may be ordered from the same organization. Names of counseling agencies in your community may be obtained from the Family Service Association of America, New York.

BIBLIOGRAPHY

AXLINE, VIRGINIA MAE: *Play Therapy,* Houghton Mifflin Company, Boston, 1947.

BAXTER, BERNICE: *Teacher-Pupil Relationships,* The Macmillan Company, New York, 1946.

BUHLER, CHARLOTTE, and OTHERS: *Childhood Problems and the Teacher,* Henry Holt and Company, Inc., New York, 1952.

DEL SOLAR, CHARLOTTE: *Parents and Teachers View the Child,* Bureau of Publications, Teachers College, Columbia University, New York, 1949.

Education for All American Children, Educational Policies Commission, Washington, D.C., 1948, Chap. 4.

KILPATRICK, WILLIAM HEARD, and WILLIAM VAN TIL: *Intercultural Attitudes in the Making,* Harper & Brothers, New York, 1947, Chap. III.

MURSELL, JAMES L.: *Successful Teaching,* McGraw-Hill Book Company, Inc., New York, 1946, Chap. 12.

OLSON, WILLARD C.: *Child Development,* D. C. Heath and Company, Boston, 1949, Chap. XI.

OTTO, HENRY J.: *Principles of Elementary Education,* Rinehart & Company, Inc., New York, 1949, Chaps. 12, 15.

SLAVSON, S. R.: *The Practice of Group Therapy,* International Universities Press, Inc., New York, 1947.

SORENSON, HERBERT: *Psychology in Education,* McGraw-Hill Book Company, Inc., New York, 1948, pp. 129-131, Chap. VII.

WALLIN, J. E. WALLACE: *Personality Maladjustments and Mental Hygiene,* McGraw-Hill Book Company, Inc., New York, 1949, pp. 97-109.

WILES, KIMBALL: *Supervision for Better Schools,* Prentice-Hall, Inc., New York, 1950.

PAMPHLETS

Better Home-School Relationships, The Department of Classroom Teachers, National Education Association, Washington, D.C., 1950. (A program consisting of two dramatizations: 1. Parents Talk It Over. 2. Teachers Talk It Over.)

BROWN, MURIEL: *Partners in Education* (A Guide to Better Home-School Relationships), Association for Childhood Education International, Washington, D.C., 1950.

Helping Children Solve Their Problems, Association for Childhood Education International, Washington, D.C., 1950.

HYMES, JAMES L., JR.: *A Pound of Prevention* (How Teachers Can Meet the Emotional Needs of Young Children), New York State Committee on Mental Hygiene, New York, 1947.

HYMES, JAMES L., JR.: *Teacher Listen—The Children Speak,* New York Committee on Mental Hygiene, New York, 1949.

It Starts in the Classroom, National School Public Relations Association, National Education Association, Washington, D.C., 1951.

Mental Hygiene in the Classroom, American Medical Association, Chicago, 1950.

Mental Hygiene in the Classroom, The National Committee for Mental Hygiene, Inc., New York, 1949.

TRAGER, HELEN: *The Primary Teacher* (A reprint of Chap. III of *Intercultural Attitudes in the Making*), The National Committee for Mental Hygiene, Inc., New York, 1949.

WICKMAN, E. W.: *Teachers and Behavior Problems,* Commonwealth Fund, Division of Publication, New York, 1949.

Index

264   ELEMENTARY SCHOOL GUIDANCE

Dramatizations, for parents, 243–244
  on proper diet, 30
  for release of feelings, 83, 95
  on responsibilities, 206–207
  on teacher-pupil relations, 257–258
Dreams, 166, 243–244

E

Eames Eye Test, 21
Environment, home, 1–16, 75, 89, 99–100,
  134, 146, 151, 163–164, 183–184, 199,
  231–232, 237–238, 254
Extroversion, 149, 153, 155

F

Failure, how to meet, 150, 213
Fair play, 112, 211–220
  films on, 218–219
  filmstrips on, 219–220
Family life, questionnaire on, 15–16
  (See also Environment, home)
Family relations, 231–248
Favoritism, parental, 122–124
Fear, 114, 120, 147–148, 166, 169–181
  of death, 236–237
  films on, 181
  questionnaire on, 177
  release treatment for, 173–174
Feelings, of anger, 80, 87–97
  of anxiety, 171
  of guilt, 111, 121–122, 125, 126, 171
  hurt, release treatment for, 150–151, 154,
    234
  of inadequacy, 55–56, 171
  of inferiority, 55–56, 113, 134–136, 150
  of insecurity, 100, 125, 175
  of jealousy, 120–128
    release treatment for, 122, 127
  of rejection, 100, 124, 160
  of resentment, 75, 80, 84, 111, 122
  of superiority, 101
Fighting, 76–78, 98, 120
Films, on aggressive behavior, 85–86
  on bullying, 107
  on dishonesty, 118

Films, on fair play, 218–219
  on family relations, for children, 242–
    243
    for parents, 244–245
  on fears, 181
  on friendship, 62
  on good manners, 228–229
  on health and safety, 33–36
  on jealousy, 130
  on responsibility, 208–209
  on teaching techniques, 259–260
  on tolerance, 219
Filmstrips, on conduct and behavior, 229–
  230
  on fair play, 219–220
  on jealousy, 129–130
  on responsibility, 209–210
Friendliness, 51–63, 104
Frustration, 52, 82, 88, 89

G

Group leaders, 39–40
Guilt feelings, 111, 121–122, 125, 126, 171

H

Handicaps, physical, 25–27, 30, 54, 136
  compensation for, 26–27, 112, 161–162
Hearing, defective, 22, 30–31
Hobbies, 66–68, 70–73, 135
Home, economic and social status of, 2–3
Home duties, questionnaire on, 204
Home environment (see Environment)
Home visits, 6–8
Hostility, 75–80

I

Ill-health, symptoms of, 20–21
Illness, 90, 136–137, 147–148, 175–176,
  187–188
  (See also Diseases, communicable)
Inadequacy, feelings of, 55–56, 171
Inferiority, feelings of, 55–56, 113, 134–
  136, 150